The Oil Market in the 1990s

Published in cooperation with
Pacific Resources, Inc.,
and the East-West Center

The Oil Market in the 1990s

Challenges for the New Era

Essays in Honor of John K. Evans

EDITED BY
Robert G. Reed III
and Fereidun Fesharaki

Routledge
Taylor & Francis Group
LONDON AND NEW YORK

First published 1989 by Westview Press

Published 2019 by Routledge
52 Vanderbilt Avenue, New York, NY 10017
2 Park Square, Milton Park, Abingdon, Oxon OX14 4RN

Routledge is an imprint of the Taylor & Francis Group, an informa business

Library of Congress Cataloging-in-Publication Data
The Oil market in the 1990s : challenges for the new era / edited by Robert G. Reed III and Fereidun Fesharaki.
p. cm. — (Westview special studies in international economics and business)
Includes bibliographies and index.
ISBN 0-8133-0819-4
1. Petroleum industry and trade—Forecasting. I. Reed, Robert G. II. Fesharaki, Fereidun. III. Series
HD9560.5.0368 1989
338.2'7282'0724—dc19 **88-20799**
CIP

ISBN 13: 978-0-367-29452-6 (hbk)
ISBN 13: 978-0-367-30998-5 (pbk)

Contents

Tables and Figures

Tables

Figures

Preface

How do you give a gift to a man who has everything? In the case of our dear friend Jack Evans, this was the very problem we faced. For a man who has given so much for so long, this festschrift by his friends and admirers is but a small token.

A Welshman who emigrated to the United States as a penniless youth, Jack Evans symbolizes the image of a tough go-getter immigrant who became a great success in his professional and personal life. As an entrepreneur, promoter, innovator, and concept man, he has always been full of ideas. In fact, his friends have a hard time keeping up with him! Although a highly successful oilman, he really is an idea man.

Jack Evans started his oil career in 1933 as a trainee for Shell Oil. By the start of World War II, he had become marketing manager for Shell in New England. During the war he was a commissioned officer in the U.S. Army, finally achieving the rank of colonel, and was involved in the allocation of oil supplies to various places in the Latin America theater. After the war, he rejoined Royal Dutch Shell as general manager in Puerto Rico, and after serving in several other overseas assignments, he became the company's representative in Washington, D.C. He retired in the early 1960s and began a career of project promotion and entrepreneurship leading him to become a founder of HIRI—Hawaiian Independent Refinery, Inc.—with which he continues to be involved in an advisory capacity.

So many of us often want to express ourselves bluntly to relieve our frustrations. But we don't. Jack does not suffer from this handicap! He is not known to contain himself if he feels strongly about anything. He is a man who speaks his mind. Although a practical man, Jack is blessed with high intellect. He travels around the globe (loves to go to conferences!), and if he likes something he hears, he will follow it up. Most of us are amazed at the flood of letters and documents that Jack can shoot across the globe to get a thought or a message across.

Jack's toughness and outspoken words sometimes might hide his very warm and soft heart—how he gives so generously to worthwhile causes, how he promotes international understanding, and how he tries to help those in need, both with love, moral support, and money. Jack is no pushover. He has earned his money the hard way and he won't just throw it away. But he is extremely generous when he sees a real need.

Jack Evans has touched the lives of many people. His friends have come together to dedicate their thoughts in this book to honor him. For us as editors of this volume, he is a very special friend, a friend whom we have come to love, admire, and depend upon. Jack Evans is a truly amazing man—one of a kind—a man who gives us hope for the future of mankind. Jack and Jean Evans are a true delight to their friends.

Robert G. Reed III
Fereidun Fesharaki
Honolulu, Hawaii

1

Structural Adjustment in the Oil Industry: Evolutionary Change and an Information Revolution

Guy F. Caruso

The world's largest industry—international oil—has undergone profound changes since 1973. Change has occurred in all sectors of the industry, from the upstream where crude oil is discovered and produced to the downstream areas of refining and marketing. International oil has gone from an industry dominated by relatively few large, fully integrated, multinational oil companies to one in which governments in both producing and consuming countries play important roles and a large number of smaller buyers and sellers have entered the market. Nevertheless, large oil companies have maintained a central role in exploration and development, investments outside the Organization of Petroleum Exporting Countries (OPEC), and in the refining and marketing of refined products in Organization for Economic Cooperation and Development (OECD) countries.

This chapter reviews some of those changes that have occurred since the early 1970s. Most changes in the industry's structure have been evolutionary, with reasonably smooth adjustments having taken place. There is one area in which change has been revolutionary: oil market information. Information available to industry participants and analysts has proliferated since the mid-1970s.

Some, if not all, of the information explosion was stimulated by governments—both consumers and producers. In 1973–1974 OECD governments found themselves in the unacceptable position of not having adequate, timely, and accurate information on oil supply, demand, and prices. The experience of 1978–1979 showed that although oil information had improved, much work remained. Since 1981, during a period of declining crude oil prices, governments of oil-producing countries became increasingly interested in better information as OPEC countries sought to set and enforce production quotas.

Role of Major Oil Companies

The role of the large international oil companies—the so-called majors (Exxon, Royal Dutch/Shell, Chevron [formerly Standard Oil of California and Gulf Oil], Texaco, British Petroleum, and Mobil Oil)—has changed substantially during the past decade. There are both myths and realities about the structural changes that have occurred and their implications.

The nature of access to crude oil for major oil companies has changed. In the period leading up to 1973–1974 almost all of their crude was acquired through equity ownership, including that oil lifted under long-term concessions in OPEC countries, with effective control over production levels. By 1988 most equity ownership by companies in OPEC countries had been sharply reduced. The majors now acquire most OPEC crude through transactions with unaffiliated parties (i.e., arm's length purchases). There are, however, continuing special relationships, such as that between the former Aramco partners (Exxon, Chevron, Texaco, and Mobil) and Saudi Arabia (although the volume lifted by the partners has shrunk considerably), continuing equity portions in Nigeria, and production sharing in Indonesia. The majors have increased equity production outside OPEC, particularly in OECD countries. Since the early 1970s, major oil company investments have increased sharply in the North Sea, in North America, and in non-OPEC developing countries.

As a result, the majors—and other oil companies, large and small—continue to have access to large volumes of oil at well below OPEC official prices: in North America, the North Sea, and many non-OPEC developing countries. Indeed the importance of lost concessions in OPEC countries has diminished as the proportion of OPEC production in total supply has shrunk.

The disposal of crude oil by the majors has also changed drastically. In the pre-1973–1974 period the majors were virtually the only crude oil marketers, selling crude to their affiliated companies, and in term-contract sales, to third-party buyers. The sales of crude oil on the cargo-by-cargo spot market was then very small and limited to balancing unexpected changes in supply and demand. In today's market, most of the former third-party customers of the majors deal directly with producer governments or national oil companies, with independent oil traders or have developed their own production. Also, affiliated companies in a number of cases buy oil from sellers other than the parent company.

As a result, there are many more buyers and sellers active in the international crude oil market. Because of the large overhang of unused productive capacity, access to oil on a long-term contract basis has become far less important. Indeed, in recent years, the persistent downward pressure on spot-market prices has led many crude-buyers to rely increasingly on spot purchases or contracts with spot-price-related indices.

Nevertheless, the major oil companies have maintained a central role. None has diversified outside energy to any large extent; the vast majority of their investments continue to be in oil. They still account for about 40 percent of the crude oil refined in OECD countries and just over 40 percent of product sales (compared with about 70 percent and 60 percent in 1973). They continue to be the main link between producers and consumers. Major oil companies' cash flow provides the bulk of worldwide investment in exploration and production. The majors retain a substantial interest in oil price stability, since a sharp decline in crude oil prices would adversely affect the value of their assets, their return on capital invested, and their cash flow.

Role of Producer Governments

Governments in most large oil-exporting countries have taken effective control over their crude oil production and marketing since 1973. In some cases, former concessionnaires such as the Aramco partners retain a special relationship under service contract or through reduced equity ownership such as in Nigeria, Libya, and Abu Dhabi. In other countries equity-like arrangements such as production-sharing contracts in Indonesia have been adopted.

Governments of some large oil-producing countries (e.g., Kuwait, Venezuela, and Saudi Arabia) have also become more involved, through state companies, in downstream operations at home and abroad. The primary objective is to ensure outlets for crude oil at a time when the demand for crude is growing very slowly. Experience so far would seem to indicate that the producer governments concerned recognize that lower produce prices could undermine the price structure for crude oil, which will continue to provide the largest share of their revenue, as well as that of other oil-exporting countries.

Developing countries as a group are eager to find economically recoverable oil and gas reserves as one means of acquiring foreign exchange to pay for imports and debt service. Some countries, such as Brazil, India, and Mexico, have used their national oil companies to develop oil and gas successfully. Apart from the Middle East and Mexico, where the proven reserve base is large relative to foreseen demands, most other governments recognize that further exploration and devel-

TABLE 1.1
World Refinery Distillation Capacity, 1960–1987 (MMB/D)

	1960	1970	1973	1980	1984	1987
OECD	16.0	31.0	38.0	48.0	39.0	36.9
OPEC	2.1	3.6	4.3	5.5	5.6	6.2
Others	3.0	7.4	11.7	10.9	14.4	14.6
Total	21.1	42.0	54.0	64.4	59.0	57.7

Notes: MMB/D = million barrels per day.
Figures given for 1987 in the conference paper were updated in 1988 by the author.

Source: Guy F. Caruso, "Outlook for Refinery Economics," unpublished paper presented at the Institute of Petroleum Conference on the Economics of Refining, London, October 1987.

opment efforts require the technology and risk capital of foreign oil companies (whether majors, independents, or national oil companies). The terms and conditions (including taxation, and production-sharing elements) must provide a level of after-tax rate of return remittable in convertible currency sufficient to attract the level of exploration effort appropriate to the geological potential of each country. Great emphasis is also put by oil companies on contract stability, which can be achieved by negotiating a fair balance in clear terms at the outset, with both parties recognizing the value of preserving a long-term relationship.

Downstream Developments

The highly competitive downstream sector of the oil industry has witnessed substantial change both in capacity and in technology. Adapting to a rapidly changing market environment, refinery capacity in OECD countries first increased by some 25 percent and then decreased by about 25 percent in the 1973–1987 period. During the same period, the typical refinery became more complex through the addition of upgrading facilities to adjust to the changing product mix.

Crude oil distillation capacity for the world (excluding centrally planned economics) doubled in the 1960s in response to an equally sharp increase in consumption. This considerable growth of world capacity (see Table 1.1) was mainly due to the rapid expansion of the industry in OECD countries, a trend that continued throughout the 1970s as refineries that had been planned on the basis of oil-consumption projections of continued strong growth came on stream.

Following the oil price increases in 1973–1974 and 1979–1980, declines in oil consumption and changes in consumption patterns led to considerable adaptation. This took the form of refinery closures—OECD countries' crude oil distillation capacity in 1987 was 23 percent below its 1981 peak—and construction of upgrading or conversion capacity, which grew from 9 MMB/D (million barrels per day) in 1977 to about 13 MMB/D in 1987, enabling refiners to enhance flexibility and to convert fuel oil, the demand for which has almost continuously declined, into lighter products.

The economic advantages anticipated when large conversion capacities were installed to improve downstream flexibility have been reduced by a combination of higher feedstock costs relative to light product prices and narrower price differentials between light and heavy finished products, both of which have been caused in part by the existence of conversion capacity. These factors may gradually become less important as construction of new conversion capacity slows down and as the share of heavy fuel oil in total consumption continues to diminish. In addition, further closure of excess distillation capacity will contribute to downstream efficiency, therefore tending to improve refinery economics. Other important factors will be future developments in crude oil and product prices, consumption growth, and net oil product imports. The near-term market outlook is for slow consumption growth and a continued need for refinery closures. Refiners will also have to continue making some investment in the light of new environmental regulations in many countries.

Market Structures

International oil market structures have also changed significantly over the past ten years and continue to evolve. Much of the change is the result of market forces operating on both demand and supply. The outcome has been a significant shift in market share away from OPEC, as consumption fell and refiners sought to reduce average crude costs by maximizing acquisitions from non-OPEC countries, where the acquisition costs were lower than OPEC prices during much of the period. Demand, supply, and price developments since 1974 have also altered the way oil is traded internationally, with an increasing emphasis on short-term transactions (largely through spot-price-related sales), the development and evolution of an influential oil futures market, and the expansion of barter and countertrade.

Demand Patterns

The nearly 15 percent drop in oil consumption in OECD countries between 1979 and 1987 was accompanied by a number of shifts in the composition and seasonal pattern of demand. Most striking is the role of residual fuel oil, which declined by 53 percent over this period and

TABLE 1.2
Annual OECD Petroleum Products Consumption (MMB/D)

	1979	1983	1987
LPG/naptha	4.7	4.0	4.5
Aviation fuels	1.8	1.7	2.1
Motor gasoline	11.0	10.6	11.3
Middle distillate	10.2	8.4	9.2
Heavy fuel oil	9.7	5.7	4.6
Other products	4.3	3.6	4.0
Total	41.8	34.0	35.7

Note: Consumption is measured as deliveries of oil from refineries, plus refinery fuel use and use of international marine bunkers.

Source: International Energy Agency, *Annual Oil Market Report 1987* (Paris, International Energy Agency, 1987).

accounted for the lion's share of the total reduction in consumption. By contrast, consumption of middle distillates declined by only 10 percent and of gasoline actually increased by 3 percent. Other products declined by 6 percent. This more than proportional decline in residual fuel oil consumption meant that its share of total oil consumption fell from 23 percent in 1979 to 13 percent in 1987. Details of the changing demand patterns are shown in Table 1.2.

Stocks

Changes in patterns of demand and supply and the price of oil have had a major effect on oil inventory management since 1979, reducing the absolute level of stocks and the amplitude of seasonal fluctuations. As shown in Table 1.3, stocks held by oil companies fell by about 106 million tons from January 1978 to January 1988. However, the 1 January 1988 level expressed in days of forward consumption was only three days lower than the level of 1 January 1978. Thus, inventory reduction over the 1978–1988 period was, in part, a correction to reflect the decline in consumption and to reduce substantial company stock build-up that occurred during 1979–1980.

The growth in government-owned and/or -controlled stocks in OECD countries has been substantial since 1978. Stocks in those categories reached 126 million tons on 1 January 1988. This change represents a major new element in the International Energy Agency (IEA) countries' emergency response preparedness. These countries have recognized the importance of a coordinated stock draw by consumer countries as an important step, particularly in the initial period of an oil-supply interruption.

TABLE 1.3
Stocks on Land in the OECD Area on 1 January, 1974–1988

	Millions of Tons[a]				Days of Forward Consumption			
	Companies	Entities[b]	Govts.	Total	Companies	Entities[b]	Govts.	Total
1974	346	1		348	71			71
1975	401	1		403	82			82
1976	396	1	3	399	73		1	74
1977	402	1	4	407	71		1	71
1978	436	2	7	444	75		1	76
1979	392	16	22	430	65	3	4	72
1980	418	17	27	463	76	3	5	84
1981	429	19	33	481	80	3	6	89
1982	395	18	57	471	82	4	12	98
1983	367	18	65	449	83	4	15	102
1984	333	16	77	426	72	3	17	92
1985	332	16	89	437	73	4	20	96
1986	314	16	97	426	70	4	21	95
1987	329	18	101	448	72	4	22	98
1988	330	21	105	455	72	5	23	100

[a]Total may not add up due to rounding.
[b]Stockholding entities established in some European countries to hold mandatory stocks.

Source: International Energy Agency, *Annual Oil Market Report 1987* (Paris, International Energy Agency, 1987).

TABLE 1.4
Shares in World Oil Supply (MMB/D)

	1973		1979		1984		1987	
	Vol.	%	Vol.	%	Vol.	%	Vol.	%
OPEC	31.3	64	31.6	60	18.5	41	19.4	41
OECD	13.9	29	14.7	28	16.7	37	16.8	36
Developing countries	3.1	6	5.3	10	8.0	18	8.9	19
CPE net exports	0.4	1	1.2	2	1.9	4	2.1	4
Total	48.7	100	52.8	100	45.1	100	47.2	100

Note: Supply excludes processing gains and nonconventional oils. Includes natural gas liquids (NGLs) and condensates.
Source: International Energy Agency, *Annual Oil Market Report 1987* (Paris, International Energy Agency, 1987).

Changing Market Shares

The diminishing share of OPEC countries in world oil production, particularly after 1979, while the shares of all other main groups of oil suppliers increased, is one of the key oil market developments of the past decade (see Table 1.4).

The MMB/D reduction in OPEC output since 1979 is explained by OPEC countries' determination to support high prices for their marginal supply by accepting a lower market share in the face of a more than 5 MMB/D decline in demand and the increased production in many non-OPEC countries over the 1973–1987 period, most importantly in Mexico, the North Sea, the Soviet Union, and Egypt.

The availability of new crude oil streams from these non-OPEC countries, generally closer to main consumer markets than many OPEC countries, also had a structural impact. It meant that significant volumes of short-haul crudes became available to markets where buyers, for a number of reasons, preferred short-term supply arrangements. Thus, this new oil production sustained and possibly reinforced the trend toward a short-term market and lower overall stock levels.

In OPEC countries the sharp output decline created considerable excess capacity, which is now estimated at about 8 to 10 MMB/D. Although this is positive from a security-of-supply point of view, most of the excess capacity, some 6 to 7 MMB/D, is located in Arabian/Persian Gulf area countries. It also should be recognized that it may take several months to bring unused capacity on stream again. Furthermore, maximum sustainable capacity is gradually being reduced, as the necessary investments to maintain it are not always made during a period of declining oil revenues and current account deficits. There is less than 0.5 MMB/D of unused capacity in non-OPEC countries.

The Information Revolution

Although much of the structural change in the international oil industry has evolved gradually, information about oil markets and oil supply/demand fundamentals has increased dramatically since 1973. Media attention to the price shocks of 1973–1974 and 1979–1980 and their aftermath was certainly a contributing factor to this information explosion. Demands from many governments for more price and price-related oil market transparency during the period of rising prices also provided a major impetus to the development of new information systems. Some of the structural changes already mentioned, such as development of oil futures and forward markets and the increasing numbers of buyers and sellers in oil markets, also contributed to information availability.

In the pre-1973 period oil analysts depended heavily on those mainstays of information such as *Petroleum Intelligence Weekly* (PIW), *Platt's Oilgram News*, and the *Middle East Economic Survey* (*MEES*). Although these remain key sources of information today, they have been joined by dozens of competitors in the oil market information business. In particular much more information is available regarding cargo-by-cargo spot-market transactions on the physical market, and price data are instantly available on futures transactions via the video screen.

Information about supply/demand fundamentals has improved markedly during the last fifteen years. National energy statistics in many countries were often unavailable, inaccurate, or both before the mid-1970s. Efforts by national governments and international organizations such as the OECD/IEA and the UN, with the assistance of oil companies, have substantially improved the timeliness and accuracy of the data. Of course, continuing efforts are still needed to improve and expand the databases, particularly in developing countries, and to maintain the progress already achieved.

The Lessons of 1979

Despite the improvements of the mid-1970s, the experience of oil market developments in 1979–1980 following the Iranian revolution clearly showed more needed to be done. Prices rose steadily during the period, despite declining consumption. Governments were to learn the hard lesson that consumption does not necessarily equal demand: The difference is inventory or stock change. The sharp build-up in stocks during the period from April 1979 to September 1980 was a major contributing factor to the demand push on spot crude oil prices from $20 per barrel to more than $40 per barrel.

Governments recognized the need for more timely and accurate information. The OECD/IEA established improved reporting systems with an emphasis on closely monitoring supply/demand fundamentals, particularly stock data. It was extremely helpful to have the improved data and better understanding of the stocks situation in September 1980 when the Iran-Iraq war commenced. The availability of better information to IEA member governments and to oil market participants in general was almost certainly an important factor in reduced oil price volatility during the period immediately following the outbreak of the war.

The principle that better information for all market participants could contribute to more efficient free market operations was an important consideration in establishing the monthly IEA *Oil Market Report.* After lengthy discussion among member countries regarding the appropriateness of making the IEA data publicly available, the report became a commercial publication in September 1983. The IEA report has been a commercial success and is considered a benchmark for data among many oil analysts and in the media. The report contains the best available supply/demand data for OECD countries. The IEA secretariat also is in a unique position, having good access to market participants in non-OECD countries. One senior IEA official described the oil market–

reporting system perhaps best when he said, "The data is not perfect but it's the best there is."

The IEA *Oil Market Report* is only one example of the proliferation of reports and analysis made possible by the oil market information revolution. Increased information has even led to the development of different schools of oil market analysis. There are the "fundamentalists," who attempt to predict current and future market behavior on the basis of supply/demand data. Oil traders generally shun the fundamentals and typically rely on day-to-day information on availability of supplies and a feel for the market through their network of contacts. Establishment of an active oil futures market with reams of trading data available has led to a school of technical analysts or so-called chartists, relying on little or no information on oil market fundamentals. Regardless of which school one believes is more accurate, one can see clearly that oil market analysts now have substantially more data to explain precisely how uncertain they are about the likely behavior of oil prices.

Proliferation of oil market information does raise some concerns. Perceptions of the meeting of a given week's American Petroleum Institute (API) statistics often move the futures markets, only to have weekly data revised substantially the following week. This clearly makes life difficult for participants in the physical market. An area of concern for governments is the necessity to maintain the commitment to improve databases. This, however, becomes harder in an era of tight budgets. Because nearly a decade has passed since the last oil supply interruption in 1979, the need for accurate oil market information may become less clearly perceived.

2

Long-Range U.S. Oil Security

Melvin A. Conant

Few topics have dominated the history of U.S. energy more than its bearing on national security. In this respect, the focus of attention has almost always been on the role of imported oil (and, very secondarily and only in recent years, on the role of natural gas). But the topic of oil security has been complicated endlessly by a widespread and deep-seated public suspicion of the motives and profits of the oil industry. This factor is of such consequence to any consideration of energy policy "in the national interest" that it virtually precludes serious discussion of sensible options for the short term and certainly for the long range.

A very large part of this public mistrust has its origins in the repeated crises that have overcome the oil industry and for which rescue has been asked and reluctantly given by a skeptical citizenry. Since long-range energy commitments will require greater acceptance by the public of the importance of the industry to national security, greatest care will be needed to ensure widespread understanding of the nation's situation.

Since the turn of the century, the oil industry has rarely, if ever, been united on an analysis of a threat to itself, much less on options for a reduction in U.S. vulnerabilities. Moreover, oil companies have been divided by their particular interests—the "majors" versus the "independents" versus refining and exploration companies of a lesser size and the service industry—all finding themselves giving support at various times to one definition or another of oil and national security and the prescription for dealing with it. The perennial cry of every administration has been "give us a united position," and quite often, in a welter of often confusing analyses and prescriptions, the cry is not heard. Of course, in addition to different company interests there have almost always been different regional interests—most notably those of oil-importing New England. Sectoral differences have haunted energy debates about who or what is threatened by what kind of energy insecurity and how best to buy New England oil votes (or someone else's) by whatever kind of vote trading is necessary.

There have been genuine concerns about oil and national security. These have arisen in times of poor finding rates, lower-cost oil imports from problematic areas, and more recently, OPEC price manipulations, which have served to reduce investments into U.S. energy resources. Any one of these causes has often put great strain on the industry. This pressure leads industry to put its peril in the context of national security. When the result of a change in the industry leads to large increases in imports, then national security may indeed be affected. There have been many instances, however, in which a sudden rise in imports has been followed only a year later by a large decrease in imported volumes, without explanation. Or a loud cry that the United States is not discovering enough new oil, and that the reserves-production ratio is declining, is followed by a period in which additions to reserves (however defined) seem to improve the outlook.

Over the past eighty years there have been nearly thirty debates over oil and security. A quick review of the record informs an analyst that probably at no time was there the elusive united oil industry view but that in virtually every case in which a powerful segment spoke, an administration, regardless of its political leanings, came to the rescue in the name of national security. Similarly, in virtually no case did Congress ultimately fail to respond somehow, through one measure or another, despite regional differences and despite general consumer opposition.

There may be no case in which an administration itself took the initiative to propose a shelter or other rescue without prodding from part of the industry. Or putting it differently, there is probably no instance in which a government initiative could ever have surfaced without its first having been supported by at least part of the industry. In either case, without some industry enthusiasm, nothing would come of a government proposal. This has been as true of the domestic oil scene as it has been internationally. It is an astonishing and disturbing fact that given the importance of oil, at very few times did an administration take an initiative to define oil security, propose actions to strengthen it, and get a plan to Congress, all of its own volition. Whereas most of the times in which rescue was given, it was to domestic oil interests (by limiting domestic production if surplus was the problem, or limiting competition from foreign oil imports), there were notable cases in which the U.S. government either intervened overseas in behalf of U.S. oil companies or quietly accepted, if not energetically supported, efforts by these companies to promote price or supply arrangements with oil companies of other nationalities.

In short, the notion that the U.S. oil industry—domestic and foreign—was opposed to government intervention in one form or another is nonsense. No one has been quicker than the oil industry to assert the need for protection irrespective of market philosophies. Help has been obtained from state governments and/or the federal government. What the companies got in response must have been beneficial to their particular interests, but more often than one might suppose, government intervention has had a way of increasing government involvement beyond the original request. And in some cases, this greater government intervention became counterproductive to all interests: the oil companies and the nation.

In every example that I can recall, the request for governmental intervention has come because of the threat from foreign imports. The threat may take the form of too low oil prices, or a "flood" of imports threatening financial devastation of domestic producers and/or refiners, or in the early years, a flood of domestically produced oil driving prices through the cellar: Controls of some kind were held essential to bring order or stability into the market. A figure sometimes used to define national vulnerability was 12 percent: When imports reached that share of total U.S. consumption, the republic was endangered. In 1988, we speak of 40–50–60 percent, or more.

In the present situation, the nation has been asked again to accept the argument that a fast-paced rise in oil imports is itself dangerous to national security, reflecting the related factors of declining, expensive domestic production (a loss of some 800,000 B/D in 1986–1987 alone and a rise in foreign lower-cost production from OPEC and non-OPEC sources. The argument is being made that oil imports from Mexico or Canada or Venezuela have the same degree of risk as supplies from the Middle East Gulf. They do not, of course.

In addition, efforts are made to define risks to U.S. national security in terms of the (rising) share of imports in total domestic oil consumption. Why is a 30–40–50 percent, or an even higher share, risk laden? Is there a distinction to be made between crude and product imports? Is one a greater risk than the other? Are there no distinctions to be made between suppliers?

Finally, how does one appraise, on the one hand, those who point to the low finding rates for additional domestic oil reserves and yet, on the other, call for stimulation of ever-greater domestic exploration efforts? There has been only one supergiant field (over 5 billion barrels) discovered in North America for the past forty years—Prudhoe Bay, Alaska. The rest have been relatively modest successes, reserves added because of reestimates of existing fields (a complex process of not altogether certain conclusions) or their extension through further drilling. By these means, additions to U.S. proven reserves have had a temporary lift, but as noted and for reasons of uncertain field evaluation, there is more than a 50-50 chance that the decline in U.S. production (from 8.3 MMB/D in 1987 to 7.6 MMB/D in 1991) may become steeper, especially in later years, causing imports to rise more sharply. What is the reason (or hope) that further U.S. exploration will change the U.S. situation? Note Tables 2.1, 2.2, and 2.3.

TABLE 2.1
Oil Discovery Finding Rates

	Non-Communist Area Barrels/Foot Drilled	U.S. (Lower-48) Barrels/Foot Drilled
1950	6,000	90
1960	2,000	70
1970	4,000	70
1980	800	60
1990(est.)	800	20
2000(est.)	200	8

Source: Unpublished data compiled by Conant and Associates, Ltd., Washington, D.C.; and Joseph P. Riva, Jr., Earth Sciences, Congressional Research Services, Library of Congress.

TABLE 2.2
Approximate Number of Barrels Discovered Per Drilling Foot

	1950	1960	1970	1980	1985 (est.)
Middle East	100,000	100,000	70,000	11,000	10,000
Latin America	2,000	700	500	5,000	4,000
Africa	600	2,000	3,000	5,000	4,000
Far East	1,000	1,000	800	700	600
Western Europe	50	200	500	500	400
North America	80	60	200	50	45

Source: Same as Table 2.1.

TABLE 2.3
Oil Well Productivity

	B/D/Well
United States	14
Canada	29
Asia/Pacific	305
Other Western Hemisphere	164
Western Europe	519
Africa	1,239
Middle East	3,247

Source: Same as Table 2.1.

If the U.S. oil situation is to improve, several compelling arguments other than brighter domestic prospects have to be presented. The requirement is to put energy in perspective.

The United States is an energy giant. Its domestic energy resources of coal, oil, gas, nuclear power, and hydroelectric power have sustained huge production increases. Oil imports constitute the only really important source of risk. Natural gas imports, overwhelmingly from Canada, and electricity imports, also from Canada, are not regarded in the United States as being in the same category as Middle Eastern or African supplies. Moreover, the U.S.-Canadian Free Trade Agreement of 1988 may remove lingering doubts about the reliability of Canada as a supplier of oil and gas to the United States.

The principal source of U.S. concern about its energy situation lies in the dependence of U.S. *allies* upon Middle East Gulf sources. The United States is not dangerously dependent on the Gulf (about 15 percent of its imports comes from the Gulf—6 percent of total U.S. consumption), whereas Europe is dependent on the Gulf for 45 percent of its imports and Japan, for about 65 percent of its imports. Although in the future, the United States may obtain more of its increasing imports from the Gulf, it is just as likely that it will obtain its larger import volume from non-OPEC sources, including those in the Western Hemisphere. The U.S. concern about oil security rests far more on the much greater vulnerability of its allies. A selective embargo on one or more of them might have a greater economic effect on their economies than would one placed on the United States. Even more serious would be a disruption of Gulf supply to allies in a time of great tension. Gulf supplies are crucial to North Atlantic Treaty Organization (NATO) mobilization, indeed vital to allies' ability to fight a conventional war. Without the knowledge that oil was coming continuously from the Gulf, they could not fight for more than a week or so. This is a different argument about oil and U.S. security than the one we have been accustomed to hearing in which it is imports to the United States that are held to be the danger.

In addition, we are accustomed to thinking in terms of a possible Gulf supplier's use of its "oil weapon" to embargo supplies to the United States and/or certain key allies. For years, this has been a principle concern, arising mainly out of the events ensuing from the October 1973 Arab-Israeli war. It should now be regarded as among the least likely of U.S. concerns—except for such an unlikely event as an Israeli destructive attack upon the Dome of the Rock in Jerusalem.

Far more likely, now and in the foreseeable future, is not the use of the oil weapon against the United States and/or its major allies but the use of the weapon by producing states of the Gulf against each other: Importing nations could be injured if key facilities were damaged. But that is a different scenario. And it is more likely that actions of producing governments against each other will take the form of economic warfare.

Of course, it is the 15 MMB/D of idle producing capacity (at least half of it in the Gulf itself) that makes for this change in threats. It was far easier to embargo oil-importing nations in 1973 when supplies and logistics were tight. Given projections of very moderate OECD gross national product (GNP) growth rates, and the resultant low increases in energy/oil demand growth, the surplus of oil may last for many years. The OPEC oil weapon has lost much of its clout.

The argument will then be heard that a U.S. strategic petroleum reserve (SPR) of 550 MMB/D is a sufficient and inexpensive protection from as much as a 50 percent cut in imported supply. The SPR could give adequate protection from even a total oil cutoff for seventy-five days. But the usefulness of an SPR depends utterly on government determination as to how the reserve is to be used. Resort to the "marketplace" in times of an emergency—with the implication of who pays the most gets the oil—would be a totally unacceptable policy (in any democratic society). In the event, oil would go to where it is most needed. Whether government is better able to allocate than it did in the 1970s is the real question. If the answer is yes, it will be because government is better prepared and because Congress lets the system work without defeating the effort through requests for preferential access to the reserve.

A new definition of U.S. energy security, especially for the long term, would be "sufficient petroleum stocks to have in place 50 percent of U.S. and other NATO imports, including Japan, for a time of mobilization, including an outbreak of conventional war." The span required is at least 180 days or double the current standard of the International Energy Agency. Assume there is confidence in these stocks' being delivered to those sectors most in need, including the armed forces; then, threats of oil disruptions in the Gulf, for whatever reason, would seem manageable.

Yet this does not altogether address the energy security interests of the United States, for there is another perspective on U.S. and allied vulnerability through their dependence on oil imports. Rarely mentioned is the energy factor in the superpower balance. The Soviet Union does not depend in any meaningful way on imported oil; the United States and especially its NATO allies and Japan are profoundly dependent on foreign oil for the effective working of their collective-security arrangements. The Soviet Union, therefore, has a large degree of flexibility in what it chooses to do in foreign areas, compared to that of the United States and its allies. There must be significance in this difference between superpowers, but it is very rarely referred to for inexplicable reasons. But because of the strategic imbalances in oil needs, allied strategic petroleum reserves may not be enough. The SPR will surely not be enough for the United States, the lead nation in security agreements. There are no shortcuts, no easy course to attaining greater oil security.

Renewed emphasis must now be placed on the long-range actions required to increase U.S. oil security and thus that of the effective functioning of its alliances. And in consideration of the oil factor in U.S. defense relationships with allies, and the use of the SPR, public understanding and acceptance is crucial. Such actions have to be considered in the long term, for none has any promise of short-term effects. It takes years to make a difference: five to seven years to exploit an oil discovery in more difficult or frontier regions, which is where such discoveries are still anticipated.

What follows is a list of priority actions. There is nothing novel about it; most items on it are wholly familiar, but some of the emphasis is different: The objective in each effort is to reduce the consumption of oil. In any case, without durable government incentives to encourage efforts to reduce energy risks, through whatever means, and without the enlistment of the U.S. private sector, nothing is likely to happen.

1. Intensification of the search for transport fuel substitutes for gasoline and diesel—transport fuel takes nearly 50 percent of the processed barrel. Success in the research and development (R & D) objective might make the largest difference in oil-import dependence.
2. High priority to the R & D effort to reduce to the least amount possible coal-burning pollution and to coal conversion into substitute fuels for oil.
3. Encouragement of oil exploration and production (E & P) in the United States, but given poor finding rates and high costs per barrel compared to other regions, overseas E & P outside the Gulf may be the most important.
4. Intensification of the search for additional natural gas reserves in the United States and Canada. If the prospect is for very sizable additional reserves at reasonable development costs, then E & P must be stepped up. But if there is concern about the degree of success, then high priority must be given to the availability of Alaskan natural gas. Highest priority must be given to the further conservation of energy and R & D into still greater energy efficiencies. It is conceivable that the United States can continue for many years to reduce its energy use per unit of GNP.
5. Another close look at the improving economics of production of heavier oils, tar sands and, more remote in time, of shale oil. Incentives to continue to use enhanced oil recovery techniques.

6. High priority to "superconductors" as a long-range means for reducing energy requirements.
7. High priority to the most publicly acceptable and economic means for generating electric power.
8. The nuclear option cannot be left unattended. For too long public concerns have been largely dismissed by a besieged industry. If construction standards and operating performances are not widely thought to have improved, there will be no meaningful increase in public confidence. A very searching look by a national independent commission at this phenomenon of public opposition is the way to begin.
9. In time, and at a pace in which circumstances and private enterprise create opportunities, research and development into nonfossil fuel energies, mainly solar, but also geothermal, have to be encouraged—especially inexhaustible sources of energy.

However, an enduring policy and commitment to the develoment of alternative fuels has to be derived from an answer to an immensely complicated question. Is the world price for oil, set mainly by OPEC, to be the major factor in determining the U.S. domestic price? If so, then the domestic oil price will be set by *governments* of producing countries. They will continue to be able to raise prices of international oil (and thereby stimulate E & P in the United States and elsewhere) or depress the international oil price (and thereby reduce E & P, conservation, and R & D commitments by the private sector). In times of increasing OPEC-defined prices, some of the private oil industry have referred to those prices as the result of market forces; when prices fall, it is said to be the result of a cartel to be countered by government action. We have to get the situation straight in our own minds.

If the United States embarks on major commitments to strengthen its oil security by reducing its dependence on oil imports, and to develop alternative fuels—all in the national interest—then commitments to an energy program have to be maintained though insulation of the national energy effort from the results of OPEC-defined price movements. U.S. energy decisions ought not to be dependent on OPEC manipulation of oil prices, but they are at present.

In addition, the United States must reconsider the option of obtaining a greater share of its imports of oil from the Western Hemisphere. The principal argument for doing so is to take fuller advantage of presumably less-vulnerable supply lanes. It is altogether possible that hemispheric supplies from Mexico (assuming its political willingness to deliver), Colombia, Ecuador, and Canada could meet some 35 percent of current U.S. imports. In the longer term, the sheer importance of petroleum

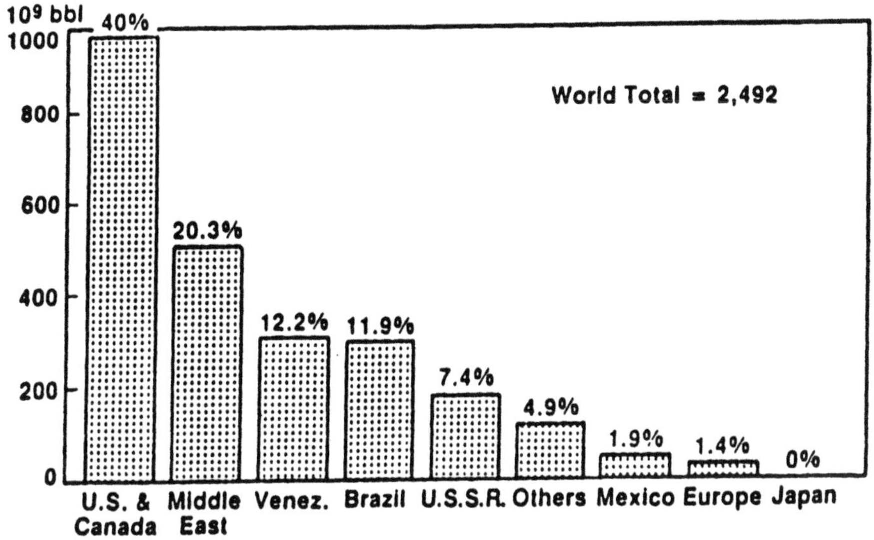

FIGURE 2.1 Proven reserves of conventional crude oil, heavy oils, tar sands, and shale oil.
Source: Based on unpublished data compiled by Conant and Associates, Ltd., Washington, D.C., and Joseph P. Riva, Jr., Earth Sciences, Congressional Research Services, Library of Congress.

reserves in North America and the Western Hemisphere as a whole should be kept in mind (see Figure 2.1).

All of these priorities are easier said than done, whether the means is a minimum "floor" price, or an oil-import fee, or some other device such as total import restrictions (letting scarce domestic oil prices rise), or preferred sources. Someone has first to define an appropriate U.S. domestic oil price and determine in which circumstances that U.S. government oil price will rise and fall to keep the domestic energy program alive. The U.S. record in setting oil prices with informed advice is no better than OPEC's. Perhaps an interagency committee, chaired by the secretaries of the treasury, of commerce, and of energy, would be a proper and sufficient group to develop a price-setting formula, with oversight of their effects. However this is accomplished, it is totally predictable that a holy row will greet each price announcement. But the objective has to be kept: U.S. long-range commitments to develop one energy fuel or another must not continue to be vulnerable to OPEC-defined price changes.

3

Oil Refining: Planning Long-Term Strategies in a Short-Term Market

Fereidun Fesharaki and David T. Isaak

Refiners tend to be justifiably skeptical when oil analysts talk about what is certain in the long term. It is safe to talk about the long term, since it is unlikely that, in the long term, anyone will remember what was predicted. Furthermore, there are statements about the long-term oil market that any reasonable person must accept. For example, oil prices will go up in the long term; oil is a finite resource. In the long term, the Gulf will return to its pivotal control of the export market; anyone who can count can see that the Gulf is where the major unexploited resources of the world are located. In the long term, sustained profitability must return to refining; if it does not, there will be no more investment, and margins will eventually rise enough that investment is more than justified.

If the analyst couches his statements about the long term in the proper language, the statements may sound profound and have a ring of certainty to them. But most refiners have become wary of such statements, not because the refiners disagree with the statements but because the refiners have a problem the analyst does not have: the refiners need to stay in business until the long term finally gets here. Furthermore, the refiner has a different time frame for decisionmaking than the typical oil analyst has. To the analyst, the short term ranges from the present moment to the next year or two, whereas the long term is typically ten, sometimes even twenty or thirty, years in the future. For the refiner, the short term is the next cargo, and the long term in today's market is the period after the current netback arrangement runs out—two months, three months, maybe a year. Knowledge of the details of the market in the year 2000 is of little use to a company that may face bankruptcy in a few months.

Unfortunately, there are certain decisions in refining that require thinking in the analyst's time frame: five, ten, or fifteen years into the future. Almost all of these center around capacity changes. Investment decisions must be made on the basis of longer-term market conditions, since most investments must pay themselves off over a long period of operation. Decisions to close capacity require equal foresight. For example, some refiners avoided some very hefty losses by moving to rationalize capacity early in the 1980s. On the other hand, many refiners "toughed it out" through the bad years of the early 1980s and got the worst of both worlds by closing in, say, 1984–1985, when the chance for a profit from netback deals or falling oil prices was right around the corner.

How can refiners plan for the long term with some certainty in a market as confused and volatile as that seen today? The answer is simple: they can't. Refiners are running out of certainty a lot faster than we are running out of oil. It is clear that, at some point, the market will firm and oil will resume its upward price trend. It is easy to make a calculation that indicates that this should happen around 1992, but it is equally easy to produce plausible assumptions that delay this until the late 1990s, or even until the turn of the century. Making the right investment five years too early can be disastrous; hesitating when the time is ripe can mean a loss of competitiveness.

We cannot claim to have the answers. In the following pages, we will review the uncertainties in the near-term market and then take a glance at some rather wild scenarios of the future of oil demand and product demand slates for the region over the next decade or so. We will then try to return to the basic question: How can intelligent planning take place under something near total uncertainty? We cannot answer this question in full, but we do have some suggestions about what we see as the emerging model for refinery planning over the next decade.

The Refining Industry in the Near Term

The world refining industry has undergone substantial changes over the past few years. The industry has been suffering from overall capacity surplus and differing government and industry policies on rationalization of capacity. Moreover, the unusual crude product price relationships have resulted in significant changes in refining margins: shifting from negative to positive in ways that are hardly predictable.

In the short term, crude price fluctuations will dominate refining margins. As product prices move in line with crude prices after the usual lags, crude prices move up or down again for a variety of reasons, leaving refining margins highly uncertain. Can any refiner seriously plan any investments or long-term policies in this environment? The answer must be no! Short of certain refiners who are in protected markets, few commercial refining operations can feel comfortable enough to invest or rationalize their operations in the near term. Netback contracts may guarantee certain margins, but can they be relied upon beyond just a few months or one year at the most?

Until and unless some crude price stability reemerges in the market, the refining industry will be in limbo. Until and unless we feel sure that netback or product realization deals are either eliminated or are here to stay on longer-term contracts, the future prospects of the refining industry remain unresolved. What may be considered as a money-losing refining operation by one company may be profitable for another with the right netback deal. Who would have thought that Exxon's abandoned Lago refinery in Aruba would be considered for reopening by another company as a potential money-maker? At the moment, it is all coming down to what kind of a crude price deal is available to the potential refiner. This is not an environment conducive to rational planning.

We all have our own theories about where the prices will go and when. Although most would agree that oil prices will rise at some point, the key factors are *when, how fast,* and the response of *product prices* to crude prices. However, a fundamental part of the equation is demand. We are often so immersed in our calculations of scenarios of OPEC and non-OPEC supply control that we forget about demand. Without increases in demand, there is little chance of price stability, irrespective of oil exporters' supply control strategies. In our judgment, demand for oil must rise by 3–4 million barrels per day (MMB/D) to, say, around 52 MMB/D for the non-Communist world before price stability returns. This level may not be reached before 1990–1991, and until then confusion in the refining industry will continue to reign. Thus, for the next few years crude price fluctuations will overshadow fundamental rationalization efforts in the global refining industry. In other words, economic decisions to close capacity or make new investments will be further postponed.

The Refining Industry in the Asia-Pacific Region

In the Asia-Pacific oil market, which is of special professional interest to us, demand has undergone a major shift away from fuel oil. Although this fundamentally is not much different from what happened in the United States or Europe during the 1970s, the speed of the shift away—particularly at the time when total oil demand continues to grow (albeit slowly)—has changed the structure of the demand barrel rather significantly.

The shift away from the heavy end of the barrel is more pronounced in power generation—owing to substitution by natural gas, coal, nuclear power, and hydroelectricity. Total regional demand for fuel oil in power generation is expected to decline over the next decade, despite a large rise in electricity demand. In many countries in the region, utilities and oil refiners have been working at cross-purposes. Government policies have encouraged the utilities to move away from fuel oil—by means of regulation, taxes, and economic incentives. While this substitution was taking place, not much attention was being paid to how the refiners (national oil companies or privately owned refineries) would fare after the substitution. Although the governments and utilities did not fully consult the refiners, the refiners themselves did not protest loudly enough that the course of their future profitability would be affected by these changes. In fact, although the governments were happy to endorse major new utility investments, very few, if any, would finance the building of cracking facilities to convert the unwanted heavy ends into lighter products.

The shift away from fuel oil is not confined to the oil importers but includes oil exporters as well. For an oil importer, reducing consumption of the heavy ends does not necessarily imply a reduction in oil imports; for an oil exporter also, substitution of fuel oil does not mean more oil exports. In both cases the critical issue is the quality of crude oil and the fuel oil destruction capability of the refineries.

The demand for oil in the Asia-Pacific region is expected to grow by 3–4 percent per annum. This estimate excludes Japan, where demand growth will be in the range of zero to 300 thousand barrels per day (MB/D) over the next ten years. We expect demand growth to be strongest for middle distillates, followed by gasoline. With the decline in fuel oil use for power generation, the share of light and middle distillates will rise significantly in the demand barrel over the next few years.

On the supply side, the average crude slate in the region has become lighter because of the higher production of light Asian crudes. Higher condensate production, resulting from recent discoveries and as a by-product of liquefied natural gas (LNG) export projects, has also helped to lighten the crude barrel. Still, we expect at least two-thirds of crude imports in the region to be made up of heavier (Arab-heavy to Arab-light types) Middle East crudes.

The regional refineries supplying petroleum products are relatively unsophisticated by world standards. A crude distillation capacity of 12.4 MMB/D is expected by 1990 (see Table 3.1). The cracking-to-distillation ratio (excluding desulfurization) stands at 19 percent—of which 4 percent is thermal cracking. Altogether this fuel oil destruction capacity is far below that found in the United States, Europe, the Middle East, and

TABLE 3.1
Structure of the Asia-Pacific Refining Industry

	Million Barrels per Calendar Day[a]
Crude distillation	12.412
Vacuum	3.161
Catalytic cracking	1.350
Hydrocracking	.301
Coking	.217
Thermal	.561

[a]Existing plus firmly planned capacity under construction.

Source: Energy Program Data Files, East-West Center, Honolulu.

even in many Latin American countries. Without the lightening of the crude slate mentioned earlier, regional refineries would have ended up with a major surplus of heavy ends. The lighter crude barrels have alleviated the situation somewhat, but the overhang of the heavy ends will still be pronounced, particularly because the major light Far East crudes yield a large volume of low-sulfur waxy resids. At the same time, the new source refineries of the Middle East could, by 1990, create a flow of as much as 150–200 MB/D of additional high-sulfur fuel oil into the region, while the fuel oil exports from the West Coast of the United States into the region are expected to be at the level of 70–100 MB/D over the next decade.

Thus, in the 1990s, the Asia-Pacific oil market will be characterized by an imbalance between the supply barrel and the demand barrel, with an overhang of fuel oil and downward pressure on fuel oil prices. In addition, new supplies of condensate and natural gas liquids (NGLs) will weaken the market for naphtha. This problem is exacerbated by the fact that most of the upgrading capacity in the region is catalytic cracking; if the fuel oil excess is disposed of by intensive cracking, the supply of naphtha, which is already tending toward surplus, will increase. Thus, there is a weakness in both the top and the bottom of the supply barrel; only the middle-distillate-range products seem to face a relatively firm situation. This by no means indicates that a middle-distillate shortage is imminent; but it suggests that middle-distillate prices will be stronger than the price trends for the top or bottom of the barrel.

Refined Products Imports into the Region

The configuration of the world oil trade in terms of crude and products has undergone significant changes. The new OPEC source refineries, the increase of processing agreements, and the rise of netback-type deals have added to the volume of product trade. In 1980, around 15 percent of the world oil trade was in the form of refined products; however, the worldwide figure for products is expected to rise to 30 percent by the end of the 1980s. The impact of this change in the crude/product ratio will also be observed in the Asia-Pacific region.

The OPEC export refineries are almost all complete, with the exception of the Rabigh refinery in Saudi Arabia and the upgrading changes in Kuwait. We continue to expect that around 300–350 MB/D of new products from OPEC source refineries will enter the region by the end of the 1980s. We had previously expected this flow by 1987, but the recent events in the oil market have again postponed the impact of underlying changes in the market. The source refineries have been plagued by technical problems (as in the case of Indonesia) and by policy problems (as in the case of Saudi Arabia). Saudi Arabia has been trying for years to come up with a price strategy to sell products on a long-term basis. Only since mid-1987 has a workable policy been adopted. In a world of spot prices and netbacks, where Rotterdam product prices can affect Asian netback prices, it is only to be expected that export refining would take a low priority. As long as the current turmoil in the oil market continues, and as long as the world is awash in market-related crude, export refining will necessarily take a backseat. Thus, once again the fundamental rationalization of the regional refining industry is overshadowed by the current uncertainties. It is our opinion that OPEC source refineries should not be written off just yet but that they will flow into the region in a slower and less disruptive manner than previously anticipated. Product prices will be set by Singapore prices and export refiners will follow these prices.

Long-Term Refining Prospects

Although we are preoccupied by short-term confusion in the oil market, longer-term refining needs need to be assessed carefully. Long-term refining prospects are heavily dependent on the future course of oil prices. We have therefore undertaken our refining investment study in the context of the different price scenarios. These could result in significant changes in the product demand pattern, which would in turn require a different refining configuration to balance supply with demand.

Oil Price Scenarios and Product Demand

Our approach to projecting the future price of oil is through constructing a number of scenarios. Scenario analysis, given present-day

TABLE 3.2
Three Price Paths

	1990	1995	2000
Case I: Low prices			
Real oil price, 1985 U.S. $	$15	$15	$15
Annual growth over previous period		0.0	0.0
Case II: Medium prices			
Real oil price, 1985 U.S. $	$18	$20	$24
Annual growth over previous period		2.1	3.4
Case III: High prices			
Real oil price, 1985 U.S. $	$23	$27	$34
Annual growth over previous period		3.3	5.0

uncertainties, is perhaps the most responsible approach we can take in giving our readers a realistic view of the range of possibilities in the future oil market.

We have selected three scenarios (see Table 3.2). The first we consider the most unlikely. It envisions a serious erosion in real oil prices, followed by fifteen years of low prices. In any case, this scenario provides what we consider to be a reasonable lower bound on oil price behavior; the scenario becomes less and less plausible after about 1995.

Our second scenario probably comes close to current conventional wisdom within the industry. It envisions an eroding price in the near future, followed by an upswing and renewed price growth as existing non-OPEC reserves are exhausted and as moderate-demand growth forces more costly frontier provinces into production.

Our third scenario is a high-price case, in which, after a readjustment of supply and demand in the near term, prices rise steeply. The difference between this case and the second case is primarily one of ultimate oil reserves; this case is rather conservative in the estimate of how much additional oil can be found at reasonable prices.

Estimating the future product demand of the region with precision would be a massive undertaking, requiring detailed computer modeling of each nation. For some countries, forecasts based on detailed studies are already available; in certain other countries, such as China, Indonesia, Malaysia, and Korea, we have already devoted considerable research to the demand picture. But unfortunately, no studies exist that cover the wide range of future prices we have adopted in our three scenarios. Therefore, to develop a picture of composite demand for the region, we have had to rely on informed judgment based on our familiarity with the major countries, extrapolating by analogy where necessary (see Table 3.3).

TABLE 3.3
Projections of Petroleum Product Demand in the Asia-Pacific Region Under Three Price Scenarios

	1987		1990		2000	
	MMB/D	% Share	MMB/D	% Share	MMB/D	% Share
Low Price						
Light	2.0	23	2.4	25	3.7	24
Middle	2.9	34	3.4	36	5.8	37
Fuel Oil	2.5	29	2.4	25	4.4	28
Other	1.2	14	1.3	14	1.6	10
Total	8.6	100	9.5	100	15.5	100
Medium Price						
Light	2.0	23	2.4	25	3.5	28
Middle	2.9	34	3.4	36	4.5	36
Fuel Oil	2.5	29	2.4	25	3.0	24
Other	1.2	14	1.3	14	1.5	12
Total	8.6	100	9.5	100	12.5	100
High Price						
Light	2.0	23	2.3	24	3.3	31
Middle	2.9	34	3.4	36	4.0	38
Fuel Oil	2.5	29	2.4	26	1.9	18
Other	1.2	14	1.3	14	1.4	13
Total	8.6	100	9.4	100	10.6	100

Notes: Light includes gasolines and naphthas; middle includes kerosene, diesel and jet fuel; other includes refinery-based liquified petroleum gas (LPG), lubes, solvents, asphalts, waxes, et cetera. Percentages may not add up because of rounding.

The table shows an estimated oil demand of 8.6 MMB/D in 1987, of which the largest portion is middle distillates at 34 percent, with the second largest being fuel oil at 29 percent. Under the three price scenarios discussed previously, demand behavior exhibits very different growth rates. The differences between the scenarios in 1990 are minimal. This is in accord with our belief that lower prices will have only minor effects on demand in the short term; the $7 per barrel differential between the high and low price for crude in 1990 makes a difference of only 1 percent in demand. However, the scenarios diverge sharply in the 1990s, and by 2000 the difference in demand between the low- and high-price cases is over 50 percent. The low-price case sees a booming demand for oil, rising 3.7 percent per annum over the period; the high-price case has an annual increase of only 0.7 percent.

In all cases, the demand for light- and middle-distillate products rises in both absolute and percentage terms. The low-price case also predicts a rise in fuel oil demand and in fuel oil's share of the market. In the

TABLE 3.4
Projected Product Imports into the Region (MB/D)

	1990	2000
Light products	200	150
Middle distillates	300	250
Fuel oils[a]	250	200
Other (excluding LPG)	50	30
Total	800	630

[a]U.S. West Coast exports of around 70 MB/D.

Source: Energy Program Data Files, East-West Center, Honolulu.

high-price case, fuel oil demand declines both in absolute and percentage terms.

The high-price case has the largest change in the composition of demand. The transport fuels (light and middle distillates) and specialty products ("other") gain substantial shares at the expense of fuel oil. In this case, by 2000 the transport fuels, a premium use of oil, account for nearly 70 percent of demand, as opposed to 57 percent in 1987.

Some analysts would question the feasibility of certain scenarios, particularly the low-price case: is it really possible to obtain nearly 16 MMB/D of oil for the Asia-Pacific region alone? Perhaps not, and probably not at the kinds of prices we have assumed here. But providing a forecast is not our goal here. We believe that, short of a regional economic collapse on a prolonged basis, most experts would agree that any likely future demands for the region will lie somewhere within the bounds of these three scenarios.

Refining Investments Requirements

To estimate the investments required, we have constructed a simple linear programming model of the region. The model has eight generic crudes available, five with primary supply from the Middle East. Production of high-quality Asian crudes was bounded at likely production levels less a small (500 MB/D) volume of exports to outside the region. Imports into the region were assumed constant in all demand cases at the levels shown in Table 3.4. It is assumed that petroleum products entering the region are mostly originating from the Middle East Gulf and the U.S. West Coast—with the latter essentially supplying high-sulfur fuel oil. This scenario assumes no construction of new export refineries in the Gulf.

In addition, excess base-year refinery capacity in Japan was lowered in accordance with present plans. Technologies included in the model were distillation, vacuum distillation, cat cracking, hydrocracking, coking, visbreaking, and reforming. The cracking technology results were aggregated because of uncertainties regarding relative costs; in some cases, the model's choice of technology was determined by small differences in economics, and we do not wish to mislead others by specifying the exact mix of technologies required in future years.

We ran two cases against our three demand scenarios: a "high-trade" case and a "lower-trade" case. The first case assumes that countries will be willing to increase product imports (from inside the region) steadily as long as major spare capacity is available in export centers such as Singapore. That is, the regional capacity (rather than the individual nations' refinery balances) is used to balance supply and demand for products, rather than individual nations' refinery balances. This case is a minimum-investment scenario.

As a matter of policy, certain countries, notably China, will not accept product imports to balance demand, and others, such as Japan, presently have limitations on certain product classes. Furthermore, some product-importing countries, such as Malaysia, are likely to construct new refineries in the longer term based on local crude supplies. The lower-trade case reflects a situation where individual countries add refinery capacity to balance their own supply and demand in addition to the needed regional expansion. Here, the refinery surplus situation of the region will continue. The economics of these new additions in most cases are roughly indifferent between product imports and domestic refining.

The results, shown in Tables 3.5 and 3.6, contain what may be some surprises. For the 1991–2000 period, the required investments are inversely related to total oil demand. This, of course, reflects the dramatic shift in patterns of product demand at higher prices; large amounts of cracking must be installed to balance supply and demand. (Note that "trade" in this context is intraregional trade. Imports from outside the region are the same for each price scenario.)

The high-trade case is probably closest to the investments required for economic efficiency on a regional basis; the lower-trade case is a more realistic assessment of the financing that is liable to be *sought* from the market by countries. The amount of investment required for balancing supply and demand varies widely in the cases discussed. First, in the high-trade/low-investment case, the following results can be observed.

1. In the low-price case, minor investments of $140 million in cracking are needed through 1990. For 1991–2000, investment of $3.9 billion is needed for primary distillation, but no cracking additions are

called for. Thus, low oil price leading to larger oil demand requires substantial investments in refining.

2. In the medium-price case, higher investments of nearly $5 billion are needed during the 1990s.
3. In the high-price case, refining investments are much larger in cracking as the demand for fuel oil declines. The investments needed are $5.8 billion in the 1990s.

TABLE 3.5
Required Investments in Refining—High Trade Case (million 1987 $)

	1987–1990	1991–2000
Low-price scenario		
Primary capacity[a]		3,860
Cracking	140	
Total	140	3,860
Medium-price scenario		
Primary capacity[a]		1,000
Cracking	140	3,980
Total	140	4,980
High-price scenario		
Primary capacity[a]		120
Cracking	140	5,660
Total	140	5,780

[a]Including auxiliary units; a "hydroskimming" configuration.

TABLE 3.6
Required Investments in Refining—Lower Trade Case (million 1987 $)

	1987–1990	1991–2000
Low-price scenario		
Primary capacity[a]	780	4,510
Cracking	1,230	1,230
Total	2,010	5,740
Medium-price scenario		
Primary capacity[a]	780	1,330
Cracking	1,230	5,840
Total	2,010	7,140
High-price scenario		
Primary capacity[a]	780	470
Cracking	2,190	8,700
Total	2,970	9,170

[a]Including auxiliary units; a "hydroskimming" configuration.

For the low-trade/high-investment case, the general pattern is similar to the previous case, but volumes are larger as each country tries to balance its own demand with supply.

An Emerging Model of Planning in Refining

First of all, back to basics: If there is any sense at all in the market, a market that requires new investment is a market where there must be a margin—at least on some products, if not on all. This fact has been masked for several years by a large number of investment decisions that were not driven by product demands' putting pressure on capacity. Since the late 1970s we have seen investments undertaken by governments in the name of energy security; investments undertaken by oil-producing countries that were riding on a vast wave of surplus funds; even some rather speculative investments undertaken by oil companies that were trying to use upstream cash flows to find some way to return profitability to their downstream operations. We have seen investments undertaken for nearly every reason except the only reliable one, which is increased demand. After staggering through the demand slump of the 1980s, most of us have forgotten that there can be something such as an increase of demand over available capacity.

Nonetheless, the previous section suggests that, even under wildly differing scenarios of demand and prices, the 1990s will see a considerable need for new investments in refining in the region, based on *demand.* Unfortunately, the types of investments vary widely between scenarios; in one case, an expansion of distillation is required, whereas in another the investments are almost exclusively in cracking facilities. Furthermore, the absolute levels of investment needed are strongly affected by government policies on product trade. Much more investment will occur if a continuation of protectionist, restrictive policies is seen in the region. This means very different things to different refiners. To a refiner in Singapore, exposed to every wind that gusts through the international market—yet denied access to many of the most profitable national markets—protectionism means that even though greater levels of investment may occur, the resulting margins may only be reflected in local markets.

A brief digression is of some importance here. At the beginning of the 1980s, we predicted the collapse of the world entrepôt centers, particularly the Caribbean centers and, to a lesser extent, Singapore. Our predictions were fairly well borne out in the Caribbean, but Singapore did much better than was generally expected. It is true that Singapore has been under heavy pressure, and that the refiners have lived more or less "hand-to-mouth" for several years. Without any of the changing factors that have kept the industry afloat (processing deals, flexible and innovative selection of a crude slate, the current netback deals, the ability of Singapore to fill in small demand imbalances as they have appeared and vanished), there is little doubt that Singapore would have undergone the kind of major contraction seen elsewhere. We have no doubt in the ability of Singapore refiners, having weathered the early 1980s, to survive in the longer term; they are simply "faster on their feet" than almost anyone else. Singapore refiners survived despite the general market trends; they ought to have been forced to shut down significant volumes of capacity but did not because of a whole series of special opportunities. These special opportunities or niches were not necessarily in harmony with the general trends or pressures of the market; they were specific to a time and place and might not have been available to a refiner on, say, the U.S. Gulf Coast or in Europe. This underlines a very important point: The special conditions a given refiner faces may frequently be more important than the general market trends. Planning based on the "big picture" has become increasingly ineffective because there are so many exceptions.

Gradually, a new model of planning for refiners is emerging, based on scenarios and probabilities. Although there is a tendency to dismiss scenario-based analysis as the work of someone who is afraid to make a forecast, scenarios are the only sensible way to deal with the vast uncertainty in the future market. In the past, the typical use of scenarios has been to produce a high, medium, and low case; everyone then proceeds to use the medium case as if it were the best prediction. This, of course, is nothing more than doing a forecast, but hedging. The new mode of scenario analysis is more quantitative and results in a more detailed menu of outcomes than the methods typically employed in the past. The new approach involves identifying the key factors that determine the profitability of the refinery. These can be large-scale market factors, such as crude prices or regional demand; they can be local factors, such as discounts on crude or government policies on imports of products.

Once the key factors have been identified, probabilities are assigned to the behavior of each variable. Although these days no one can tell you what the price of crude will be in 1995, most people can comfortably estimate how likely it is that the price will be below $8/barrel (b) or above $50/b; most people can even decide how likely they think it is that the price will be below or above $20/b (say, 50–50?). Once the probabilities are assessed, the variables are assembled into a decision tree where the probabilities are applied to the various strategies the company is considering. The result is a probability distribution of profits from the various options. At this point, executive judgment takes over; a gambler may go for the strategy that offers a high probability of large profits but has a significant downside risk; a conservative may opt for the strategy that appears to offer almost no downside risk but that does not promise great profits.

A number of companies in the energy industry are now using this type of approach in dealing with the wide range of possible market conditions seen in the future; it is no longer a matter of betting on a forecast, but instead a matter of selecting a strategy that performs as desired over a range of outcomes.

This change in approaches to planning is causing changes in the relations between consulting analysts and their clients as well. The consultants and firms that are most active in this kind of planning do not tend to be the major consulting firms, because many of the tools that the major consulting firms use—macroeconomic models, econometric forecasting equations—are not well suited to the scenario-type of analysis. Moreover, there is considerably less opportunity to sell basically the same research over and over to a series of clients. Instead, the scenario analysts tend to be smaller groups that work closely with the corporate management in identifying key driving variables and assembling probability distributions that reflect the management's perception of local factors that the analysts understand in depth. It is an arrangement where there is a great deal of give-and-take and debate between the company and the consultants, and where the direction of the course of work is often changed by insights that occur during the course of the research. It is the opposite of the multiclient study, where a vast array of data is assembled and the consultants form some judgment as to the future trends; instead, it is a type of study that is tailored to the most important factors facing an individual company.

It is our belief that this scenario-type of planning, especially for investment planning or decisions to reduce capacity, will become the dominant method of analysis over the next decade. As stated in our "Introduction," one cannot plan with any certainty in a volatile and unpredictable market; but it may be possible to get a fairly good grip on the range of possible market conditions and the implications that they may have for the profitability of various strategies. In the long term, such wide-ranging planning may not be necessary; but in the near term, planning on the basis of forecasts will continue to be a disappointing business.

Conclusions

The Asia-Pacific oil market promises to be the most dynamic in the world in coming years, with many changes occurring simultaneously. Differing government policies, rules and regulations, and structure of demand will make the region the most complicated to analyze. While many are preoccupied with near-term changes, fundamental underlying changes in the structure of this market continue to take place. The region's dependence on petroleum imports from the Middle East will continue indefinitely. Though this may be a problem in times of shortage, it can be turned into a major advantage in times of persistent glut. Oil demand can rise substantially in the region in the face of continuing low prices. The demand for fuel oil—the weakest part of the price barrel—can rise significantly from the late 1980s as the first round of substitution comes to an end.

The imbalance between the demand barrel and the supply barrel will worsen over the next few years, giving rise to significant expansion of product trading. This will put further pressure on product prices and may create additional room for refining margins.

The issue of supply/demand imbalance and of the relative simplicity of Asia-Pacific refining systems raises the question of trade-off between product imports and investments in refining. Investments in refining are highly dependent on oil prices and oil demand. Lower oil prices require additional investments in primary distillation because of demand increases across the barrel. Higher oil prices, on the other hand, will create the need for more upgrading investments—as fuel oil is further backed out. In both cases, there is unlikely to be much investment before 1990. Cooperation in exchange of information or plans for refinery construction can significantly reduce regional investments in this sector.

Given the uncertainties surrounding the refining industry in the short term, traditional means of planning may have lost their relevance. A flexible approach based on a range of outcomes may be the only rational way to approach investment planning over the next decade or so.

4

The Changing Structure of the Oil Industry

Paul H. Frankel

Fundamental Features of the Oil Industry

Some of the fundamental features of the oil industry have a virtually permanent impact upon its structure. Changes in the economic and political climate do influence the way these features are allowed to fashion actual developments, yet the basic concepts do shine through the passing clouds even if these tend at times to obscure what really matters.

The central factor in the oil industry's life is its being investment oriented, hence the extreme relationship of fixed and variable cost. In all phases of the industry—exploration and production, refining, transportation, and even marketing—the need to put down the money "up front" has far-reaching repercussions: First, there is the fact that once the initial investment has been made, it makes sense to strive for full employment of plant, since the attributable cost of marginal capacity is extremely low. This feature inhibits the working of an acceptable floor to the price curves: Elasticity of supply is low (that is, reaction to lower or even higher prices makes itself felt slowly), and also the reaction to price changes on the demand side is limited to fuel oils, since motor fuels have no competitors. Moreover, a result of the vulnerability of investment is the search for security of tenure, provided inter alia by vertical integration, which assures controlled outlets for the producer and refiner and, incidentally, a safe line of supply for refiner and marketer, should there be a shortage of supplies.

Finally, due to the need for reducing the risks faced by isolated enterprises, there is an abiding tendency toward spreading risks by extending activities on a wider front, making it possible to average out the different profit and loss levels, thus extending an enterprise's life expectancy.

Growth of Oil Companies

The oil industry's history does bear out the results of fundamental analysis: All along there has been a strong drift toward formation of large managerial units, tending, once they have reached a certain size, to cover more than one and most likely all phases of the industry and to cover, where possible, a substantial number of regions and countries. Beyond this there was a tendency of big companies to establish a modus vivendi with like-minded competitors in order to achieve—whenever and wherever legally possible—a form of shared control of the market and to achieve and maintain a profit margin that included a certain degree of "rent."

Alongside these big-unit arrangements there always developed, in one form or another, a welter of smaller-size enterprises, originally in the United States called independent of Standard Oil, and existing in the gaps between the majors. Although living dangerously, they sometimes thrived, making good use of the philosophy Small Is Beautiful and, with luck, growing into substantial entities. There is an irresistible trend against control by Big Brother. An advantage opposite to that of the big enterprises can be derived, moreover, by implanting oneself in a limited area of above-average profitability rather than averaging out profits across a broader range with lesser prospects (which inevitably dilutes profit margins).

The Role of Government

Another almost permanent feature consists of the governmental impact on oil affairs: Ever since the beginning of the twentieth century, when the importance of oil became evident, governments could not help taking an interest in what was going on in this sector. Oil, it was said, was too serious a matter to be left to the oilmen. Originally, in the United States, governmental agencies confined themselves to curbing the tendencies toward monopolistic or cooperative market control—the general term *anti trust* evolved from the opposition to the Standard Oil "Trust." It is interesting to realize that, at the time of the Great Depression of the early 1930s, the absence in the United States of any possibility of regulating the market by cooperative means inevitably led to the government itself having to handle the job: The Texas Railroad Commission was the only point to which the Department of Justice had no access.

Subsequently, when the global dichotomy became more apparent—the main industrialized countries were bereft of indigenous oil, but it was found in massive amounts in faraway lands where there was little demand for it—that is, when oil became a truly international problem—governments could not fail to take a direct interest. Hence the predominence first of a British and French role in the Middle East, only later shared by the United States. After World War II, when the imperial holds weakened, the empire of the oil companies survived that of their governments by a couple of decades. Nevertheless, the inevitable happened and it was the governments of the main producing countries that took it upon themselves to handle their oil affairs by way of wholly owned national, that is, government-run, oil companies.

Downstream Changes

What is the landscape of the oil industry now and what might it be in the foreseeable future? The traditional large-scale companies that operate internationally still occupy center stage, but their modus operandi has fundamentally changed. The almost exclusive control that the Seven Sisters (five U.S. and two British companies, plus the Compagnie Française des Pétroles, which was once called the "eighth" of the Seven) enjoyed for several decades as a result of their position in the Middle East has been lost. They no longer control the "commanding heights." But they still control the traffic in the plain; they still have their points of intrinsic strength—or at least some of them have. They also now have less in common with each other than they used to have in their heydays.

The essential new element, as far as the international companies are concerned, consists of the fact that their downstream establishment is—to a great extent—no longer intrinsically linked to a substantial upstream position of their own. Although in some producer countries the major oil companies have retained vestiges of their erstwhile positions, even "equity oil" is now in fact *bought* by those entitled to it.

The result is that their downstream positions are no longer fashioned to meet the need for disposal of their "own" crude oil, hence their tendency to "decouple" refining and marketing from the upstream sphere, which means they need to be considered profit centers on their own. Consequently, what was originally an organic structure, closely linked by what each sphere could offer to the others, has now become something of a conglomerate, its policies progressively determined by administrative and financial considerations. This involves some degree of centrifugal tendencies; the future of these entities mainly depends on the quality of their management. It is then that we behold a parting of the ways: First U.S. oil companies as a group have been affected by the fact that they achieved their international prominence in the period, lasting for virtually three-quarters of a century, during which the United States was the fountainhead of world oil; now the tables have been turned and the United States is the world's biggest importer of oil. True enough, in a buyer's market, the customer has a vital role; to play and can help to determine policies, but there is no longer a full justification for the Americans to occupy a top place in the worldwide oil industry.

Hence, the less well structured U.S. companies with lower than average managerial skills—Gulf and Texaco—were the first to disappear or to be gradually dismembered. Exxon, of course, has a momentum of its own due to its size, which carries it over the humps, but it cannot be denied that Exxon's top management has for some decades been less than inspired. Its two recent trends, which one can discern, consist of the buying up of the company's own shares and of the brutal thinning out of its organizational setup—both are signs of deliberate retrenchment. Mobil and Chevron are holding their own; the former still smarting from its catastrophic endeavor to diversify out of oil, the latter being a long way down from the time when it was the sole concession holder in Saudi Arabia.

The European majors are in a different position. Royal Dutch/Shell, originally a coalition of Dutch upstream and British downstream talents and strength, were from the beginning not, like the Americans and Anglo-Persians, rooted mainly in their own national culture but being binational, were more open to the intricate demands of a multinational world. Raised to the top rank by the near genius of Henri Deterding, they had ample opportunities to savor also the drawbacks of having an outsize figure at the top and have ever since seen to it that their decisions are made in a rigidly collective fashion. It is due to the overall managerial quality at the top and of the rank and file, that despite the deceleration that their system involves, the result tends to be more than adequate. Yet, it is in the case of Shell that one can best detect the intrinsic problem of such large-scale and diversified enterprise: Lately Shell has prided itself on having a genuinely decentralized management, leaving a great deal of freedom to its widespread network of affiliates. There remains the eternal dilemma: If that freedom goes very far, the cohesion of the group becomes fatally weakened, whereas if control by the center is operationally effective, the vitality of the affiliates may be seriously impaired.

What is now British Petroleum (BP) was securely rooted upstream and owed its position to concessions in Persia and Kuwait, which were acquired mainly due to that area's belonging at the time to the British sphere of influence. This upstream fixation may have helped in the team's developing a remarkable knack of finding oil, a distinction that, much later still, led BP to a premium position in the North Sea and in Alaska. Yet, having been the first one to lose its main position in the Middle East, BP managed to become proficient generally and, under the present management, has infinitely improved its managerial skills.

An analysis of the position of the outsize oil enterprises on the whole shows that if they had not been forged in a period vastly different from out own, they would not have seen the light of the day. Since, however, they do exist and occupy such a wide field of endeavor, they tend to hold on, provided that their management is of a caliber to be at the same time forceful and subtle—a difficult blend to maintain consistently.

Power Shifts in the Industry

The decades of the 1950s and 1960s saw a steady but progressive shift of the decisionmaking centers from the concession-holding oil companies to what became known as their host governments. First the volume of offtake and the posted price, which formed the basis of the country's tax take, originally the prerogatives of the concessionaire companies, became matters for negotiation with the government—one remembers the annual palaver with the shah—and there developed the concept of a 50-50 participation by the government. Finally, in the early 1970s, the main concessions were extinguished, and their governments became the sole arbiter of volume on offer and of price demanded. Through most of that decade demand followed the (by then customary) trend of doubling every ten years or less. Meanwhile, it was fashionable to concentrate on the natural limitations of human existence. Spaceship Earth and all that gave the impression of oil's being essentially and perhaps permanently a scarce commodity.

In this atmosphere only temporary supply interruptions, or even only the fear thereof, were needed to put upward pressures on prices. At least in 1980 it was the buyers' panic that led to the bidding up of prices. OPEC only inhibited a subsequent prompt and sharp fall of the kind for example previously witnessed in the unregulated tanker market. It is now easy to appreciate that OPEC overreached itself, misled as its members were by the erroneous assumption that oil and especially *OPEC* oil was unique and irreplaceable.

It is worthwhile at this point to trace the very origin of OPEC. Its architect, the great Venezuelan oil minister J.-P. Pérez Alfonso, saw his country's predominance endangered by the oncoming Middle East competitors: Venezuela then had limited reserves and (comparatively) high cost whereas, say, Saudi Arabia had virtually inexhaustible reserves and low cost. Venezuela's interest was to optimize by margin, whereas Saudi Arabia could have afforded to optimize by volume; in other words, the

Saudis could have made a lot of money by flooding the market even at much lower prices than were current.

Pérez Alfonso managed to convince the then–Saudi oil minister, Sheikh Abdullah Tariki, to accept the Venezuelan program, and it has remained in essence the basis of OPEC thinking to this very day. The unjustifiably high oil price level of the early 1980s resulted, however, in the steep fall of the OPEC countries' world market share, relegating them—and especially the Saudis—to the role of the swing producers, and in the end they all not only lost volume but also, due to external and internal competitive pressures, a sizable part of their margin or rent.

It was inevitable that to stem the progressive deterioration of their collective and individual positions, the OPEC countries should resort to the classical methods of apportioning what there was of a market, an endeavor that previously, in easier times, had always eluded them. Yet, again as in all cartels, an agreement was only possible because of sacrifices made by the strongest members, who have to "carry the can" simply because they are the ones who can afford to do so and also because they are the premier beneficiaries of market control. Due to the inevitable lack of discipline among several of the members and the limits to the endurance of the biggest, the proration system does work only intermittently and the tendency of relying on the system is wearing thin as time goes on.

Producer Countries and Downstream Outlets

By evolving from the role of a tax collector to the one of an entrepreneur, in fact by becoming oil companies of sorts, the producer countries were and are forced to behave as oil companies have been doing since they were formed. As long as they operated in a sellers' market and later, when each member expected to be secure within its allotted quota, there was no real incentive to do it the hard way and to look for security by extending into refining and marketing. Yet once these countries saw the tables turned against them, it became mandatory for most of them to play safe by securing downstream outlets. Obviously, any such move, which at the time of this writing is still in its early stages, is bound to have substantial repercussions all along the line and inevitably will affect the shape of things to come for other entities in all spheres of the industry and of related governmental circles.

The two OPEC members that so far have been the pioneers, Venezuela and Kuwait, have chosen different paths: The former decided to operate in partnership with existent downstream operators, whereas the latter, more courageous in fact, went all the way and established itself, brand name and all, right down to the ultimate consumer. Whereas both of them are now active in foreign lands, Saudi Arabia confined itself so far to going massively into refining at home, in partnership with two major internationals, only one of them belonging to the charmed circle of its original concession holders. It is worth recalling that these and other investments by foreigners were attracted by the assurance of acquiring rights to incentive oil, thus securing preferred treatment on oil supply. *Tempi passati* indeed!

It is understandable that there are quite a number of problems with which the newly and only partly integrated operators have to cope. There is first the need to put down substantial amounts of cash to acquire control of going concerns, at times when the integrated operators' own cash flow has been reduced substantially and is, in most cases, needed to cover political and social commitments and the continuation of projects for creating infrastructures at home. (To overcome the problems of putting down vast sums of cash, an alternative might be considered: There could be a swap of upstream and downstream positions, bringing foreign oil companies partially back to the exploration/production sphere. A similar device was in essence the famous Gulf/Shell deal in respect of Kuwait crude oils.)

More serious still is the blatant fact that downstream profitability, per dollar invested, is traditionally lower than profitability in their home-ground upstream domain; thus what is taking place is in fact integration into losses, eating into their already compressed upstream margin or rent. Such a state of affairs would, incidentally, be still more adversely affected by the most likely sharpened refining and marketing competition, engendered by the emergence of more and more acute, and likely to be less experienced, participants in the marketplace. If OPEC members turn themselves into major operators downstream, the control of their quotas and, when applicable, of their pricing becomes progressively unmanageable. In fact positions downstream involve the producer into a kind of "netback" pricing—the very system introduced massively, if temporarily, in 1986, which had in itself some features of "cold" integration.

It is likely that of several such projects in the pipeline early in 1988, a limited number will actually come to pass and a still smaller number will be considered as being successful or even viable. There is inter alia the sheer human element: Scarcity of indigenous and experienced talent will involve importing substantial numbers of foreign personnel, and mutual understanding and confidence may not reach the standard required for industrial and commercial success.

The obvious targets for such transactions are ex-majors and minimajors, essentially of U.S. ownership, firms that, as pointed out earlier, neither feel nor in fact are justified in keeping up the whole network of corporate operations that dates from their status in earlier periods. In fact the low dollar eases such takeovers, just as the high dollar in previous days helped the extension of U.S. enterprises in the rest of the world.

Low-Cost Producers and Higher-Cost Operators

Another striking feature of the current readjustment of positions is the radical scaling down of the units of operation and the emergence of entirely new types of transactions.

- Whereas previously the integrated operations of the majors never actually appeared in the market, their disintegration and the concept of each affiliate's being a profit center on its own have transformed them into what are in fact outsize traders, whose individual transactions may be quite small.
- Whereas the spot market could be considered marginal in the previous round, it has now taken the center of the stage and so-called term contracts have become nothing more than a mutual first refusal. They are an understanding that the parties would not only actually deal provided the current price was not too different from the stipulated one. Should that be the case however, the obligation would lapse if the other party was not prepared to align itself to a market-oriented level.
- The basic reason for this state of affairs lies in the fact that during the past few years oil prices have fluctuated to an extent not known in the postwar period and adherence to preset contract prices could not be enforced by either seller or buyer.

Such fluctuations have become more critical by oil's being considered as just another commodity with a new type of player of a genuinely speculative nature: the so-called Wall Street refiners. True enough, such increasing volatility has bred some degree of antidote, the futures market, in which a party can hedge, provided it finds another party that takes the opposite view of developments to come. The relief thus achieved is of but a short-term nature. It fails to cover the longer-term aspect, altogether the relief is critical for investment decisions.

It is tempting to assume that the vast number of individual transactions and the fact that even larger and more solid, so-called term, contracts are becoming market related as far as price is concerned are proof that market forces have now been allowed to work fully and directly. In this context, where governmental interference is shunned, it is, somewhat surprisingly, being forgotten that the market, as we now know it, is being structured by the most effective governmental interference: the legal, political, and moral antitrust concept.

We are all so imbued with the prevailing approach, which tries to stamp out monopolistic and oligopolistic tendencies and which has resulted in outlawing any endeavor of competitors to align their policies to each other, that we don't realize that, without such governmental veto, the market would present itself in a shape quite different from the one to which we are accustomed. The economic landscape or market structure has for such a long time been fashioned by antitrust philosophy that its result is considered to represent the industry's and trade's natural habitat. We have forgotten that it stems from deliberate—if sometimes admittedly justified—governmental interference in the shape of things as they would otherwise develop if the market were really left to its own devices.

This state of affairs is generally relevant but especially so for the energy industries in which, as was pointed out at the outset, the prevalence of the investment element does result in a quest for security of tenure, which only some degree of market control can provide. If it is accepted that the oil industry is not self-adjusting and thus needs some elements of order and continuity in order to escape the trap of built-in self-destructive tendencies, then it is not surprising that the leadership role has devolved upon an association of oil-exporting countries' governments in OPEC. They, as the Texas Railroad Commission was in its time, are beyond the reach of antitrust agencies. Still classified as developing countries, they are to some extent immune even to the criticism of world public opinion. Even the oil companies—after an initial period of antagonism—have long since realized on which side their bread was buttered and accept the fact that OPEC's existence provides for a kind of market management.

The OPEC countries have had to pay a high price for having decided, as pointed out earlier, to try to optimize by margin: By maintaining a high price level after supply crises had faded out, they encouraged the development of higher-cost oil and gas, opened the gates for alternative sources of energy, and created a climate conducive to the deliberate conservation of energy. By thus shattering the concept of oil's uniqueness and by putting an end to the spectacular annual rise of demand, they have weakened to some extent the erstwhile relevant idea that oil's price elasticity of demand (and for that matter of supply) was minimal and that they could write their own ticket for what they wanted to sell to the world. Consequently, the share of OPEC oil came down from 65 percent in 1973 to 43 percent of a reduced total in 1987. Still, the OPEC countries cannot shake off the role of swing producer, whose turn comes only when all other claimants for market share have been satisfied.

The two kinds of suppliers' interests are intertwined: The low-cost producers, in order to preserve a useful part of their "rent," have to pitch their prices at a level at which higher-cost competitors can compete; thus the low-cost producers have to give up market share; the higher-cost operators (and for that matter consumers afraid to become altogether dependent on the lowest-cost suppliers) have, short of introducing import fees, to stop begrudging the low-cost producers a substantial rent. It appears that this delicate equilibrium is nowadays in fact positioned lower down in the price scale than was previously considered workable: Technical progress, and most important, the squeezing out of the fat from the inflated cost of services and of the degree of upstream tax imposition have somewhat narrowed the hitherto enormous gap between the two cost levels.

Future Trends

What, after all, does such a sketch of the current situation presage for the future, short and longer term? With so many different interests in play it is easy to assume that we have to face a prolonged period of uncertainty. Yet the need for some sort of overall management is so strong that there is every likelihood that somewhere or other there will reemerge, now and again, forces bent on securing a degree of continuity, which is the only way of providing the incentive for investment. The very fact that OPEC, despite its substantial built-in handicaps (variations of size and weight and even an eight-year war between two of its founder members), has proved to be well-nigh indestructible shows the intrinsic need for some cooperative policies.

Moreover, despite the regular occurrence of near dissolution, the OPEC members so far have always stopped at the brink and have, more or less successfully, kept their ship afloat. The elements of the present situation and of what can be detected as short-term trend are simple: Upstream there is a sizable, if high-cost, supply stream almost fully utilized, whereas the low-cost potential is substantially greater than the outlets available to the swing producers. Both refining and to some extent marketing still suffer from overcapacity resulting from an earlier overestimation of demand growth. In spite of considerable sacrifices made in the course of the inevitable thinning out of the networks, this state of affairs is likely to persist for some time. The situation is made more critical by refining capacity's tendency to move back to the producer areas from the consumer regions to which it had shifted after World War II.

Consequently, short of political events of great magnitude in the Middle East, there is every likelihood that the buyer's market prevailing in late 1988 will continue to determine the flow of oil and its price. It is unlikely however that the several centers of decision will allow the price to fall for any length of time as low as it did in summer 1986. The instinct of self-preservation is likely to bring the interested parties within OPEC together whenever prices fall significantly. Also the non-OPEC producers, and for that matter the oil companies, have means at their disposal to stem the price declines should they threaten to undermine the whole fabric of the energy-related economy.

The more difficult question remains: Will there be sufficient sources of energy at acceptable cost so that it will be unnecessary to rely altogether on low-cost oil—mainly originating in the Middle East—to a degree to make it inevitable for the world to pay for it whatever its rulers see fit to demand. Lately, informed opinion appears to veer away from the generally held expectation that, with the progressive exhaustion of U.S. and other sources of supply, the dependence on the Middle East will become more critical sooner rather than later.

It is true that although it is not likely that any further agglomeration of reserves at minimal cost is going to be within our reach, that very fact provides incentives for moves to find solutions that are considered viable at a somewhat higher price level. Also the palpable progress toward lower cost of a number of procedures and the ingenuity of technological research and management are likely to reduce the degree of energy intensity of all processes as well as increase the ways and means of providing units of energy by more sophisticated methods.

It is also more than likely that the decisionmakers among the low-cost producers will keep in mind that they can no longer count on keeping their central position if they underrate the forces they unleash by going too far too fast. Consequently, although prices toward the end of the century may tend upward, there is every likelihood that there is a de facto ceiling, which is not going to be pierced any time soon.

5

Medium- and Long-Term Energy Outlook

Herman T. Franssen

Forecasting Energy Demand and Supply

The track record of energy forecasts in the 1970s and early 1980s has been rather poor, and the people still engaged in an occasional exercise of estimating the future path of every demand and of supply and prices have become very cautious. Gone are the days when oil industry management and governments confidently committed billions of dollars based on studies predicting that scarcity of oil in the 1980s would cause prices to rise to multiples of today's reality. Aside from the fact that major external events such as the 1973–1974 and 1979 energy crises could not be predicted, the magnitude of the impact of the two price explosions on oil consumption and production was not fully understood until the mid-1980s. It is therefore not inconceivable that the full impact of lower oil prices of the mid-1980s—reinforced by dollar depreciation—will not be fully understood until several years in the future.

Energy forecasters have moved from simple methodologies largely based on extrapolation of past trends to ever more sophisticated sectoral energy models. In the end, the sophisticated models proved no more accurate in predicting demand and supply trends than the less-sophisticated earlier methodologies. One major company pioneered the scenario approach, providing different future outcomes based on different assumptions. This methodology did not gain widespread recognition in an industry wanting a clear view of the future on which to base investment decisions. Industry and government have no choice but to continue with the art of estimating medium- and long-term trends, but decisionmakers pay far less attention to these exercises than they did in the past. The so-called bottom-up approach of estimating sectoral energy demand trends, combined with conventional assessments of supply based on geological and engineering studies (oil and gas) as well as cost analyses (coal, nuclear, and alternative fuels), is still predominant in industry.

Past Perceptions, Current Realities

Prior to the mid-1970s, there appeared to be a close relationship between gross domestic product (GDP) growth and energy demand. They seemed to grow at about the same pace throughout the 1960s and early 1970s. However, even prior to the first oil shock of 1973–1974 there was some indication that structural changes were beginning to alter this relationship. The oil price increases of the 1970s speeded up ongoing structural changes in the industrial sector, reinforced government conservation and fuel switching policies, and stimulated technological development aimed at using energy more efficiently. High oil prices had an equally stimulating effect on the cash flow–rich energy industry, turning numerous previously uneconomic ventures into realities. On the demand side, the "linkage" between energy consumption and economic activity had been broken. Between 1960 and 1973, energy demand closely followed GDP growth; in the following decade GDP in the OECD countries grew at an average annual rate of 2.3 percent, whereas primary energy demand grew by a mere 0.2 percent per year.

Following the price fall of 1986, OECD oil consumption grew somewhat faster than predicted by industry analysts. In 1988, for example, OECD oil consumption is expected to average 36 MMB/D versus an estimated 1990 range of 34 to 37 MMB/D in the IEA's *World Energy Outlook* of 1982. Assuming a continuation of the oil-consumption growth rate of recent years, OECD countries are projected to consume close to the high end of the range forecasted by the IEA in 1982 for 1990.

By contrast, analysts have overestimated oil consumption trends in the developing countries. IEA's *World Energy Outlook* of 1982 projected that oil consumption in those countries would rise from 10.8 MMB/D in 1980 to 16–19 MMB/D in 1990. Low economic growth (negative growth in many countries) as well as improved fuel efficiency and fuel switching caused oil consumption to stagnate through the early 1980s and grow modestly thereafter to about 13 MMB/D to date. Even buoyant growth in 1988 and 1989 would keep oil consumption in the developing countries well below the 16 MMB/D (low case) projected in the IEA's *World Energy Outlook* of 1982. Predicted "inevitable declines in oil production outside of the Middle East" did not occur. On the contrary, higher prices stimulated investments in exploration and developing, causing a surge in non-OPEC supplies and a gradual retrenchment of

OPEC's market share. The reality of the 1980s—a chronic oversupply of oil—was one of the best kept secrets of the 1970s.

A Sectoral Close-up of Energy Demand Developments in the OECD Countries

To understand recent energy demand trends, the declining role of oil, and prospects for future oil demand, it is necessary to take a closer look at developments in three major sectors of the energy economy: industry, the residential/commercial sector, and transportation. Although not an end-use sector by itself, electricity deserves to be treated separately because of its importance in turning fossil fuels and nuclear and hydro power into electricity.

Industry

Declining energy consumption per unit of output is not an entirely new phenomenon of the post–1973–1974 energy crunch. Industrial energy data for the OECD countries show a steady decline of industrial energy use per unit of output during the 1960s, when energy prices declined in real terms. New technologies, more rationale use of production input, and more efficient management techniques were the prime reasons for these developments. Price, convenience, space limitations, and environmental reasons were behind the switch from solid fuels to oil in this sector.

The post-1973 oil price increases resulted in an almost one-third decline in industrial energy intensity in the industrialized countries between 1973 and 1985. Recession and industrial restructuring contributed further to reductions in energy growth in the industrial sector. Energy consumption in the OECD's industrial sector fell by almost 20 percent, and the share of the most expensive fuel, oil, fell from 48 to 28 percent in favor of coal, natural gas, and electricity.

By far the bulk of industrial energy consumption is concentrated in five to seven industries: iron and steel, aluminum, chemicals, nonmetallic minerals, paper and pulp, textiles, and food. Future energy demand in the industrial sector of the OECD will depend on long-term structural change, shifts within industries (from bulk petrochemicals to higher value-added products), industry rationalization, capital stock rotation, changes in the structure of the boiler stock, and future autogeneration. Modest growth in OECD industrial consumption is expected, with the share of natural gas and electricity growing at the expense of oil.

Residential/Commercial

Historically, energy demand in this sector grew in line with economic activity in the OECD countries. After the oil price rises of 1973–1974, energy demand in this sector grew at only half the rate of OECD economic growth. It is true that much of the growth in consumption prior to 1973 was based on the income effect. Higher incomes encouraged a move toward central heating (and air conditioning), hot running water, and growing use of appliances. Some degree of saturation was noticeable by the mid-1970s but the big fall in per unit energy consumption was caused by higher prices. Initially, consumers reacted by reducing comfort levels and investing in less expensive and simple improvements of energy efficiency. Gradually such short-term measures were followed by major efficiency improvements of new houses, heating and cooling systems, and appliances.

Historically, the residential/commercial sector has been dominated by one fuel, based on price and convenience. Cheap oil replaced solid fuels in the 1960s; cheaper and even more convenient natural gas and electricity increasingly replaced heating oil after the mid-1970s. Heating oil use in the OECD declined 30 percent between 1975 and 1980 and by another 20 percent in the early 1980s (from 4.8 MMB/D in 1975 to 2.8 MMB/D in 1982). This trend is still continuing in particular in Europe, but at a slower pace. It is actively encouraged by government subsidies, taxes, and other measures. In the United States and Europe, the share of oil in the residential/commercial sector may stabilize to around one-fifth of the 1973 level. In Japan, kerosene may stabilize at more than 40 percent of total energy used in this sector. Overall oil use in the OECD residential/commercial sector is expected to fall between 0.5 and 1.5 MMB/D by 2000.

Electricity

Although electric utilities are not an end-use sector, they deserve special attention because of the large use of primary fuel in the production of electricity. In contrast to the declining growth of primary energy in the OECD countries after 1973, demand for electricity continued to rise above the growth rate of GDP. Electricity grew faster because it was cheaper, cleaner, and more efficient than oil. After 1973, the share of nuclear power and, to a lesser extent, coal increased at the expense of oil and natural gas. The share of nuclear power increased from 4.4 to 15.7 percent in the ten years following 1973. By contrast, the share of oil fell from 25.1 to 11.6 percent. By the mid-1980s oil was largely used for peak shaving (meeting peak electricity load), with the exception of Italy and Portugal, where oil still presented a large share of base load.

Future OECD consumption of oil will to a large extent depend on peak demand. This in turn is highly sensitive to the total electricity demand growth rate. Oil use could be either declining substantially or increasing by as much as 50 percent, depending on the future growth rate of total electricity demand. An unpublished IEA study completed in 1985 suggests that oil consumption for electricity generation in the OECD by 2000 could be anywhere between 1.5 and 5 MMB/D.

Whereas the basic trend in industry and the residential/commercial sector is away from oil, in the transportation sector, oil has gained in importance: Its share of overall OECD oil consumption grew steadily after the mid-1970s. Oil consumption in the transportation sector increased by about 1 percent per year between 1973 and 1983, when oil consumption in other sectors fell by 3.5 percent per year.

Transportation

Almost all energy used in the transportation sector is oil (99 percent), and for the remainder of the century oil will certainly keep its dominant role. Road transport—divided into passenger cars and commercial vehicles—takes up to 80 percent of all transportation fuels. In this subsector, oil use is a function of the size of the fleet; average distance traveled, and average efficiency of the fleet. The size and composition of the fleet are determined by car prices, growth of the driving population, taste, and the price of gasoline.

Higher gasoline prices after the two oil shocks had both short- and long-term effects. Whereas higher gasoline prices led to improved fuel efficiency of new cars, the recessions following the two oil shocks slowed the turnover of the fleet, which was still dominated by less-efficient cars built in an era when oil prices were lower. On the other hand, higher gasoline prices and economic slowdown encouraged the trend toward smaller cars. Recession and higher prices also had a significant impact on distance driven, in particular in North America, where the difference between high and low proved to be as much as 1,000 km per year per car.

The medium-term countervailing trends of stable to lower gasoline prices and continued efficiency improvements of the car fleet have resulted in a small net increase in motor fuel demand for passenger cars in the OECD. By the early 1990s, when passenger car saturation is expected in the OECD, the degree of improvement in fuel efficiency could determine whether motor fuel consumption in the OECD will stabilize or decline modestly through most of the decade. Until then, the growth in the size of fleet (estimated at 2 percent per year) is expected to outweigh projected improvements in fuel efficiency of 1 to 2 percent per annum.

Depending on the rate of economic activity and price developments, OECD fuel demand for passenger cars could grow between 0.4 and 1.3 MMB/D by 2000.

Fuel demand for commercial vehicles is subject to some of the same variables as the passenger car subsector, but economic factors are more dominant here. Short-term alterations in fuel prices have less effect on consumption, and fuel efficiency improvements have been slower than for the passenger fleet. Fuel consumption in this subsector, which uses about 60 percent as much as the passenger car sector, is estimated to increase by about 1.0 to 1.4 MMB/D in the OECD by the year 2000.

Although small in comparison with that of road transportation, aviation fuel use has been the fastest growing transportation fuel. Fuel consumption depends on average airplane fuel efficiency, the number of planes in operation, and the average number of kilometers flown. Fuel efficiency improvements have been considerable in the past. The switch from narrow- to wide-body aircraft improved efficiency per passenger kilometer by 20–40 percent. Technology used in the new generation of airbuses and the Boeing 757 and 767 series will again improve fuel efficiency substantially over that of aircraft being replaced. Fuel efficiency improvements are offset by the rapid growth of both passenger and freight travel. In the past air traffic grew at about three times the rate of GDP. Depending on economic growth and the above variables, aviation fuel in the OECD is estimated to grow between 0.2 and 1.0 MMB/D by 2000.

Maritime transportation, the third-largest user of transportation fuels, is greatly influenced by the use of oil tankers, which make up more than half of the fleet. Fuel efficiency, the size of the fleet, and average distance traveled are again the main determinants of fuel use in this subsector. A significant improvement in fuel efficiency has come about in the gradual change from steam turbine to diesel engines, a trend which is likely to continue. Fuel efficiency is expected to increase at a rate of about 1 percent per year. Tanker traffic will grow gradually in the 1990s, when oil trade is expected to increase faster than in recent years. Growth in dry cargo shipments is closely related to growth in world trade, which tends to expand above the rate of world GDP. Marine bunkers, which stood at about 1.3 MMB/D in 1986, could expand by up to 0.5 MMB/D by the year 2000.

The smallest transportation subsector, the railroads, use about 0.4 MMB/D of fuel oil. Stagnation of both freight and passenger travel, coupled with modest further electrification, will keep fuel use by 2000 at best at current levels.

In total, OECD transportation fuels could grow by some 2–4.5 MMB/D by 2000, depending on economic activity, oil prices, and efficiency trends. This assessment of OECD sectoral energy consumption trends and the expected role of oil in future overall energy use shows that over a period of about fifteen years there is a range of oil demand trends that is rather large but difficult to narrow down unless input assumptions are specified.

There is clearly more room for efficiency improvements in all sectors of the OECD energy economy. Superinsulated houses currently on the market are about ten times more efficient than the average house. In every industry, existing and new technologies can significantly reduce energy per unit of output, and there is considerable scope for further fuel switching. In the road transportation sector, new small cars on the market are about three times as efficient as the average car used, and even more efficient cars are being developed. And even larger savings per passenger mile are being realized from replacement of older aircraft with the latest wide-body aircraft. What is unknown is the speed and the extent to which end-users are willing to invest in higher-cost energy-saving equipment as long as real oil prices remain significantly below the level of the early 1980s.

Developing Countries

Historically, all non-OECD countries have been put into two groups: the developing countries and the centrally planned economies. The developing countries consist of a very diversified group of about 100 countries, representing nearly half of the world's population and accounting for 25 percent of world economic output and 15 percent of world commercial energy consumption. They differ widely in per capita incomes and in socioeconomic and political structures. In the world of oil they are frequently divided into net oil exporters and importers. Although some 40 percent of the energy consumption of these countries consists of noncommercial sources such as firewood, this chapter will only discuss prospects for commercial fuels.

Since high energy consumption is generally associated with economic development, consumption has risen sharply in the developing countries throughout the past thirty years. The close relationship between rising incomes and energy consumption has continued despite the sharp oil price increases of the 1970s and early 1980s. There is, however, some indication that among the more advanced developing countries higher prices have resulted in a reduction of energy per unit of industrial output. Energy efficient machinery, cars, and aircraft are available in all markets, but the rate of penetration tends to be slower in the developing countries. Moreover, population growth offsets such efficiency gains. It has been estimated that with a 2.5 percent annual increase in population, the mere maintenance of current per capita levels of energy use would require 60 percent more energy over the fifteen years from 1985 to 2000. Moreover, since per capita energy use is very low, any increase in real per capita income will result in further growth in energy demand in all sectors of the economy.

World Oil Supplies

In the decade of the 1970s, when world demand for OPEC oil was close to the productive capacity of the group, the general perception in the oil industry was that non-OPEC supplies would decline in the 1980s, causing demand for OPEC oil to rise to such high levels that another supply crisis could be expected sometime in the mid-1980s. Supply tightening would cause oil prices to rise above the peak level of 1981 in constant dollars.

Despite oil price projections for the mid- to late 1980s that were a multiple of today's reality, the industry expected production in mature areas like the United States and the North Sea to decline. Throughout the late 1970s and early 1980s it was also generally accepted that Soviet oil exports would either decline or cease altogether by the mid-1980s. Some analysts believed that the Soviet Union might become a small importer of oil from the mid-1980s on. By contrast, industry expectations of both Mexican and Chinese production and exports were higher in the early 1980s than the current reality. Few serious industry analysts predicted that OPEC might have to struggle for market share in the late 1980s at prices considerably lower than those of 1974 (in dollars of 1974).

Oil Production Developments: The Decade Since 1978

Worldwide distribution of crude oil reserves has not changed much in the decade since 1978. The Middle East still contains close to 60 percent of world reserves and the OECD countries still about 15 percent. The biggest changes have been in speedy development of new production in a few areas such as the North Sea and Mexico and in a large number of other non-OPEC developing countries. Moreover, North American oil production is considerably higher today than was thought possible at substantially higher prices a decade ago.

In 1978, the industry expected U.S. oil and gas production to decline sharply in the 1980s. In reality, production of crude oil was 8.1 MMB/D in 1976; it peaked at 8.9 MMB/D in 1985 and fell after the price collapse of 1986 to 8.6 MMB/D and 8.3 MMB/D in 1987. Industry

TABLE 5.1
Oil Production, 1976–1986, Selected Countries (MB/D)

	1976	1986
Brazil	167	593
Mexico	831	2,430
Colombia	167	305
Oman	366	560
Angola	108	280
Egypt	330	813
Malaysia	165	501

Source: Data base provided by Petroleum Economics, Ltd., London.

sources expected an even more modest production decline in 1988. The large, precipitous fall predicted in the 1970s has not yet occurred, and U.S. oil production in 1990 is expected to be 1 to 1.5 MMB/D higher than the industry consensus of the early 1980s.

In 1978, some analysts predicted a steep fall in Soviet oil production in the 1980s, turning the USSR from a net exporter to a net importer of oil. In reality, Soviet production rose steadily in the 1970s to about 12 MMB/D in 1984. Thereafter, production fell for two years and recovered again in 1986 following increased investments. In 1988, analysts predicted a record level of Soviet oil production above 1987's 12.8 MMB/D; further production growth, following new large oil discoveries in the Caucasus, was not excluded. Instead of a Soviet production of 9–11 MMB/D in 1990, as projected by some U.S. sources in the early 1980s, Soviet production could top 13 MMB/D in 1989.

By contrast, developments in the People's Republic of China (PRC) have belied industry expectations in the early 1980s. Prior to the disappointing offshore drilling results, the PRC was expected to produce 3–4 MMB/D by the end of the 1980s. Current production is 2.6 MMB/D.

North Sea oil production had reached 0.5 MMB/D in 1976 and it was expected to peak at around 2.5 MMB/D in the 1980s. Twelve years later the North Sea produced close to 4 MMB/D and production is still rising, albeit slowly. Mexico, a net oil importer through the mid-1970s, was producing less than 1 MMB/D in 1978. Production in 1988 was close to 3 MMB/D, of which about half was exported. Whereas the North Sea and Mexico are among the big success stories of the 1970s, production increased by 1986 in a large number of non-OPEC oil-importing and -exporting countries on every continent (see Table 5.1). In 1987, production rose again in each one of these countries and 1988 will show further growth. In addition to developments in older producing areas, new discoveries are being developed. North Yemen has recently begun producing at a rate of 150 MB/D and is expected to expand steadily. Some sources estimate production in North and South Yemen could reach more than 0.5 MMB/D within the next few years.

In summary, OECD oil and NGL production, which a decade ago was projected to decline from about 15 MMB/D in 1980 to 13–14 MMB/D in 1990, has in fact risen to 16.8 MMB/D at the beginning of 1988. Centrally planned economies (CPEs), which a decade ago had been expected to cease exporting oil after the mid-1980s, are still exporting 2.1 MMB/D to the market economies. At 9 MMB/D, oil production in developing non-OPEC countries today is pretty much in the middle of the 8–11 MMB/D range projected a decade ago. Whereas the current perception of 1990 world oil demand (about 50 MMB/D) is in line with IEA estimates made in 1982 (low case), non-OPEC production is some 7 to 9 MMB/D higher than projection only half a decade ago.

OPEC

The thirteen countries belonging to OPEC control three-quarters of the non-Communist world oil reserves. In the 1960s OPEC reserves doubled from 218 to 434 billion barrels, and despite a cumulative production of more than 200 billion barrels between 1974 and 1986, year-end 1986 OPEC reserves still stood at 480 billion barrels. Despite the worldwide upsurge in oil exploration and development since the mid-1970s, OPEC succeeded in maintaining its reserve base.

The 1970s were the decade of OPEC. Producing countries gradually took control over their own petroleum resources, causing major restructuring of the world oil industry at a time when world consumption pushed demand for OPEC oil very close to capacity. In such a world the relatively mild and short-lived supply interruptions of 1973 and 1979 caused prices to triple twice within one decade.

Throughout the 1970s OPEC had followed market forces, and it became an active cartel only after 1981 when the unforeseen fall in world oil consumption coupled with rapidly rising non-OPEC production caused a major decline in demand for OPEC oil. OPEC's market share, which had remained fairly stable through the turmoil of the late 1970s, was almost halved in the next five years, that is, from 60 percent in 1979 to 30 percent in 1985. The "fat" years of the late 1970s, when OPEC production averaged close to 31 MMB/D, were followed by lean years, when conservation, recession, fuel switching, and non-OPEC oil production reduced the demand for OPEC oil from 31.5 MMB/D in 1979 to just below 20 MMB/D in 1982. In March 1982 OPEC decided to manage prices by controlling production. An overall production ceiling was set at 17.5 MMB/D, but because there were no individual country quotas, it proved ineffective. The Gulf and in particular Saudi Arabia acted as the de facto swing producer when demand fell.

A year later, in March 1983, OPEC agreed on country quotas and an overall ceiling of 17.5 MMB/D. OPEC also adjusted to market realities and cut official prices by $5 per barrel to bring the official selling price (OSP) in line with prevailing spot prices. Market analysts were surprised that an agreement was reached at all between countries with often fundamentally different views. The OPEC price and volume adjustments of 1983 proved inadequate when stagnant demand and stock draw coupled with rising non-OPEC supplies further eroded OPEC's market share. Quotas were reduced to 16 MMB/D by the end of 1984 in the hope that demand for OPEC oil would gradually increase. Saudi Arabia, acting as OPEC's swing producer, saw its production fall to 3.5 MMB/D in 1985—almost one-third of its peak production five years earlier.

It became apparent that at $28 per barrel demand for OPEC oil was still falling, and several OPEC members felt forced in 1985 to offer discounts in order to maintain production. Saudi Arabia, faced with the prospect of further erosion of its market share upon the completion of the 0.5 MMB/D pipeline from Iraq to Yanbu, signaled that it was no longer willing to act as OPEC's swing producer. OPEC decided to regain some of its market share lost to non-OPEC producers; one of the vehicles used was the so-called netback deals, based on the value of oil products in the marketplace. Refiners were guaranteed a certain margin built into the products yield or into the fee, providing an incentive to buy crude oil on a term basis. OPEC exports increased rapidly in spring and summer 1986, and prices fell below $10 per barrel in July, although few industry analysts had predicted that prices would fall much below $18 to $20 per barrel. OPEC, shocked into action, called for an ad hoc meeting in July and decided to cut production initially for two months and set a target oil price range of $17 to $19 per barrel.

Later in the year Sheikh Ahmed Zaki Yamani, minister of petroleum and mineral resources, preferred to continue with quotas and a flexible price target but King Fahd decided that the Saudi position would be to advocate specific country quotas coupled with fixed prices around a basket of OPEC crudes valued at $18 per barrel. The quote for the first quota was set at 15.8 MMB/D in order to mop up excess world stocks. The December 1986 agreement would not have been possible without a Saudi-Iranian agreement. The outcome pleasantly surprised veteran OPEC watchers, and oil prices firmed quickly.

Assisted by rising world consumption, the new system worked remarkably well during the first half of 1987 when all but one OPEC country observed the production quotas and Saudi Arabia allowed its own lifting to fall below its quota. The June OPEC meeting decided to roll over the earlier agreement, but external events and nonobservance of production quotas by at least two OPEC producers set the stage for a hardening in the Saudi position later in the year. Responding to considerable market pressures to build stocks in the summer and autumn following tension in the Gulf and the Mecca incident (in which many deaths were caused by the removal of armed occupiers from the holy sites), the United Arab Emirates (UAE) and Kuwait together exported more than 1 MMB/D above their quotas. When tension eased later in the year, discretionary industry stocks were estimated once again substantially in excess of projected industry requirement.

Unhappy with persistent quota violations by some OPEC members and the reality of still-rising non-OPEC and Iraqi production, Saudi Arabia signaled its determination no longer to act as a swing producer. Moreover, after the Mecca incident, serious discussions on oil policy between Saudi Arabia and Iran were no longer possible. The December 1987 OPEC meeting failed to solve the issue of raising the Iraqi production quota, leaving Iraq outside the quota system despite its ability to expand exports. OPEC also failed to reduce first-quarter 1988 quotas in line with expected demand for OPEC oil and instead left the overall annual quotas unchanged. Saudi Arabia clearly registered its unhappiness with quota violations and higher non-OPEC production by refusing to cut production below its quota of 4.3 MMB/D.

OPEC-Non-OPEC

Market reactions were negative: Prices fell by several dollars per barrel below the early December level, and there were renewed fears of another price collapse. In March 1988 seven non-OPEC oil-exporting countries met at the technical level in London to discuss the world oil market and ways to improve it. The meetings of the seven countries, Angola, China, Colombia, Egypt, Malaysia, Mexico, and Oman, resulted in a proposal to OPEC to jointly cut exports by 5 percent in order to restore oil prices to the level of the $18 OPEC basket. At a meeting of its Pricing Committee OPEC decided on April 9 to invite the seven independent oil producers for discussions with the committee at the ministerial level later in the month. Results of the meeting would be reported by the Pricing Committee to a consultative meeting of all OPEC members.

The meeting of the OPEC Pricing Committee with seven independent oil exports took place on April 26. The seven proposed to cut exports by 5 percent for the remainder of the second quarter and if necessary to meet again with OPEC at its regular June biannual meeting to discuss further cooperation. The Pricing Committee presented the proposal of the independent oil exports to the OPEC Consultative Conference two days after the meeting with non-OPEC countries. Eight OPEC countries favored the concept of an OPEC–non-OPEC production cut but suggested a 1.5 B/D cut for every barrel cut by the independent oil exporters. The Gulf OPEC countries preferred a barrel-for-barrel cut equally divided among OPEC countries. The differences within OPEC could not be solved at the April meeting, and thus it was decided to postpone a decision on the non-OPEC proposal until the next OPEC meeting in June. Whatever the outcome of the debate between OPEC and independent oil exporters, the April meeting was a historical event, highlighting the fact that the independent oil exporters have recognized the need to cooperate with OPEC in order to achieve price stability.

Future Energy Outlook

The future of energy supply, demand, and prices in both the industrialized and developing countries remains uncertain for the following principal reasons:

- World economic activity. While it now appears that the high growth rates of the world economy of the 1960s and early 1970s were the exception rather than the rule, it is by no means certain whether the world economy will grow at closer to 2 or to 3 percent in the 1990s. The difference between 2 and 3 percent growth will have a major impact on the energy outlook.
- Energy and oil intensity fell sharply between the mid-1970s and mid-1980s, but there are signs that both are declining less in recent years, due to lower prices. Hence, energy and oil consumption may rise more rapidly than previously foreseen if prices remain around the current level.
- Nonoil fuels added more than 10 MMB/D in the OECD between 1975 and 1985. Environmental, safety, socioeconomic, political, and behavioral factors could cause a reduction or an increase in the growth rate of nonoil energy resources.
- Uncertainty about the future non-OPEC oil production outlook and the ability of OPEC to manage the transition from world oil surpluses to a better balance between oil demand and supply.

Medium Term: Managing the Surplus

After OPEC continued to lose market share and it became clear that the world oil surplus could not be managed at $28 per barrel, OPEC strategy changed in 1986. Initially, prices fell sharply, due to pricing policies and rather unconstrained output, but by 1987 prices had stabilized some $10 below the pre-1986 level. OPEC had managed to survive the greatest challenge to its existence. The consequences of a dissolution of OPEC could be a prolonged period of oil prices below $10 per barrel and through domestic taxation a long-term shift of resources from producer to consumer governments. The pressures on OPEC have been intense and the fact that the organization has survived six years of production quotas is a sign of remarkable strength. In five years after 1979 OPEC as the residual supplier reduced output almost 50 percent; oil income fell by more than 50 percent in the same period: from $280 to $130 billion.

The short-lived abandonment of surplus management in 1986 caused OPEC revenue to drop 42 percent in one year to $75 billion and the revenue decline was compounded by dollar depreciation. Although lower prices increased demand, actual world oil consumption rose by only 0.8 MMB/D, and the expected boost to world economic growth did not materialize for reasons not related to oil. But however small the increase was in comparison with the price cut, 1986 showed that lower prices do stimulate consumption at the margin. Higher prices also led to a production fall in the United States of about 0.5 MMB/D; it has been estimated that other non-OPEC production would have been several hundred thousand B/D higher if prices had remained at $28 per barrel.

OPEC's ability to manage the surplus, however imperfect, is the more remarkable when one realizes the extent of the diversity of OPEC members geographically, economically, politically, and culturally. Despite the Iran-Iraq war, the consistent overproduction by some members, and non-OPEC's rising market share, OPEC has nevertheless managed the surplus rather well in all those years of falling demand for its oil. Excess productive capacity will persist for several more years until growth in world demand and leveling off of non-OPEC output combine to increase the call upon OPEC production to levels that are closer to capacity. The current OPEC–non-OPEC dialogue suggests a possibility that a broader group of oil exporters may be needed to help stabilize the world oil market in the medium term.

The price level required to manage the surplus must be low enough to discourage fuel switching, a new wave of conservation, and large-scale investments in exploration for oil and natural gas in high-cost areas. On the other hand, the price must be high enough to meet minimum foreign exchange requirements of most oil exporting nations, OPEC and non-OPEC. Most petroleum analysts believed that the $18 price for the so-called OPEC basket met the above criteria, but others have argued that lower prices are needed to achieve those targets and cause the demand for OPEC oil to rise to a more comfortable level of some 22 MMB/D, which could satisfy OPEC's minimum volumetric needs. The $18 price chosen for the OPEC basket at the December 1986 OPEC meeting was not a "scientific" price calculated to ensure that OPEC would regain part of its lost market share within a certain time. Instead it was a political compromise between those who wanted substantially higher prices to meet revenue needs and those whose priority was early restoration of OPEC's market share.

There is no clear evidence that relatively modest price changes from this level will have a significant impact on final consumption in the short run. For example, the almost 50 percent reduction in average crude oil prices in 1986 caused only a modest 3 percent increase in oil consumption in the industrialized world (0.8 MMB/D) and in the developing countries (0.4 MMB/D). A modest price increase of about $3 per barrel in 1987 resulted in an increase of 0.5 MMB/D in the industrialized countries (1.5 percent) and 0.3 MMB/D in the developing countries (2 percent). Preliminary estimates for this year suggest that prices will average $2 per barrel below last year's but OECD oil consumption is expected to rise by 1 percent (0.3 MMB/D). Although some analysts subscribe to the thesis that at $15 for the OPEC basket, world consumption will rise much faster than at $18 per barrel, there is no evidence to prove it. This is in part due to the fact that more than one-half of the product barrel in the industrialized world is used for transportation fuel, where a significant part of the consumer price consists of taxes. Also, at $15 per barrel, only a small amount of fuel switching from nonoil fuels to fuel oil is expected to occur. This volume is too small to have much of an impact on the market in the short run.

On the supply side, a 50 percent drop in the price in 1986 caused U.S. oil production to fall by 0.5 MMB/D, but elsewhere production continued to grow. The industry has learned to reduce costs by employing new cost-cutting development technologies in such high-cost areas as the North Sea. Overall non-OPEC supplies in 1986 were only 0.2 MMB/D below the level of 1985, and they rose again in 1987 (0.7 MMB/D) and probably will in 1988 as well.

Price Assumption for the Outlook

The assessment is based on the assumption that oil-exporting countries can and will limit production to the degree required to maintain a maximum price for the OPEC basket of $18/B price through 1990, gradually increasing to $20 per barrel (1987 dollars) by 1995. At that price level, exploration for oil and natural gas worldwide is expected to continue at the 1987–1988 level, resulting in a modest reduction in U.S. oil output, partially offset by gains in the North Sea. Production potential in non-OPEC developing countries would continue, as would exports from centrally planned economies. At $15 per barrel through 1995, exploration and development outside of OPEC would slow and production would peak a few years earlier. At least one OPEC producer would prefer prices to move in a band around the OPEC basket with periods of higher and lower prices in order to keep industry guessing about the price level and thus reduce investment in new exploration and development.

Impact on Conservation

Energy intensity fell 20 percent in the OECD countries between 1973 and 1985, saving the industrialized countries the equivalent of 18 MMB/D yearly. The average gain in energy efficiency of 3 percent per year for this period has slowed substantially (to between 0.5 and 1 percent), due to lower energy prices. However, new buildings, vehicles, and machinery, will continue to be more energy efficient than the equipment and buildings they replace, and new energy-efficient technologies will continue to be introduced. At $18 to $20 per barrel, energy consumption will be slightly higher than at $15 per barrel, but the difference is expected to be small. Most of the future conservation is likely to come from replacement of buildings, cars, and capital equipment with built-in improved efficiencies. This kind of substitution will continue, whatever happens to oil prices. Higher prices will only speed up substitution to more energy-efficient equipment.

Fuel Substitution

Tables 5.2 and 5.3, based on IEA data, clearly show what has happened to oil demand since the first and in particular since the second oil crisis of 1979. Heavy fuel, which constituted one-fourth of the demand barrel or 10.68 MMB/D in 1973, fell to 15 percent or 4.61 MMB/D in 1987. The decline was strongest in Japan (63 percent) and smallest in Italy (38 percent). All end-use consumer sectors were almost equally affected.

Subsequently, the growth of nonoil fuels in the industrialized countries has, with few exceptions, been high across the board between 1980 and 1987 and was achieved at the expense of oil consumption (see Table 5.4). Oil to coal substitution has been significant, increasing the share of coal from 19 percent of primary energy in 1973 to 22 percent in 1985. This total number masks the fall in metallurgical coal due to a declining steel industry. In the industrial sector, coal made important inroads in the cement industry and has penetrated paper, pulp, chemicals, and nonferrous metals in recent years. When oil prices fell in 1986 there was some fuel switching away from coal to oil, offsetting some of the

TABLE 5.2
OECD Consumption of Heavy Fuel Oil (HFO) and Other Products (MMB/D)

						Percent Change		
	1973	1977	1979	1983	1987	1979–83	1983–87	Peak Yr. To 1987
OECD countries in:								
North America	3.16	3.51	3.23	1.72	1.46	−46.7	−15.0	−58.4
Europe	5.15	4.37	4.46	2.76	2.27	−40.7	−17.7	−55.9
Pacific	2.37	2.10	2.01	1.19	0.88	−38.0	−26.7	−62.9
Total OECD HFO	10.68	9.98	9.70	5.68	4.61	−41.5	−18.8	−56.8
Other products[a]	29.78	30.85	32.08	28.36	31.13	−11.6	+ 9.8	− 3.0
Total products[a]	40.45	40.83	41.78	34.04	35.74	−18.5	+ 5.0	−14.5

[a]Total may not add up due to rounding.

Source: Data Base Provided by Petroleum Economics, Ltd., London.

earlier substitution. Prospects for coal substitution in the industrial sector remain poor in the medium- and even long-term future due to technical considerations, high conversion costs, and environmental constraints. Steam coal use will continue to increase in the electricity sector, in particular in the United States. There was some substitution to oil in the United States in 1986 in areas where coal transportation and delivery costs were relatively high and where there was idle oil-fired capacity.

Natural gas has and will continue to make progress in substitution for heating oil and industrial fuel in Western Europe for environmental and economic reasons. In Japan rising LNG imports are largely used

TABLE 5.3
Heavy Fuel Oil (HFO) Consumption by End-User Sector (MMB/D)

	Utilities		Industry		Other[a]		Total[b]	
	1973	1986	1973	1986	1973	1986	1973	1986
OECD countries in:								
North America	1.45	0.61	0.83	0.41	0.88	0.59	3.16	1.61
Europe	1.59	0.69	1.97	0.76	1.58	0.92	5.15	2.36
Pacific	0.87	0.51	0.89	0.16	0.62	0.26	2.37	0.92
OECD	3.91	1.80	3.69	1.32	3.08	1.77	10.68	4.89

[a]"Other" includes mainly refinery fuel, bunkers, commercial, and public service heating.
[b]Totals may not add up due to rounding.

Source: Data base provided by Petroleum Economics, Ltd., London.

TABLE 5.4
Energy Demand by Fuel in Non-Communist World (NCW) (MMB/D oil equivalent)

	Solids		Natural Gas		Hydro		Nuclear		Oil	
	1980	1987	1980	1987	1980	1987	1980	1987	1980	1987
U.S.	7.5	8.5	10.0	8.2	1.4	1.6	1.3	2.3	17.1	16.2
W. Europe	5.5	5.9	3.9	4.4	2.3	2.5	1.0	3.3	13.9	12.2
Japan	1.0	1.3	0.5	0.8	0.5	0.4	0.4	0.9	4.9	4.4
Other OECD	1.0	1.2	1.0	1.3	1.4	1.7	0.2	0.4	2.6	2.2
Total	15.0	16.9	15.4	14.7	5.6	6.2	2.9	6.9	38.5	35.0
Non-OECD	2.6	4.4	2.3	4.1	1.8	2.9	0.1	0.4	11.3	12.8
Total NCW	17.6	21.3	17.7	18.8	7.4	9.1	3.0	7.3	49.8	47.8

Source: Data base provided by Petroleum Economics, Ltd., London.

for power stations in environmentally sensitive areas and city gasworks. Only in the United States did gas consumption fall, but most of the decline was limited to power generation and industry and was due to cost considerations and structural change.

Electricity demand growth has continued unabated throughout the past decade. Since 1973, electricity consumption in the OECD was up by 40 percent or 300 million tons of oil equivalent (mtoe). Oil has continued to lose market share in this sector to nuclear power, hydro, coal, and natural gas. The future of electricity capacity is difficult to plan because of high capital costs and the considerable political constraints. Although the industrialized countries currently enjoy surplus electricity capacity, in the 1990s spare capacity will be reduced gradually in many OECD countries unless more new plants are built. The use of oil will depend on the extent of further fuel switching in base-load plants and peak-shaving demand, which is usually met by oil and natural gas.

At $18 to $20 per barrel, substitution from oil to natural gas, coal, and electricity is projected to be higher than at $15 per barrel, but the difference is not expected to be great since most investment decisions affecting the period up to 1995 have already been made. If, however, oil prices were to fall substantially below $15 per barrel and stay at that level for a few years, substitution back to fuel oil would be significant in particular in the United States.

Non-OPEC Oil Supplies Through 1990

In the medium term U.S. oil production is projected to decline by about 0.3 to 0.4 MMB/D by the end of 1990. Canadian and European oil production is expected to remain stable. Unless production is slowed by cooperation with OPEC, production in non-OPEC developing countries may grow by 0.3 to 0.4 MMB/D per year over the next two years. Exports from centrally planned economies have risen in recent years and are expected to stabilize or grow slightly over the next few years.

Medium-Term Price Outlook: Stability or Volatility?

OPEC supply management and seasonal demand factors are assumed to cause oil prices (OPEC basket) to hover somewhere between $14 and $18 per barrel. This assumption is based on the belief that no producer would like to see a price collapse and most large producers will see to it that prices will not surpass $18 per barrel for the OPEC basket in order not to lose market share. The most important variables in projecting the price outlook for oil in the medium term, that is, 1988–1990, are the status of the world economy and OPEC behavior.

Since the miraculous 1983 U.S. economy recovery, the United States has been the prime engine of growth in the world. Unbalanced domestic demand in the OECD economies enabled continued world economic recovery but at the expense of a major trade imbalance between the United States and the rest of the industrialized world. The United States soaked up a significant part of the industrialized world's savings to balance its persistent budget deficit, thereby balancing the deficit on the current account. The reluctance of the world banking system to continue the generous lending of the 1970s to developing countries has caused a net flow of foreign exchange from the debtor nations to the industrialized countries, reducing growth potential in the debtor countries.

Economists have wondered for years how long the status quo could persist before the financial bubble would burst. In each of the three years prior to 1988 a U.S. recession and/or a financial crisis was among the plausible forecasts for the world economy, but to the surprise of many economists the world economic system showed an amazing ability to adjust to massive exchange rate fluctuation, trade imbalances, huge U.S. budget deficits, and the gigantic debt burden of the developing countries of Africa, Latin America, and to a lesser extent, Asia. Many serious economists have predicted that a major U.S. recession will occur following the election in 1988 or a year later with the introduction of the 1990 budget. We cannot prove or disprove the validity of the recession predictions and have therefore assumed two possible futures for 1989 and 1990.

As shown in Table 5.5, if the world manages to avoid a recession in 1989 and 1990 because of a considerable improvement in OECD coordination of economic policies, the future for oil price stability looks rather promising. Based on the demand/supply assessment shown, the

TABLE 5.5
Medium-Term Oil Market Outlook: Two Scenarios (MMB/D)

	1987	1988	1989		1990	
			I[a]	II[b]	I[a]	II[b]
Consumption						
OECD	35.7	36.0	36.3	35.3	36.6	35.6
Non-OECD	12.9	13.2	13.5	12.9	13.8	13.2
Total consumption	48.6	49.2	49.8	48.2	50.4	48.8
Supply						
OECD	16.8	16.7	16.5	16.5	16.3	16.3
Developing countries	8.9	9.2	9.5	9.5	9.8	9.8
CPE net exports	2.1	2.3	2.2	2.2	2.2	2.2
Processing gain	1.1	1.2	1.2	1.2	1.2	1.2
Total non-OPEC	28.9	29.4	29.4	29.4	29.5	29.5
OPEC NGL	1.7	1.7	1.7	1.7	1.8	1.8
OPEC crude oil	17.7	18.1	18.9	16.8	19.3	17.3
Total OPEC	19.4	19.8	20.6	18.5	21.1	19.1
Total supply	48.3	49.2	50.0	47.9	50.6	48.6
Stock changes and miscellaneous adjustments	−0.3	0	+0.2	−0.3	+0.2	−0.2

[a]Scenario I assumes 2 percent growth in oil demand.
[b]Scenario II assumes a recession-induced 2 percent fall in oil demand.

demand for OPEC oil (assuming other countries produce close to capacity) could increase from 17.7 MMB/D in 1987 to 18.1 MMB/D in 1988 and 18.9 and 19.3 MMB/D, respectively, in 1989 and 1990. Although the task of dividing such volumes among the OPEC members would by no means be an easy one, a small quota increase for all members, coupled with fairly stable production in Iraq and some Gulf states, would make the problems manageable.

If, however, the long awaited recession were to occur in either 1989 or 1990, the "call on OPEC" could be below 17 MMB/D in 1989 and below 17.5 MMB/D in 1990. In both instances, assistance from a large number of non-OPEC oil exporters would be essential in order to stabilize the market. In case a recession were to reduce world oil consumption by, let us say, 2 percent, inclusion of even some currently reluctant large non-OPEC exporters might be required in order to stabilize the market. Hence, at a minimum, OPEC–non-OPEC cooperation could avoid the likelihood of a major fall in oil prices during the next recession. Oil exporters would be better served, however, if they succeeded in coordinating their policies even in case of continued economic growth. The aim of such cooperation would be to restore and maintain a reasonable oil price level that would gradually restore the equilibrium between world demand and supply and simultaneously provide sufficient income to promote development in most oil-exporting countries.

Such policy would in the end also serve the interests of the industrialized countries. Allowing a reasonable and fairly stable oil price in the medium term would avoid misallocation of world resources, secure past investments, and promote stability in oil-producing countries. Violent oil price swings, on the other hand, make it difficult for oil exporters to maintain stable economic development and for oil importers to plan a long-term economically viable energy policy.

Energy Outlook Through 2000

A recent U.S. Energy Information Administration (EIA) assessment of the long-term energy outlook stated that long-term prices are determined by the following factors:

- The cost in real resources of developing alternative energy sources. Attempts to raise oil prices above the long-term development cost of alternative fuels will result in additional fuel switching and thus reduced oil demand.
- Prospects for non-OPEC oil supplies. If non-OPEC production peaks over the next few years, OPEC's market share will grow, allowing for upward price adjustments. If the consensus view proves wrong—as it has so many times in the past—and non-OPEC supply keeps constant or rises, OPEC's ability to raise prices will be limited.
- OPEC's willingness to increase productive capacity whenever demand for OPEC oil rises. This could be done with limited costs to the producing country and improve its long-term market share.
- Expectations of consumers and governments. If they believe that prices will rise, investments will be made in demand-reducing equipment and nonoil fuels (as well as oil exploration). Such action will keep a lid on prices.

The long-term outlook, however, is also impacted by short-term developments of the world economy and OPEC policy.

Transition from Short to Long Term

World economic developments and OPEC's ability to manage the oil supply surplus over the next few years will not only affect the short-term energy outlook but will also have an important bearing on longer-

TABLE 5.6
World Energy and Oil Demand and Supply 1987–2000 (in MMB/D)

	1987	1990	1995	2000
Consumption				
World primary energy demand	105.4	112.8	124.5	137.5
Nonoil production	56.8	62.4	71.5	81.8
Total oil consumption	48.6	50.4	53.0	55.7
Oil supply				
Industrialized countries	16.8	16.3	14.2	13.2
Developing countries	8.9	9.8	10.0	10.3
CPE exports	2.1	2.2	2.1	2.0
Processing gain	1.1	1.2	1.2	1.2
Total non-OPEC	28.9	29.5	27.5	26.7
OPEC NGL and Condensate	1.7	1.8	2.0	2.5
OPEC crude oil	17.7	19.3	23.5	26.5
Total supply	48.3	50.4	53.0	55.7
Stock changes	−0.3	+0.2	0	0

Sources: Data base provided by Petroleum Economics, Ltd., London, and author's projections.

term investment decisions and thus impact market development beyond the mid-1990s. A relatively strong world economy, resulting in modest growth in world oil consumption, will facilitate OPEC's ability to manage the supply surplus and thus stabilize prices around the OPEC basket of $18 per barrel. By contrast, a serious recession in the West in either 1989 or 1990 would reduce world oil consumption and severely test OPEC's ability to cope. A recession scenario could lower oil prices, leading to postponement of oil and nonoil supply investment decisions. Energy surpluses in a recession could turn into shortages later when the impact of postponed investment decisions are felt. A stable price in the short term, on the other hand, will facilitate investment decisions and lead to a smoother long-term price path for oil and other fuels.

Assuming no major recession during the next few years and fairly stable medium-term oil prices in the range of $18 to $20 per barrel (1987 $) between 1990 and 1995, energy demand and supply in the non-Communist world may develop as shown in Table 5.6. Short- and medium-term energy supplies have already been determined by investment decisions taken in the 1980s, when consumers and governments remained convinced of future oil supply crises leading once again to much higher world oil prices. It will take many more years of relative price stability to alter these strongly held views. Even then, past price increases have triggered energy savings technologies, which will reduce energy intensity of the world economy throughout the period of the forecast. The decline in energy intensity is expected to slow from the 2 to 5 percent per year in the 1975–1985 period to between 0.5 percent and 1.0 percent in the 1990s.

Oil Demand in Developing Countries

Oil consumption in the developing countries doubled between the mid-1960s and mid-1970s and except for 1984 and 1985 continued to grow—albeit at a slower rate—throughout the period of high oil prices between the mid-1970s and 1980s. Following the price fall of 1986, consumption rose sharply in Asia and modestly debt-ridden Latin America. The more advanced industrialized developing countries are following patterns of conservation and fuel substitution of the heavy end of the barrel not dissimilar to the experience of the industrial countries of the West. But despite improvements in energy efficiency and fuel substitution, oil consumption in developing countries has once again resumed growth at an average of 2.6 percent annually since 1985.

Much of the growth is taking place in the transportation sector. Studies by Massachusetts Institute of Technology (MIT) and OECD suggest that the number of automobiles in the developing countries will more than double between the mid-1980s and the end of the century, requiring more gasoline and diesel oil. In the household sector, kerosene and LPG are rising rapidly even in countries producing natural gas (with undeveloped gas grids). Diesel oil use is growing steadily in the industrial sector, and despite rapid substitution of heavy fuel oil in many of the more advanced developing countries, overall fuel oil consumption in the developing countries is still rising.

One of the serious constraints is capital to build new hydro, nuclear, or coal-fired power plants or to construct natural gas grid or infrastructure for coal storage and transportation where such fuels are regionally available. Capital constraints are likely to show fuel substitution in all but the richest developing countries. The modest growth rate in oil consumption of 2 percent per year through 2000 projected in this study would seem to be conservative and implies continuation of relatively low rates of economic growth in those countries.

The Use of Natural Gas

In the industrialized countries, natural gas is likely to maintain its current market share of about 18 percent. In Europe, natural gas penetration will continue in the home-heating sector when gas commands a premium price. Natural gas use for steam raising in power stations and industry was supposed to be phased out in the Common Market, but current environmental concern coupled with technological developments (combined cycle power plants) and potentially adequate long-term gas supplies could change this policy. The adverse effect of the Chernobyl accident on public opinion might add additional weight to the argument for switching to safe and clean natural gas. Diversification of supply entered a new phase with the agreement of continental European buyers to purchase additional Norwegian gas. Supply security has been enhanced further by interconnecting the European natural gas grid. In Japan, long-term contracts with Asian and Middle Eastern suppliers will guarantee a further small increase of the share of natural gas in primary energy through the end of the century. Most of the gas is used as town gas and to generate electricity in environmentally sensitive urban areas.

In the United States, energy analysts have changed the perception of long-term availability of natural gas in recent years. For a number of reasons natural gas use fell from 22 thousand cubic feet (TCF) in 1973 to a low of 16.2 TCF in 1986, but gradual deregulation and a surprising ability of industry to cope with lower prices has resulted in a gradual increase in natural gas consumption. Industry analysts now project ample availability of domestic and Canadian gas through the 1990s to meet expected growth in consumption to 20 TCF by 2000. These supplies are expected to be forthcoming at prices gradually increasing from $2 to $4/TCF by the turn of the century. At these prices, gas would remain competitive in industry and in combined cycle electric power plants, which are expected to use two-thirds of incremental demand in the second half of the 1990s. In the residential/commercial sector consumption is expected to grow slowly, with the increase in new houses and buildings partially offset by efficiency gains. The current view on U.S. gas availability differs from the prevailing view a few years ago when gas production was expected to decline sharply in the 1990s and large-scale substitution to fuel oil was held possible.

Coal

The share of coal in primary energy consumption of the industrialized countries may not grow much above the current 25 percent. Although many studies in the early 1980s foresaw a large potential for coal use in industry, environmental concerns, coupled with structural change in industry and lower oil and gas price expectations, have reduced earlier predictions. In fact, coal use in industry may hardly grow at all through the end of the century.

Coal's promise remains in the electricity sector, where further growth is projected in particular in the United States. Decisions on using coal, nuclear power, or combined cycle units for future electricity generation will depend on considerations of cost and policy, which differ from country to country. The contribution of coal for electricity generation has pretty much been determined for the period through 1995 (long lead times), and decisions over the next few years will determine the future of coal in this sector for the remainder of the 1990s. Most of the growth in coal use is projected for the United States, where the nuclear power industry is faced with serious regulatory problems and public opposition. However, the high cost of meeting increasingly stringent environmental regulations may postpone investment decisions for new base-load coal-fired power plants in favor of gas-based combined cycle power plants, which are characterized by shorter lead times and lower capital costs.

Nuclear Energy

In contrast to stagnant overall energy demand growth in the industrialized countries since the oil crises of the 1970s, electricity demand continued to grow, albeit at a slower pace. The share of oil and natural gas for base-load electricity generation fell sharply, and nuclear power was the big gainer. Slower growth of electricity, higher than expected costs due to technical and environmental factors, and the aftershocks of the Chernobyl accident have reduced prospects for growth of nuclear power. At the minimum, Chernobyl caused further delays in lead times (now eleven years in Europe and higher in the United States) and additional costs to meet safety and environmental standards.

In Europe, France has been the big success story for nuclear power, raising its contribution in electricity generation from about 10 percent in 1975 to 70 percent in 1986. The other extreme is Austria, where the only nuclear plant ever built was closed down in 1978 and dismantled in 1986. Despite all these problems, plants under construction are expected to be completed, raising Europe's nuclear contribution from an oil equivalent of 2.5 to 3.0 MMB/D by mid-1990s and some further expansion thereafter. In Japan, the nuclear power program has been very successful, and electricity from nuclear power is expected to increase by another 50 percent in the 1990s, raising nuclear energy from 4 percent of primary energy in 1980 to 19 percent by the turn of the century. In the United States no new nuclear power plants have been ordered since 1979, but plants under construction will still add another 0.5 MMB/D of oil-equivalent to electricity supplies.

Throughout the industrialized countries, environmental problems, the high capital cost of new base-load power plants, and public opposition to power plant siting has forced management to look at alternative options, such as improving the efficiency of electricity use and load management, reducing spare capacity requirements, extending the life of existing power plants, purchase electricity from industrial producers, and, where possible, buying electricity abroad.

Oil Production

For years, highly qualified petroleum geologists and engineers have predicted the peaking and subsequent decline of non-OPEC production. In reality, non-OPEC production has continued to grow, reducing OPEC's market share. Again, most experts believe that non-OPEC production will soon peak and begin to decline in the early 1990s. It is generally agreed that oil production in developing non-OPEC countries will continue to grow at least through the mid-1990s at prices of $15 to $18 per barrel (1987 $) or more. It is also generally accepted that at much lower prices investment in exploration and development will be postponed, leading to stagnant and lower production in those countries.

Views on the production outlook of the United States, North Sea, and the USSR have been altered many times in recent years due to actual recent production experience and the development of new cost-saving technologies for the development of new fields and maintenance of the production ceiling in existing fields beyond the original plan. In 1987–1988, for example, the U.S. Department of Energy increased its estimate for U.S. petroleum production in 2000 by 0.7 MMB/D and natural gas by about 1 TCF. Similar changes have been made by other analysts related to North Sea production. Whereas only a few years ago, the consensus view was for North Sea oil production to decline sharply in the 1990s, new cost-saving technologies for smaller fields and continued reserve additions from improved recovery of oil-in-place in producing fields have changed analysts' perception about the timing and the extent of oil production declines even in the United Kingdom (UK) sector. Recent developments in the USSR have led to increased oil production and exports, and analysts now doubt if Soviet oil exports will decline at all in the 1990s. The consensus view still holds that non-OPEC oil production will peak and decline in the 1990s, but later and in a less-pronounced way than previously predicted.

Impact on OPEC

The frequently predicted oil crisis of 1985 was postponed a few years ago to the late 1980s or early 1990s. Although there is considerable uncertainty about actual developments of world oil demand and supply over the next decade, most scenarios now indicate that the world oil surplus will persist through the mid-1990s, and that the major task ahead for OPEC and independent oil exporting countries is to manage the supply in such a way as to optimize revenues without triggering a new burst of oil substitution and large-scale exploration and development. Unless there are major surprises such as a sudden unforeseen and prolonged burst in world economic activities and/or major reductions in either nonoil fuels or non-OPEC oil production, it seems unlikely that the oil market will tighten much until the mid-1990s or even thereafter when the demand for OPEC oil will move closer to the volume OPEC is willing and able to produce on a long-term sustained basis. Thereafter, prices are expected to increase gradually, leading to new developments of nonoil fuels, more expensive oil, and the introduction of new energy-efficiency technologies.

Aware of these potential developments, oil exporters are unlikely to repeat the mistakes of the late 1970s and early 1980s and instead revert to a strategy of gradual and modest price increase to keep supply and demand in balance. Expected price increases in the late 1990s will make it increasingly economically attractive to develop the vast heavy oil reserves in the world.

Security of Supply Revisited

Recent energy publications in the United States and Europe continue to refer to the next energy crisis of the 1990s, which, it is said, could have a worse impact on the world economy than the previous oil shocks because the easy conservation and fuel switching have already been accomplished. Some authors have gone as far as to call OPEC's desperate attempts in recent years to prevent a price collapse through supply management as "deliberate manipulations of world oil prices" by OPEC's forcing a major reduction in exploration and development.

Supply security remains a valid concern for oil-importing countries, but one may question the implied urgency of the problem as stated in recent assessments in particular in the United States, as well as the medicine prescribed to cure the problem. Deliberate attempts to cut off oil supplies, as was the case in 1973, are unlikely to be repeated by major oil exporters because they are still suffering from the consequences of the first attempt and because large oil exporters have acquired—or are in the process of acquiring—major downstream and other financial interests in the importing countries. Moreover, deliberate oil-supply interruption cannot continue for long, due to financial constraints of producers and possible counteractions by consuming countries. The industrialized countries now have adequate strategic storage—and the will to use it—to cope with supply interruptions of up to six months or more.

Incidental supply interruptions can of course occur. The Iran revolution and the outbreak of the Iran-Iraq war are examples of such supply interruptions. In case of the Iran revolution, world supplies were down about 2 MMB/D for about one quarter. If the industrialized countries had had the current strategic oil storage, releasing up to 2 MMB/D (including the use of futures options to reduce short-term price increases) for that period would have reduced the problem to more manageable proportions. The net effect of the Iran-Iraq war was to prevent oil prices from falling more rapidly between 1981 and 1985 than they actually did. In recent years the tanker wars and continuous attacks on transportation and storage facilities have had little measurable impact on supplies and prices. The construction of oil pipelines from Iraq and Saudi Arabia to the Red Sea and Turkey as well as pipelines under construction or in advanced planning stage will further reduce the impact of the "Hormuz factor."

Energy-supply security should not be belittled as a potential problem, but the changes in world oil demand and supply and trade patterns, coupled with changes in transportation outlets and interests of now vertically integrated oil exporters, have affected both the scope and the urgency of this potential problem. In view of changed circumstances and long-term interests of producers and consumers in avoiding extreme volatility in oil prices, it would appear that instead of confrontation there is ample room for future cooperation.

6

World Oil and U.S. Imports: Is the Past Prologue?

John H. Lichtblau

As we move toward the end of the 1980s we can look back on almost a decade of rising world oil surpluses and falling oil prices, both trends accelerating in the post-1985 period. The trauma of physical shortages and exploding prices that occupied center stage in world economics and politics from 1972 through 1981 has receded into a historic nightmare as we contemplate the complete reversal of the buyer-seller relationship between then and now.

Yet, in the midst of plenty, the Cassandra warnings of another oil-supply crisis in the early to mid-1990s are heard once again and are, in fact, becoming louder. In the face of OPEC's desperate battle to stem the avalanche of surplus capacity within and rising production without, we are told that within five years the organization will once again have the power to raise prices at will and can be expected to do so. Those who make this prediction in the United States argue that the interests of national security require the government to act now to prevent such a development or, at least, to mitigate its impact. Since the proposed policies and measures would help the domestic oil-producing industry, it is legitimate to ask whether the new doomsday warnings are not, at bottom, self-serving industry pleas. The answer is partly yes, but that does not invalidate them.

The U.S. oil-producing industry and the industry that services it are indeed in serious trouble as a result of the 1986 price collapse. In the two years since then they have remained too low for U.S. producers to drill enough wells to replace their depleting reserves. To wit, oil discoveries in 1986 and 1987 were just half of the 1.1 billion barrels annual average of the 1980–1985 period.

Thus, absent a substantial and sustained increase in foreign oil prices in the near future, the commercial resource base of the domestic oil industry will shrink inexorably and probably fairly rapidly. No new public policy could arrest this decline. But the industry believes that administrative or legislative support measures could at least slow it down. There is much debate over what form this support should take. Like all special interests seeking public support, the oil industry must formulate its case in terms of the national interest to receive a serious hearing. It is beginning to get attention because oil imports are growing again, domestic oil production is declining, and both trends are expected to continue into the 1990s.

In other words, it is plausible, though by no means inevitable, that during the 1990s the dependence of the United States and the rest of the world on OPEC oil will once again rise to the level at which OPEC can temporarily dictate oil prices. The organization succeeded twice in using temporary price explosions, caused by brief extraneous supply disruptions, to maintain for extended periods oil prices vastly above their free market value. Thus, the argument goes—and must be taken seriously—that under similar circumstances, or even without an extraneous trigger, OPEC would do so again. However, it must also be recognized that this proposition contains the facile assumptions that history repeats itself, that the 1990s will essentially resemble the 1970s, that technology stands still, and that none of the major players on the supply or demand side has learned a lesson from the past, all of which is unlikely.

The strongest point underlying the present warnings is the almost certain return to the Middle East for incremental world oil supplies after 1990. How rapidly this will take place depends primarily on the future price of oil as well as the present perception of the future price. The lower the price or the price perception, the faster the return will occur, and vice versa. But at any realistic price assumption, the share of Middle East oil supplying the world's import markets will grow significantly from 1988 through the 1990s. This should not come as a surprise. OPEC Middle East crude oil production dropped from a peak of 21.6 MMB/D in 1977 to 9.5 MMB/D in 1985, thereby absorbing the bulk of the global decline in oil demand as well as the increase in non-OPEC supply throughout that period. Now that world demand is starting to rise again and total non-OPEC supplies are likely to level off within four to five years and probably decline thereafter, this process will be reversed. In fact, by 1987 OPEC Middle East crude production had already risen to 11.7 MMB/D.

The Department of Energy (DOE) study, *Energy Security*, published in April 1987, projects under its *low* price scenario total OPEC Middle East crude production of not quite 21 MMB/D in 1995. This seems unrealistically high, since it assumes sustained low prices and high demand. But it could easily be met, with capacity to spare, if the region's producers want it. Thus, resource constraint will not pose a problem for oil supplies by the mid-1990s nor by the end of the century.

However, once the Middle East has reestablished its position as the world's incremental producer, with control over virtually all actual and potential spare capacity, its exporters would collectively be in a position by the mid-1990s to raise prices temporarily almost at will if they so choose. In a market characterized by rising demand and falling spare producing capacity the marginal supplier has this power.

To what extent Middle East exporters will actually use this power is of course the $64 billion question. If they take a long-term rational approach, based on their current 100-year reserve/production ratio, in planning their revenue optimization, they will not let prices rise to the point of depressing world consumption once again and stimulating high-cost oil and other energy production, particularly since such production will continue once the investment has been made, even if prices decline again. Thus, the short-term gains of cartel price maximization could well be more than offset by medium- to long-term market losses. This is not just a theoretical possibility, as OPEC has learned.

How successful the Middle East countries will be in this rational economic approach depends to a significant extent on political and strategic factors and considerations that have little to do with the economics of oil. In other words, the very low cost and superabundance of Middle East oil may not be the principal future determinants in setting its price, just as they were not in the past.

How will the U.S. oil industry fare under these conditions? U.S. crude production will of course decline for the foreseeable future. The aforementioned DOE report illustrates this. Even under its high-price case, in which the price is approximately back to the *nominal* 1985 level by 1990 and to the *real* 1985 level by 1995, U.S. production in 1990 will be almost 1 MMB/D lower than in 1985 and an additional 1.2 MMB/D lower in 1995. Yet these prices would be considered very attractive by post-1985 standards.

What this suggests is that over time the potential for oil discoveries and production is quite limited in the United States and only up to a point sensitive to higher prices. It is important that this is probably less true for domestic natural gas production, whose reserve/production ratio and production potential are higher than those of crude oil. Thus higher prices may do more to stimulate gas production than oil production.

The limited upward price sensitivity of oil production is probably not a mirror image of its downward price sensitivity. In other words, a substantial price increase would at most postpone the production decline for a number of years. On the other hand, if domestic crude prices were to fall back to the mid-1986 low of about $11 and remain there for several years, most exploratory oil and gas drilling would cease, given the fact that direct domestic finding and development costs are in the $12–15 range. Development drilling would also drop sharply, as would flowing stripper well production. The result would be the phase out of much of the domestic producing industry and its ancillary service industry over this period.

Technically and physically a price decline of such magnitude and duration is entirely possible. There is enough readily available oil and oil resources that can be developed in the world to meet all requirements at a positive cash flow at this price for four to five years, perhaps longer. Of course, such a scenario could only come about if OPEC were to collapse totally and its members then engaged in maximum competition with each other and if no reconstitution of the organization in any form became possible for this period. In other words, prices would have to be determined in a fully competitive, totally free, unfettered market. This is highly unlikely, given the overwhelming economic and political self-interest of all oil exporters to prevent it or, if it should happen, to quickly reverse it.

Now let us move from these hypothetical speculations to an appraisal of future oil imports under what we might call a midpoint price scenario. This assumes that the 1988 average price stays flat in nominal dollars to 1990 and then rises slightly faster than inflation to 1995. First, a look at production: We know that lower-48 production, which had remained approximately flat from 1980 to 1985, fell as a consequence of the price drop by 800,000 B/D, or 11 percent, from 1985 to 1987. In the last quarter of 1987 the year-to-year decline leveled off to about 200,000 B/D. It will continue to fall, perhaps at a somewhat slower rate, even under a somewhat higher price than we assume.

Alaskan production, which is far less sensitive to price declines because of its much lower production cost, has moved in the opposite direction. It rose by 40,000 B/D in 1986 and nearly 100,000 B/D in 1987. It is now reaching its production plateau of 2 MMB/D, will stay there until 1990, and then enter its long-term phase of declining production with a projected drop of 500,000 B/D in the first half of the 1990s. Thus, from 1990–1991 on, Alaska will contribute to the decline in U.S. production. By 1995 this may result in a total U.S. production level about 2 MMB/D below the 1985 level.

U.S. demand, which was at 15.7 MMB/D in 1985, rose by a hefty 3.5 percent in 1986 and a further 1.5 percent in 1987. Assuming annual increases below 1 percent to 1995, demand in the latter year would be about 17.5 MMB/D. Imports would therefore have to rise sufficiently between 1985 and 1995 to offset the decline in production and provide

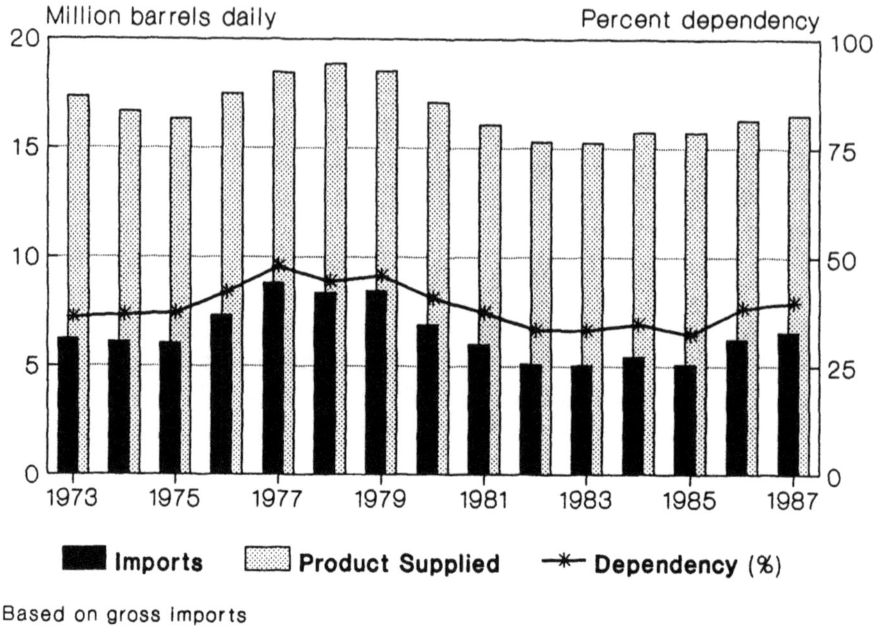

FIGURE 6.1 Total petroleum imports and import dependency, 1973–1987.
Source: Energy Information Administration, *Monthly Energy Review* (various issues).

the increase in demand. This might require a 4.0 MMB/D increase in imports from the 5 MMB/D level of 1985. About 1.5 MMB/D of this increase has already occurred. It has raised the gross import dependency from 32 percent of total U.S. demand in 1985 to nearly 40 percent in 1987 (see Figure 6.1). By 1995 it is likely to exceed 50 percent under our assumptions.

Can the United States afford such a ratio of import dependency? There are as many answers to this question as there are definitions of the term *afford.* One can of course point out that many other industrial nations, including such major ones as Japan, Germany, and France, have always been more than 90 percent dependent on imported oil. Yet this has not hurt their economies nor raised their energy cost above that of the United States. However, these countries do not have to cope with the huge U.S. balance-of-trade deficits, of which oil imports are a large part.

Up to now, the oil price decline has actually helped the U.S. trade balance because it has lowered the oil-import bill. In 1986 the oil-import bill was $15.5 billion lower than in 1985. In 1987 it rose but was still $9–10 billion below 1985 despite the substantial increase in the volume of imports (see Figure 6.2). By 1989 the oil-import bill will exceed the

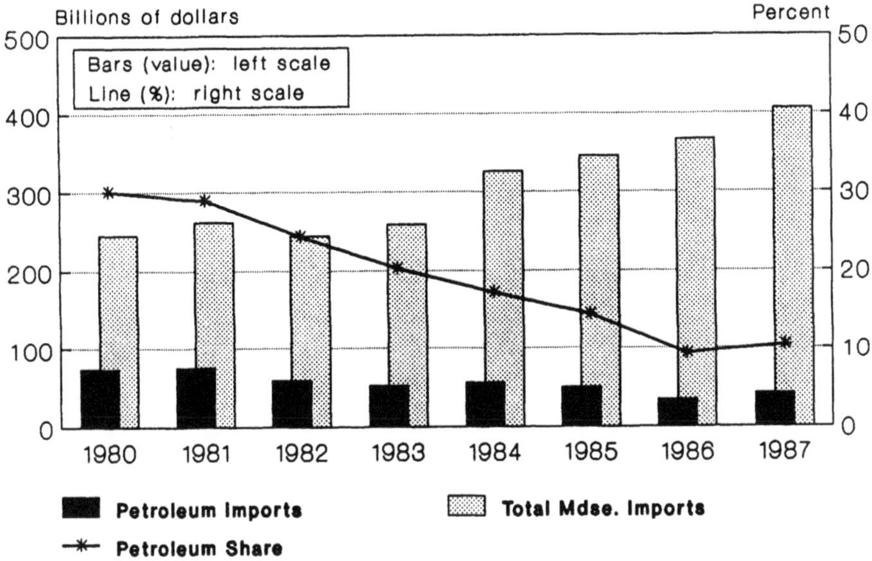

FIGURE 6.2 Value of petroleum imports and merchandise imports, 1980–1987. *Source:* U.S. Department of Commerce, *Survey of Current Business* (various issues).

1985 level. Thereafter it will keep growing. But even in the early 1990s oil's share of total U.S. merchandise imports will still be below the 20–30 percent ratio of the early 1980s. Japan and the oil-importing nations of Europe do not face this problem. Their oil imports will rise much less than that of the United States to 1995. Hence, their oil-import bills could well remain below the 1985 level throughout this period.

What about the security of foreign supplies? Can the United States count on sustained ready commercial access for its growing import requirements? As pointed out, the physical availability of projected U.S. import volume by 1995, or more if needed, is not in question. Purely economically, the geographic sources of these imports are of limited importance. Since oil is a fungible commodity, oils from various sources are largely interchangeable and oil prices are generally interrelated and competitive. Thus any price change initiated by one major exporter either is transmitted to all others or is unlikely to be sustained. However, there are political-strategic implications to certain foreign oil dependencies. The most obvious is of course the Middle East. Between 1980 and 1985 the Middle East's share of U.S. oil imports dropped from 30 to 6 percent. In 1987 it was back to 16.5 percent (see Figure 6.3). By 1995 it may well account for 25–30 percent of U.S. oil imports.

In analyzing the security of these supplies we must differentiate between long term *dependency* on foreign oil and the risk of short-term

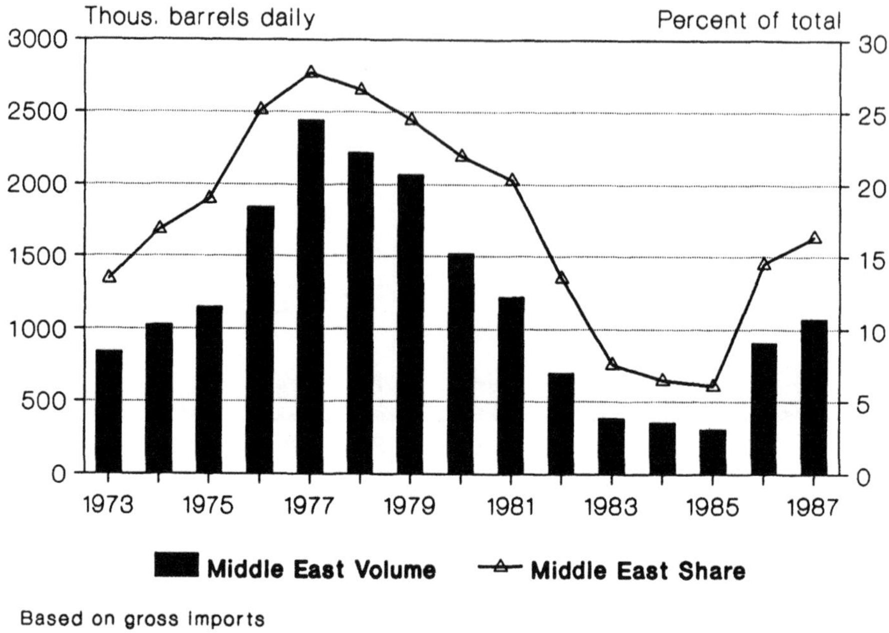

FIGURE 6.3 Middle East share of total U.S. petroleum imports, 1973–1987.
Source: Energy Information Administration, *Monthly Energy Review* (various issues).

foreign *disruptions.* It is important to keep these two concepts apart, since they are essentially different and require different policy responses.

A disruption that is temporary in nature can occur at any moment or may never happen again. For the foreseeable future a disruption could have a serious effect on world oil supplies only if it occurred in the Middle East. The reason is the region's excess producing capacity. Currently it accounts for 65–70 percent of OPEC's total excess producing capacity. By the mid-1990s it is likely to exceed 90 percent. Thus, if export supplies outside the Middle East became unavailable at any time, importers could readily draw on the Middle East's excess capacity. But if any of the major Middle East producers' exports became unavailable, so would their excess capacity, which would make the disruption more serious and require the importing countries to deal with it on their own.

They can do so through various readily accessible and pretested emergency measures. The most important of these is the strategic petroleum reserve (SPR) in the United States and similar noncommercial reserves in all other industrial countries. Clearly, the increasing level of U.S. imports requires it to keep filling the SPR as rapidly as possible until it reaches the congressionally mandated level of 750 million barrels. Another measure to assure continued access to oil supplies during a disruption is contained in the recent U.S. trade agreement with Canada, currently the largest foreign oil supplier of the United States.

The long-term growth in U.S. dependency on foreign oil is inevitable, as has been pointed out. However, the rate of this growth can be affected positively or negatively through government action or inaction. The pros and cons of these policies have been widely discussed. I would just like to touch on a few. Until recently the government's most negative existing policy in this area has been the windfall profit tax. The tax was obsolete in concept and created a potential disincentive to development drilling and exploration. It was finally abolished in August 1988. Another negative public policy is the long-standing prohibition on drilling in the Arctic National Wildlife Refuge. The oil industry considers this the most promising unexplored area in the United States.

Regarding new governmental action, import fees and drilling tax incentives are the most widely discussed measures. Per dollar of expenditure, a tax incentive is much more cost-effective since it concentrates the support where it is actually needed: the drilling of new wells. An import fee might achieve a similar result for new production, but it would also raise the price of all flowing production (including natural gas, whose price is determined by parity with certain oil products), even though at current prices flowing production obviously does not require any price boost, nor is there a significant volume of shut-in production. A fixed import fee would of course have an inflationary impact on the economy and could also hurt the U.S. trade balance, both by raising the U.S. cost of energy relative to that of other countries and by inviting trade retaliation from oil exporters who all strongly oppose the fee.

An oil-import fee would of course help reduce the U.S. budget deficit and encourage energy conservation. However, since there is no causal connection between the price or import volume of oil and the federal budget deficit, singling out oil as an instrument for deficit reduction would be an arbitrary act, devoid of logic. Furthermore, the oil-import fee is not an efficient revenue-raising instrument. Regarding the conservation effect, if this is desired, an increase in the existing consumer tax on transportation fuels would be far simpler, more effective, and less distortive.

Another currently discussed concept is a *floor price* for crude oil, supported by a flexible import fee or a special consumer tax whose revenue could be used to subsidize the chosen floor price. A tax reduction tied to a floor price has also been suggested. The policy question here is whether the floor price is intended to raise existing prices or to provide a safety net under them for longer-term investment purposes. In the latter case the floor price might provide tangible benefits at very little cost. The concept dates back to 1975 when the International Energy

Agency adopted a $7 floor price, which remains in effect though it has never been adjusted.

In conclusion, I would like to reiterate my basic points: Public action or inaction can affect the pace but not the direction of the post-1985 trend. Over the next seven years domestic oil demand will rise modestly, production will decline moderately to substantially, while oil imports will account for at least half of total supplies by 1995. Meanwhile, the Middle East's share of world oil production will rise. By 1995 its output could be up at least 35 percent above that of 1987. There will be enough oil to provide the required volumes without straining the supply system. Its price will be determined by the interaction of the OPEC cartel and market forces. If OPEC ignores market forces, it is likely to damage itself irreparably over time. If market forces destroy OPEC, U.S. oil production would be severely and probably irreparably damaged over time, unless it receives effective government support.

7

Drill Rigs and Battleships Are the Answer! (But What Was the Question?)

Oil Efficiency, Economic Rationality, and Security

Amory B. Lovins and L. Hunter Lovins[1]

Cyclical concern about U.S. oil depletion has for many years drawn forth almost every kind of reasoned or tendentious argument save one: serious exploration of a *least-cost oil strategy* based on pursuing the best buys first.[2] Just as no corporation can long survive in the marketplace unless it uses its resources economically, so no nation, however richly endowed, can long remain secure and competitive if its energy strategy ignores the market's cost-minimizing imperative. Today's oil problems are a harbinger of the far more severe ones that will arise if costly options continue to be pursued to the virtual exclusion of cheap ones.

U.S. oil policy has long emphasized depleting oil reserves in the United States first, other regions later, and oil-rich parts of the Middle East much later. Three responses are available to the resulting depletion of cheap domestic oil:[3] protectionism, trade, and substitution. Protectionism, and the various policy options subsumed under trade (friendly relations, diversification, stockpiling, military force), seek to mitigate some of the consequences of depleting different provinces at different times. Neither protectionism nor trade, however, seeks to slow domestic depletion or to provide replacement supplies. Paradoxically, many proposed "strength-through-exhaustion"[4] policies, which could be classified under protectionism, respond to domestic depletion only by accelerating it.

In contrast, substitution would gradually replace oil by a judicious combination of more efficient use and alternative fuels. Only substitution looks beyond the petroleum era. Only substitution can avoid the serious problems inherent now in protectionism and later, if not now, in large-scale oil imports. And substitution—of higher oil productivity for burning oil itself—is, we shall suggest, at the core of an energy policy that takes economics seriously.

This chapter examines how the efficient use of energy, particularly of oil, can help to create and smooth a transition beyond oil. It analyzes the dynamics of how the United States used efficiency to improve its oil supply/demand balance throughout the period 1977–1985. It also explains the unusual events that in 1986 reversed this steady decline in oil imports. Finally, it quantifies the approximate size and cost of the least-cost technical and policy options available to reduce or eliminate oil imports while stretching domestic resources in the years and decades ahead.

Lopsided Policy Emphasis

Misdirected emphasis on supply expansions is now becoming not only wasteful but also dangerous. As will be shown, cheap oil-saving opportunities offer practical, presently available ways to run today's U.S. economy with about a fourth as much oil as now, at an average cost of savings probably under $10 per barrel—far less than the finding cost of new domestic oil. Despite this, official policies continue to emphasize supply options that cost about *ten to a hundred times* more than readily achievable, less risky ways to save oil through more efficient use. The Reagan administration's military intervention in the Gulf, for example, increased the effective cost of imports from that region (neglecting all the military risks involved) to a FY1985 level of about $495 per barrel—eighteen times as much for the military force as for the oil itself.[5] Yet the same administration rolled back auto-efficiency standards whose societal marginal cost, if it exceeds zero,[6] is at most a few dollars per barrel saved. Those U.S. new car standards alone—one of the most effective oil-saving programs the world has ever seen—accounted for a fifth of *all* oil saved (6.2 MMB/D) during 1979–1983 by the twenty-one IEA nations.[7] Rolling them back starting with 1986 cars is shown below to have doubled 1985 U.S. imports from the Gulf.

The asymmetry between supply and efficiency initiatives continues to dominate public policy and many private-sector attitudes. After the oil crises of 1973–1974 and 1979–1980, the federal government sought to spur supply with public subsidies and removal of procedural or environmental constraints.[8] Both times, however, those efforts collapsed and the overbuilt supply industries faced insolvency as the market instead produced a largely unforeseen gush of efficiency. The Reagan administration seems to have been determined to make this mistake a third time.[9]

Many policymakers continue to be slow to learn that energy demand is not fate but choice, an enormously flexible choice. Customers can and do buy energy-saving devices at need. This flexibility is often overlooked, in part because efficiency options are less familiar and come less readily to mind than supply options. Insulation installed out of sight and out of mind in millions of attics is somehow less impressive than one huge power plant, even though the insulation provides larger, cheaper, and more reliable energy services. The striking successes of efficiency are less well known than the more limited successes of supply expansions, are not promoted by lavish public relations campaigns, and hence are given less credence. The risks and uncertainties of supply versus demand options are seldom compared fairly and symmetrically. This chapter, by sketching basic elements of the "supply curve" of available oil savings, seeks to make efficiency easier to discuss on the same footing as supply.

Implications for the Oil Industry

Most thoughtful oil analysts now foresee fairly flat long-term real oil price trajectories. In these circumstances, upstream rents are scarce. Downstream rents were long ago squeezed out. The only big rents left to be captured are the spread between the cost of extracting barrels and the cost of *saving* barrels, which might be called "producing 'negabarrels.'"[10] (This rent represents the difference between the supply curves of extracting oil and those of saving oil.) An oil company wishing to stay competitive should consider selling a mix of barrels and negabarrels, altering their proportions to suit current market conditions.

This strategy offers important advantages. For example, when real oil prices fluctuate unpredictably—as many analysts believe they will for at least the rest of the twentieth century[11]—between, say, $15 and $25 a barrel (with odd spikes now and then as war or peace breaks out in the Middle East), smart oil companies will find that it is much easier to make their margins selling negabarrels that cost $5 to produce than barrels that cost $15. To be sure, the mix of oil and efficiency that one sells can and should vary with current market conditions; but including in that mix a hefty dose of efficiency yields cheaper energy services—a better buy for the customer—and virtually eliminates downside price risks. (Avoidance of other kinds of risks is discussed at the end of this chapter.)

Saving oil, too, does not just stretch supplies further and hold down prices, as it did so dramatically in 1986; it also helps to bring sorely needed stability to world energy markets. The basic reason that prices fluctuate for oil, as for copper, wheat, and sowbellies, is that consumers' and suppliers' response to surplus or scarcity is not instantaneous: It is delayed by lags of both perception and logistics. Even if politics did not affect oil prices at all, lagged responses by buyers and sellers would still make prices volatile, like a driver who reacts too late and oversteers a car. Amid short-term price fluctuations, however, two "slow variables" are also operating: depletion, which raises the price, and more efficient use, which lowers the price. If depletion proceeds faster than efficiency, price will become more volatile. But if efficiency proceeds faster than depletion, it will tend to dampen price volatility, moving long-term markets toward stability and predictability. That is certainly in the interest of any capital-intensive business such as the oil industry.

For any oil company wishing to survive, paying careful attention to oil-saving opportunities is not a luxury but a necessity. The world is already irreversibly in an era of relatively costlier fuel and cheaper efficiency. Customers will increasingly want to get their energy services by buying less fuel and more efficiency. Energy companies that sell them that altered mix will prosper; those that only seek access to ever-costlier oil will falter.

Since before the first oil shock, such success as we have had in foreseeing the evolution of energy markets has come from careful attention to economics, from faith that, given the choice, customers will seek the best buys in each end-use. The energy industries can choose to aid or inhibit the spread of efficient energy use, to embrace or ignore, facilitate or stall, the flowering of the energy service marketplace. But in the long run, their choice is only between participation in the efficiency revolution and obsolescence. Efficiency options are increasingly available and will sooner or later be bought, with or without fuel vendors' foresight, blessing, and participation. The only choice is who will make money on efficiency, and who will use it cannily to hedge against the remaining, much reduced, risks in the ever less dominant supply-side markets.

Oil Savings Achieved

Virtually unnoticed, efficiency improvements have outperformed all efforts to expand energy supplies. It is vital to understand how and why this occurred. The United States in 1987 used a third less oil to produce a dollar of real GNP than it did in 1973. A minor part of this reduction was due to small changes in behavior. The average U.S. passenger car was driven 6 percent fewer miles in 1986 than in 1973, despite 4.5 percent lower real gasoline prices;[12] surprisingly, only 4 percent of the 1976–1987 gain in car-fleet efficiency was the result of shifts to smaller cars.[13] Probably more of the reduction was due to changes in the composition of economic output (less steel[14] and cement, more computers and financial instruments). The majority of the savings—by most estimates more than three-fourths—was due to technical gains in energy productivity. These gains came chiefly from such mundane measures as caulk guns, duct tape, plugging industrial steam leaks, and modestly raising car efficiencies.

Even such simple means yielded vast benefits. The 1979–1985 reduction in oil/GNP intensity corresponded by 1985 to annual savings equal to three times the 1986 U.S. imports from the Gulf. Just the 1973–1986 improvement in the efficiency of the U.S. car fleet, from 13.3 to 18.3 miles per gallon (mpg), provided in 1986 more than twice as much oil as the United States imported from the Gulf in that year, or as much oil as Alaska provided.[15] As will be seen, the additional potential for future vehicular efficiency improvements similarly dominates future oil savings—indeed, dominates all oil options on both the supply and the demand side.

In terms of market share, efficiency has quietly swept the field. During 1979–1986, the United States got:

- Fifteen times as much new energy from savings as from all net increases in supply from nuclear and fossil fuels
- Seven times as much new energy from savings as from all net increases in domestic supply combined[16]
- More than four times as much new energy from savings as from the increased gross output of coal and of nuclear steam[17]
- More new net supply from renewable than from nonrenewable sources

Specifically, the Energy Information Administration's *Annual Energy Review 1986* showed, from 1973[18] and 1979[19] through 1986, the absolute amounts (in q, or quadrillion Btu, per year) and percentage shares of increased total effective supply (see Table 7.1). ("Effective supply" includes both new energy production and improved energy productivity—wringing more economic activity out of energy already being used.) The percentages of the total increase in effective supply are shown in two ways: including in that total (INCL) and excluding from that total (EXCL) the changes in output of domestic oil, gas, and natural gas liquids. The following table *ex*cludes renewable sources, such as wood, not shown in EIA's summary statistics; these sources' contributions will be partly accounted for later.

These data show, for example, that of the actual net expansions in effective primary energy supply (counting the decrease in fossil-hydrocarbon output), savings accounted for 92 percent of the total since 1973

TABLE 7.1
Effective Energy Supply Gain, 1973–1986, Excluding Renewable Sources

	1973–1986		1979–1986	
	q/y	INCL/EXCL[a](%)	q/y	INCL/EXCL[a](%)
Savings[20]	26.21	92.1/74.3	18.78	92.8/81.3
Coal[21]	5.52	19.4/15.6	2.87	14.2/12.4
Nuclear[22]	3.56	12.5/10.1	1.45	7.2/6.3
All other EIA supply[23]	−6.84	−24.0/na	−2.85	−14.1/na
Total[24]	28.45	100.0/100.0	20.25	100.0/100.0

[a]Including and excluding oil/gas/NGLs.

Source: Energy Information Administration, *Monthly Energy Review*, September 1987.

and for 93 percent since 1979. (Komanoff's analysis, with which we concur, indicates a slight *acceleration* of savings during 1984–1986—contrary to the conventional wisdom that energy savings have recently slowed if not halted.) Expansions of nuclear power and coal combined accounted for only the remaining 32 percent and 21 percent of the total during the same periods.[24] As fractions of *gross* supply expansion, ignoring the declining oil and gas output, the coal-plus-nuclear fractions were smaller—26 percent since 1973 and 19 percent since 1979–while savings accounted for 74 percent and 81 percent of the respective total increases in effective supply.

An even more realistic assessment of absolute and relative contributions can be obtained by disaggregating "All other EIA supply" into fossil hydrocarbons, hydroelectricity,[25] and geothermal heat, and by adding very conservative estimates of output from some of the other renewable sources that are omitted from EIA's summary statistics[26] (see Table 7.2).

Thus the much-touted claim that nuclear power, for example, has been the key to displacing oil is clearly exaggerated. Since 1973, savings have outpaced nuclear expansion by sevenfold; since 1979, by nearly thirteenfold. Even the expansion in coal plus nuclear power combined was responsible for only 25 percent since 1973, and for only 18 percent since 1979, of the total gross expansion of U.S. energy supply. Komanoff noted that, during the two-year period 1985–1986, there was a further decrease in the coal-plus-nuclear share, to a mere seventh of the energy savings.[30] (In terms of opportunity, cost, indeed, coal and nuclear investments, far from contributing to oil displacement, have undoubtedly *retarded* it, as will be noted below.)

It might be objected that comparisons between savings and net increases in supply are between a large number and a very small one, since decreases in oil and gas output have been of the same order of

TABLE 7.2
Effective Energy Supply Gain, 1973–1986, Including Some Renewable Sources

	1973–1986		1979–1986	
	q/y	INCL/EXCL[a](%)	q/y	INCL/EXCL[a](%)
Savings	25.13	85.5/68.8	18.39	87.9/76.6
Coal	5.52	18.8/15.1	2.87	13.7/12.0
Nuclear	3.56	12.1/9.7	1.45	6.9/6.0
Oil/gas/NGL	−7.16	−24.4/NA	−3.07	−14.7/NA
Hydroelectricity[27]	0.75	2.5/2.0	0.34	16./1.46
Geothermal	0.18	0.6/0.5	0.16	0.7/0.6
Wood and wood wastes[28]	1.125	3.8/3.1	0.62	3.0/2.6
Other renewables[29]	0.28	1.0/0.8	0.18	0.9/0.7
Total	29.38	100.0/100.0	20.93	100.0/100.0

[a]Including and excluding oil/gas/NGLs.

Source: Energy Information Administration, *Monthly Energy Review*, September 1987.

magnitude as increases in conventional supply. But no such objection applies if the efficiency bonanza is expressed in *absolute* terms. The data in Table 7.2 show that the "efficiency industry" built during the fourteen-year period 1973–1986 is now producing each year about two-fifths more primary energy than the century-old U.S. oil industry is extracting.[31]

Moreover, the efficiency industry has expanding reserves, output rising by several percent per year, and falling real costs, while the domestic oil industry has shrinking reserves, dwindling output, and rising real costs. Which industry merits, and is receiving, the marginal dollar of investment—the one scraping ever nearer the bottom of the old-province barrel, or the one just starting to tap a newly discovered and nondepletable barrel? In which industry can an investor make more profit, at less risk, over a longer period? That is the challenge, and the business opportunity, for the oil industry.

These data also show that since 1973, the United States has gained 3.5 times as much new energy from savings, or 3.8 times as much from savings and renewables combined, as it has lost from the decline in fossil hydrocarbon output. That is, the new "oilfields" being discovered in U.S. buildings, factories, and vehicles have been coming onstream several times as fast as the aging oilfields were petering out. In 1986, therefore, the energy already being saved each year (25.1 q/y), compared with 1973 levels of energy productivity, was equivalent to:

- 6.4 Alaskan North Slopes (each of 3.95 q/y) or
- 12.8 times U.S. imports from the Gulf (1.93 q/y) or

- 2.2 times total U.S. net imports of crude oil and refined products (11.5 q/y)

Even the inevitable minor corrections for behavioral and compositional changes, to isolate the effects of purely technical gains in energy productivity, can hardly change the conclusion: Energy efficiency represents an extraordinary and largely unrecognized bonanza. Because of it, the share of U.S. oil consumed that was imported (net) fell from 46.5 percent in 1977 to 27.3 percent in 1985; the absolute amount of imported oil fell by half. Since stock changes were immaterial, this means that *oil was being saved faster than more oil was being needed.*

So What Happened in 1986?

Both of the periods just analyzed, 1973–1986 and 1979–1986, reflect increased domestic energy efficiency elicited by price shocks. To understand whether the great savings achieved in those periods can be expected to continue—whether, for example, it is safe to extrapolate from the abrupt (if minor) reversal of aggregate national oil saving in 1986—we should examine more closely the behavior of U.S. oil productivity gains over time.[32] Accepting for heuristic value the extremely aggregated measure of gross national product, with all its well-known faults, we see that those gains are conveniently represented by the annual percentage decrease, compared with the previous year, in the ratio of total petroleum consumption to real GNP[33] (see Figure 7.1). Real oil prices are summarized by one surrogate—leaded regular gasoline—because cars represent the largest single use of oil. Figure 7.1 reveals a striking correlation between price movements and oil-productivity movements. Of course, the detailed causality is vastly more complex than consumers' merely watching price movements, but even this simple correlation appears to have some explanatory and even predictive value.

Figure 7.1 shows how energy users' and suppliers' responses at first stuttered in the mid-1970s. Falling real prices after the initial 1973–1974 shock, and confusion about how best to respond to that unique transformation of global energy markets, led to incoherent responses. Regardless of what policymakers said or did, however, increased energy efficiency gradually emerged as a major force in the marketplace. Further stimulated by the second price shock in 1979–1980, national oil productivity gains accelerated steadily during 1978–1981, reaching an impressive pinnacle with the 8.4 percent/y gain in 1981. This sustained success contributed significantly to softer prices. The gradually decreasing annual falls in real oil prices during 1982–1985 were correlated with a gradual decrease in the rate of oil savings—but the 1982–1985 average

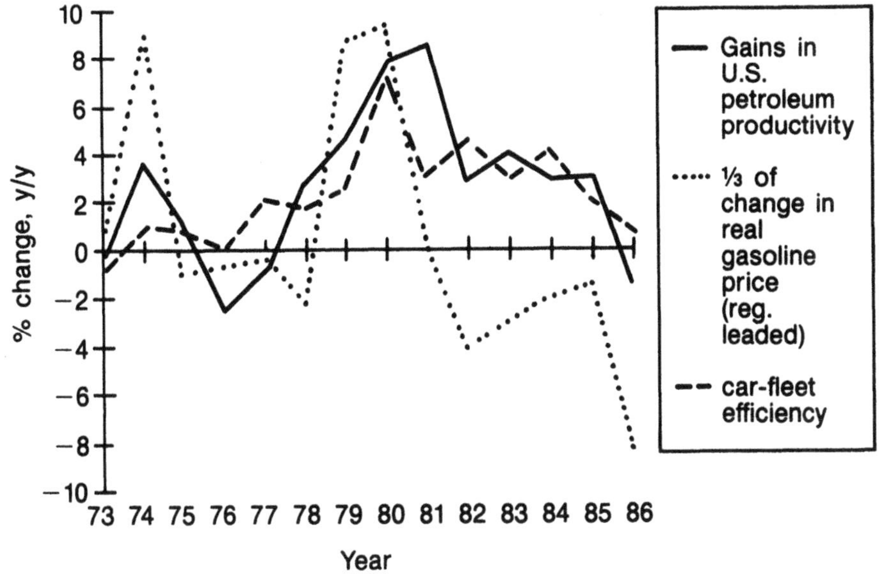

FIGURE 7.1 Gains in U.S. petroleum productivity and change in real gasoline price. *Source:* Adapted from data in Energy Information Administration, *Monthly Energy Review*, September 1987.

savings rate was still an important 3.2 percent/y. Only in the single year 1986, with prices crashing to below their real *1973* levels, did the nation slip from this plateau of steady progress into the first actual *de*crease in oil productivity (by 1.5 percent) since 1977.

A closer look at what drives improving oil productivity reveals that 1986 combined many extraordinary and uncharacteristic events. Figure 7.2 shows a generally strong correlation between movements in oil savings and in the average efficiency of the passenger-car fleet. Overlain on this variable, however, with about half its weighting, is the far more volatile productivity of oil in industry. The extreme volatility of this factor is due in substantial part to short-term fuel switching impelled by the changing marginal cost relationship between residual oil and natural gas. In 1986, the average untaxed end-user price of residual oil fell to a phenomenal 34¢ a gallon—27 percent below its real 1978 level (the earliest comparable data available). Not surprisingly, while 1986 real industrial output rose by 1.1 percent, industrial gas use fell by 5.5 percent and oil use spurted ahead by 3.0 percent, yielding a (3.0 − 1.1) = 1.9 percent loss in industrial oil productivity. Bargain-hunting utility fuel buyers likewise bought 36 percent more heavy oil in 1986 than in 1985, reversing a decade-long pattern that had seen a steady 73 percent decrease in utility oil burning during 1978–1985.

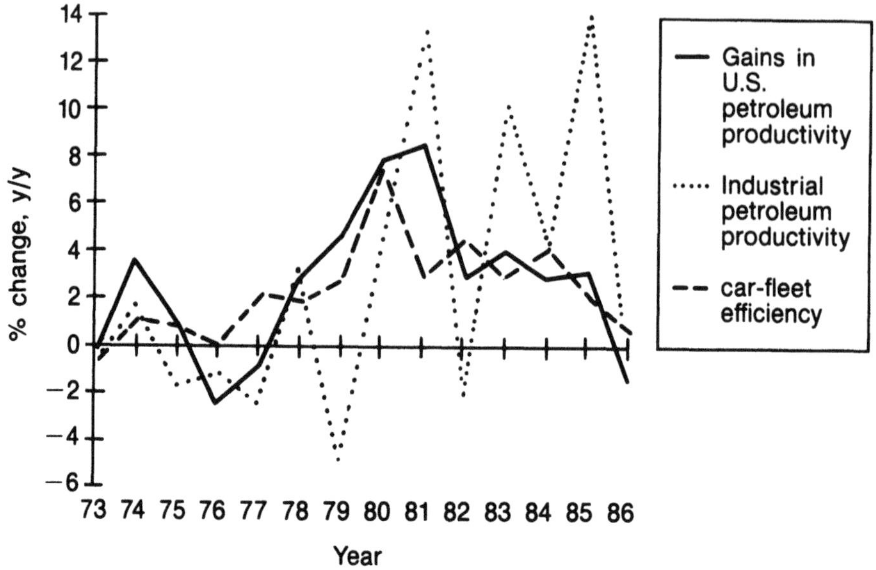

FIGURE 7.2 Gains in U.S. petroleum productivity and industrial petroleum productivity. *Source:* Adapted from data in Energy Information Administration, *Monthly Energy Review*, September 1987.

At the same time that industrial and utility oil productivity was thus falling, the Reagan administration stalled the previously steady improvement of the 18.2-mpg car fleet, on which virtually *any* new car was an improvement: Average new 1986 domestic cars had an mpg rating of 26.9 mpg, imports 30.9 mpg, and their mix 28.1 mpg, nearly 10 mpg above the whole-fleet average. The stall's proximate cause was a rollback of 1986–1988 new car standards: an action apparently meant as a mere favor to General Motors (GM) and Ford, but with serious results for the nation.

The rollbacks arose because Ford and General Motors have failed[34] ever since model year 1983 to meet Congress's 1975 sales-average efficiency standards, which Chrysler has met every year. Ford's and GM's model-year 1984 (cars released in fall 1983) noncompliance incurred no penalty because they used a 1979 amendment to "carry forward" offsetting credits for earlier "overcompliance." When their continued model-year 1985 noncompliance was then penalized, the Reagan administration, by regulatory decision out of public view, obligingly rolled back the model-year 1986–1988 standards to levels they could beat, so they could retroactively offset the uncollected penalties with new credits. (This still was not enough to bail out GM, so a retroactive rollback of the model-year 1985 standard is now also being considered.) This rollback:

- Cost the Treasury more than $1 billion (a direct gift from taxpayers to GM and Ford shareholders)[35]
- Told both firms they could defy Congress with impunity
- Penalized Chrysler for obeying the law
- Most importantly, signaled Ford and GM to intensify their ferocious marketing of less efficient (but more profitable) models

The resulting sales crusade of Ford and GM did much to cut the 1985–1986 gain in U.S. whole-car-fleet efficiency to a ten-year low of 0.12 mpg—89 percent below the 1979–1985 (post-CAFE—U.S. car fleet efficiency standards) average—while similar light-truck rollbacks cut the new truck efficiency gain by 67 percent. This stall in previously steady progress directly accounted for an increase in crude oil imports of ~295,300 B/D—equivalent to a doubling of 1985 imports from the Gulf.[36]

Simultaneously with this blunder, threats of terrorism in Europe and a 1985–1986 drop of ~27 percent in real gasoline prices contributed to 0.7 percent heavier summer driving in 1986—barely noticeable, but the highest level since 1978. Together with a 2.7 percent one-year increase in car registrations (probably spurred by the automakers' aggressive rebates), half again as high as normal, the net result was a 3 percent increase in 1986 sales of motor gasoline.

Are the circumstances that conspired to convert the unprecedented 1986 price collapse into a 1.2 percent decrease in national oil productivity a harbinger of an emerging supply/demand imbalance in the years ahead, as many industry observers insist? Based on the most recent two-year record currently available, just the opposite seems likely. During 1985–1986,[37] many stripper wells were lost, the domestic output of oil and gas fell by 1.96 q/y, and total net oil imports rose by 164 q/y. Yet simultaneously, energy savings soared by 3.90 q/y, with 3.48 q/y of those savings being achieved directly in the use of oil and gas.[38] Thus Americans saved 78 percent more oil and gas in those two years than was lost in domestic output.[39]

The only reason net oil imports rose during 1984–1986 is that GNP grew by more (6.0 percent) than oil productivity improved (2.3 percent—a 3.5 percent gain in 1985 offset by a 1.2 percent loss in 1986), so oil consumption rose by 3.5 percent—essentially equal to the difference between these figures. But meanwhile, domestic crude output fell by 2.5 percent, increasing imports by nearly the sum of rising consumption plus falling output. This increase in imports was 2.58 q/y—only 8 percent of 1986 oil consumption, but a more dramatic-sounding 29 percent of 1985 imports.

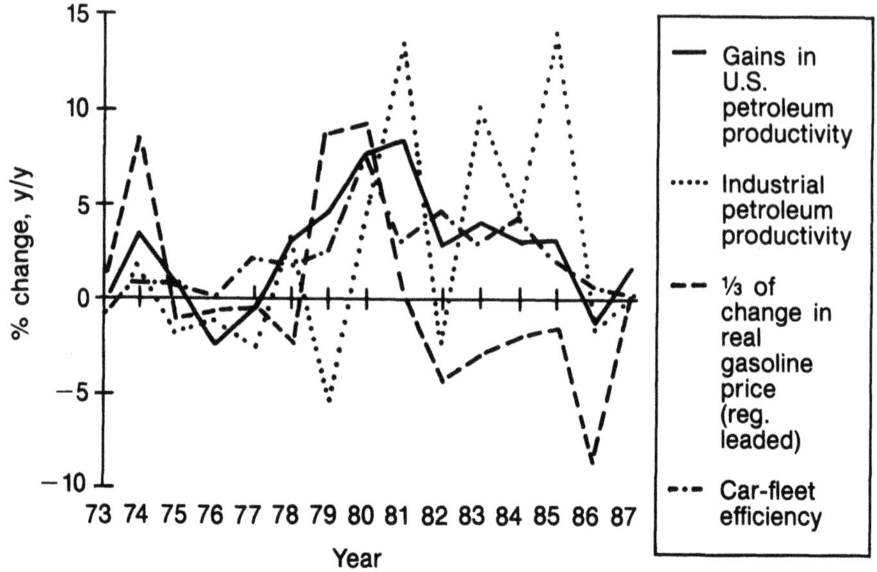

FIGURE 7.3 Gains in U.S. petroleum productivity, industrial petroleum productivity, and change in real gasoline price.
Source: Adapted from data in Energy Information Administration, *Monthly Energy Review,* September 1987.

It should be remembered, however, that during 1977–1985 the average rate of improvement in oil productivity was an impressive 5.0 percent per year. Nothing has fundamentally changed the causal relationships and processes underlying this trend. It therefore appears highly likely that 1986's *minus* 1.2 percent oil-productivity change was an artifact of a coincidence between a unique price movement (itself largely a consequence of past efficiency gains) and the administration's ill-advised effort to help GM and Ford escape the consequences of their persistent noncompliance with the 1975 CAFE standards. Though reliable statistics are not yet, at this writing, available for 1987, we venture to predict that as prices rise again, even if slowly, and even with relatively stable real prices at pre-1966 levels, oil productivity will again rise on much the lines shown for the past decade in Figure 7.1. Preliminary EIA data for 1987[40] (see Figure 7.3) seem consistent with this hypothesis: U.S. oil productivity rose more in 1987 than it fell in 1986.

It is hard to avoid the conclusion that even under the exceptional circumstances of 1986–1987, despite federal indifference or antagonism to efficiency, America's oil supply/demand balance has been getting better, not worse. It is gaining efficiency faster than it is losing field output: The country is seeing a *shift* of energy "source," not a loss of its ability to "produce"—as either barrels or negabarrels—enough effective supply to meet its needs. The fundamental causes of this are not immutable, but they *are* durable, as will be shown next.

During 1979–1986, real GNP grew at an average rate of 2.12 percent/y, while domestic oil output fell at an average rate of 0.03 percent/y. Together, these trends would require an increase of 2.14 percent/y in oil productivity to hold imports constant. Yet over the same period, the United States saved oil four-fifths faster than that (averaging 3.88 percent/y), significantly increasing its ability to live within its domestic oil budget. Moreover, this was achieved more in spite of than because of national policy: The period 1979–1986 was replete with federal neglect of efficiency ranging from benign to possibly malign, and with often misguided and counterproductive government messages that confused efficiency with curtailment, discomfort, and privation. The United States has never mounted a thoughtful, systematic policy commitment to an energy-efficient economy. As will be shown below, *much* better performance can be achieved with high confidence by simply making high oil productivity a policy goal and using proven methods—market, regulatory, or both—to apply what is now known.

Transportation: The Dominant Term

In 1985, a year representative of the mid-1980s, 65 percent of all oil consumed in the United States (roughly twice the Japanese and Western European share), or 19.56 q, was used for transportation. This transportation fuel use was equivalent to *thirty times* that year's imports from the Gulf (0.64 q), or 7.6 times the total net petroleum imports from all sources (2.57 q). An efficiency gain of 3.3 percent, therefore, would have eliminated 1985 oil imports from the Gulf. Only 4 percent of all U.S. transportation energy in 1984 was provided by forms other than oil. Of the oil thus used, approximately[41] 75.5 percent went to highway vehicles—47 percent of the total to cars and 14 percent to light trucks,[42] 14 percent to 40 million heavy trucks, 0.7 percent to 0.6 million buses, and a negligible amount to 5 million motorcycles and other small vehicles. Constituting the 24.5 percent of 1985 transportation oil used by non-highway vehicles was an estimated 8 percent of the total for ships, 8 percent for commercial and private aircraft, 3 percent for trains,[43] 2 percent for pipelines,[44] and 3.5 percent for "other (including military)."[45]

It is interesting that the Department of Defense (DOD) in FY1986 consumed 83 percent as much oil as the total annual U.S. imports from the Gulf (averaged over 1984–1986)—mainly for the aircraft and ships on which theater operations in places like the Gulf are highly dependent. DOE stated that a major conventional conflict would increase DOD's oil use by two- or threefold. Thus a major conflict centered on the Gulf could plausibly *use* more oil than the United States *gets* from the Gulf.[46]

DOE reported[47] that total U.S. freight energy intensity would have declined by 13 percent during 1972–1986—slightly more than passenger energy intensity's 11 percent—if there had not been a shift toward the less fuel-efficient modes. (Passenger travel would have shown a 12 percent energy-intensity decline at the 1972 mode mix, but there was a shift from surface to less-efficient air travel.) It is interesting to note that, during 1972–1986, the economy became no more travel intensive: Passenger miles traveled by all modes per dollar of real GNP was constant, but the number of tons of freight shipped per dollar of GNP declined by an impressive 30 percent. Since the number of ton-*miles* per dollar of GNP fell by only 3 percent, one can infer that the average number of miles shipped per ton rose by some 27 percent, reflecting the rapid increase in air freight services and an increase in imports through coastal gateway cities requiring reshipment inland (imported tonnage grew by 100 million tons, while domestically generated tonnage fell by 176 million tons or 3.6 percent of the 1986 domestic total). Thus of the 8 percent reduction in freight energy consumption per dollar of GNP, five percentage points came from improved efficiency and three from structural change; the efficiency gain would have been twice as great had a shift to less-efficient modes not simultaneously occurred.

The U.S. transportation sector has so far achieved by far the smallest intensity reduction of any end-use sector: Its share of U.S. oil rose from 51 percent in 1973 to 65 percent in 1985 as other sectors saved or substituted more. Yet transportation has far from the smallest savings *potential*. For illustration, a marginal improvement of 1 mpg in the productivity of a single average U.S. light vehicle translates into a gasoline saving of about 0.8 barrel per year. With 136 million passenger cars and light trucks registered in 1986, and conservatively assuming the product slate is all gasoline, that 1-mpg fleet gain corresponds to ~0.30 MMB/D—essentially equal to total 1985 imports from the Gulf (0.31 MMB/D), or to a third of the unusually high 1986 Gulf imports (0.91 MMB/D).

It is therefore especially bewildering that the Reagan administration places such emphasis on using oil more quickly and saving it more slowly. Just the above-mentioned rollback of 1986, 1987, and 1988 new car efficiency standards from 27.5 to 26 mpg,[48] carried through the next replacement car fleet, will waste more oil[49] than currently forbidden lease areas in the Arctic National Wildlife Refuge (ANWR) or offshore California might yield, if they turned out to contain any oil, during the same period.[50] Indeed, the 1986 light-vehicle-standards rollbacks may

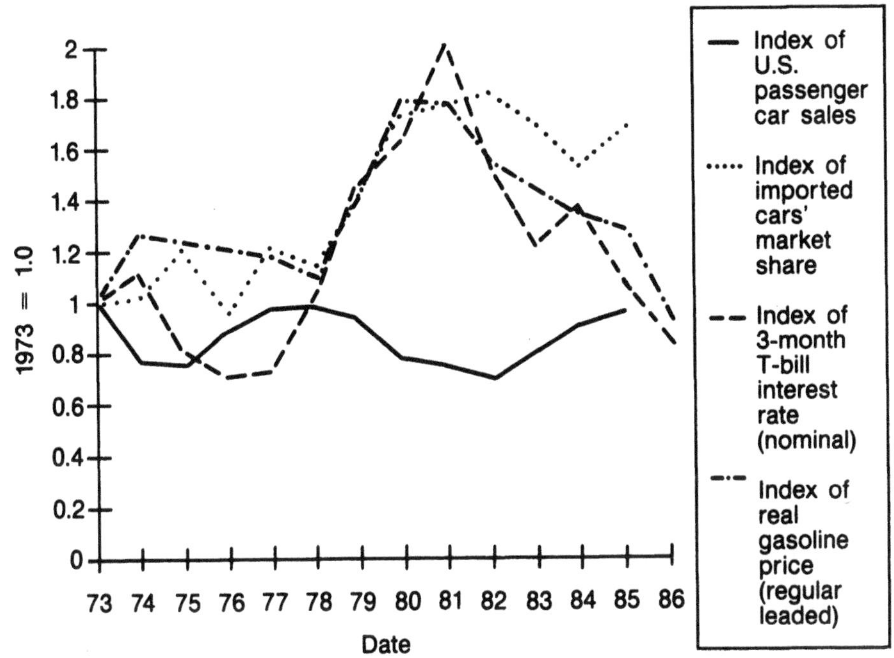

FIGURE 7.4 U.S. passenger car purchasing behavior and interest rates.
Source: Adapted from data in Energy Information Administration, *Monthly Energy Review*, September 1987.

be said to have *un*discovered the equivalent of the hoped for mean ANWR reserve: the resulting ~295,300 B/D increase in crude oil imports (counting the 1.88:1 crude:gasoline ratio) happens to equal the average output of a 3.23 billion-bbl reserve extracted over thirty years.

The historic behavior of U.S. car buyers, while complex in detail, is surprisingly simple in broad outline. Figure 7.4 shows the correlations between real gasoline price and imported cars' market share; the inverse correlation between the rate of car purchases and nominal interest rates; and a suggestive correlation between those interest rates and the real price of gasoline. The relationship between the speed of additions to the car fleet and the improvement in fleet-average efficiency (Figure 7.2) is weak; the *efficiency* of the new cars, and the rate of scrapping the worst old ones, is more important than the turnover rate. This is not surprising, since fleet-average efficiency is a geometric, not an arithmetic average: The worst cars drag down the fleet average disproportionately.[51] Moreover, there is a strong correlation between car efficiency and household income: Gas-guzzlers have trickled down to the poorest people, who can afford neither to run nor to replace them.

Potential Light-Vehicle Efficiency Gains

Car-fleet efficiency is widely recognized as the most important single variable in U.S. oil prospects. For example, the Department of Energy assumes a "market" scenario in which, with no policy intervention,[52] new cars and light trucks will average 30 and 25 mpg respectively by 1990 (the level currently planned by only one of the three major U.S. carmakers), with no improvement thereafter. Compared with constant new vehicle performance through 2020 averaging 27 mpg for cars (close to Congress's prerollback 1975 standards of 27.5 mpg for 1986–1988 cars) and in the low 20s for light trucks, the cumulative saving would be 1.3 billion barrels by 2000 and *6.0 billion barrels* by 2020.[53] The former figure is about twice, and the latter about ten times, the risked mean oil reserves, undiscovered and economically recoverable at implausibly high prices under favorable (pre-1986) tax law, beneath the Arctic National Wildlife Refuge.[54] The 2020 figure is also equivalent to about two-thirds of a Prudhoe Bay supergiant field of 9.4 billion bbl.

How much more could be done with straightforward extension of the CAFE standards? If new cars and light trucks achieved respectively 45 and 30 mpg in 1998, rising to 60 and 45 mpg in 2008, then the fleet would save 2.9 billion bbl by 2000 and a staggering *22.8* billion bbl by 2020 (both compared with the 27- and 19.5-mpg base case). Even if the DOE "market" assumption of 30/25 mpg by 1990 were subtracted, the standards' cumulative *net* savings by 2000 (2020) would still total 1.6 (16.8) billion bbl. This 2020 net saving is three times the mean risk undiscovered oil officially estimated to be economically recoverable at very high prices (if present) offshore Alaska plus California. That 16.8 billion barrels is also 27 times the risked, or 5.2 times the unrisked, mean reserve hoped for in ANWR.[55] It would be like discovering a whole new ANWR every thirteen months. Yet the rhetoric about how crucial ANWR oil (if it exists) would be to national security seems not to carry over to the 27-fold larger (when also risked) oil resource sitting untapped in the inefficient U.S. light-vehicle fleet—or 51-fold larger if adjusted to reflect the 1.88:1 ratio of crude oil input to gasoline output.

Nor would 60/45 mpg standards push existing technology in the least.[56] A glance at the annual *Gas Mileage Guide* reveals that the 40- to 55-mpg efficiency range, often achieved with the help of smart-chip-controlled fuel computers, is now commonplace from a variety of U.S. and foreign vendors. Aerodynamics, tires, suspensions, lighter weight materials, engine designs, finishes, clutches, transmissions, bearings, lubricants—all are continuing steady incremental improvements. Such once implausible technologies as continuously variable transmissions, "idle-off" engines (which turn off when idling and instantly restart when needed), ultralean-burn engines, variable-displacement engines (which deactivate some cylinders at low loads), variable valves, composite leaf springs and wheels, plastic body panels, composite and light-alloy drive shafts, and liquid-injection-molded tires—all are already on the market.[57]

DOE's July 1985 conservation plan projects a 28-mpg car fleet—0.5 mpg worse than the average 1988 car being sold that year, and exactly half as efficient as the most efficient U.S.-made 1988 car—*in 2010,* two fleet-turnover intervals from 1988. DOE further asserts an estimated "potential" to achieve a 39-mpg fleet in 2010 "with successful R & D effort." Yet acting out early-1980s projections that existing technologies could achieve 70–80 mpg,[58] most leading carmakers *have already tested* four- or five-passenger prototypes, similar in size and performance to many ordinary cars now on the road, but getting *~70–100+ composite mpg.*

Bleviss[59] cited seven manufacturers whose prototypes have on-road composite ratings >67 mpg. Volvo, for example, has a 71-composite-mpg LCP-2000 ready for production. It accelerates 0 to 60 mph in 11 seconds—2.1 seconds faster than the average new U.S. car (rated at only 28 mpg) could do in 1986. It would be one of the most crashworthy cars on the road and would meet all U.S. emissions standards. Volvo expects that at break-even production of only 20,000 units a year, the LCP-2000 would cost *about the same* as an average subcompact today. This illustrates a surprising but apparently general finding: In many lightweight car designs, the saving on the amount of materials, number of parts, and fabrication labor (since large, previously complex parts can be molded in one unit) can make up for the higher cost of the lighter and stronger materials.

Furthermore, Renault, Peugeot, Ford, and Toyota (with a 56-hp, 98-mpg prototype compact) all have >71-mpg prototypes. Their experience confirms that such efficiency can come with comfort, performance, safety, and environmental standards at least equal to those of the inefficient cars of 1988. One of the most impressive new prototypes, a Renault Vesta 2 four-passenger prototype outwardly akin to the standard R5 model, did 146 mpg highway at 62 average mph in recent 311-mile road tests.[60] Its U.S. on-road city rating (as computed from European-standard city tests) is 101 mpg, for an on-road composite rating of 121 mpg. It has a top speed of 87 mph, a 27-hp/4250-rpm three-cylinder four-stroke engine displacing 716 cc, and a curb weight, by various accounts, of a mere 1043–1146 pounds. Its drag coefficient is only 0.19, compared with 0.48 for the average U.S.-made car in 1979 and with ~0.3 for "slippery" production cars today. (Ford, however, measured a draft coefficient of only 0.137 in its Probe V prototype—lower than for an F-15 jet.[61]) One could do even better than the Vesta 2 with a continuously variable transmission instead of the manual 5-speed, more exotic materials such as lightweight but very crashworthy metal foams (the current model uses an all-steel frame and hood with composite roof and floor), or other developmental technologies such as ceramic engines (announced by Isuzu for 1990 models) or oxygen-enriching membranes on intake air.

Still further savings could be had by introducing small commuter vehicles, perhaps more advanced than the two million-odd "minicars" (no more than 4.5 × 10.5 feet and 550 cc) that hold a fifth of the Japanese domestic market. General Motors, for example, has invested more than $50 million in developing a one- or two-passenger, ~¾ liter "Lean Machine," which typically gets 150–~200 mpg, is said to be safer than a normal car because it is highly maneuverable, has an extraordinarily small turning radius, and occupies in driving or parking less than half the width of a normal car. Although its manufacture and marketing have been licensed to Opel (Europe) and Suzuki (United States), its release is held up by regulatory uncertainties. (Is it a car, a motorcycle, or what? What sort of license, registration, and insurance does it need? Is it legal to drive it two abreast? And so on.) Any state could probably choose to remove these barriers.

Though variously derided and neglected, mass transit, too, shows impressive progress in certain sectors. U.S. buses, perhaps because so many are operated by the public sector, were no more energy efficient in 1984 than in 1974:[62] Their average 5.90 mpg was 1.3 percent worse than in 1976–1977. (This often reflects poor operation and maintenance practices.) Yet striking advances have been made elsewhere in the technical efficiency of buses and, notably in Brazil, in managerial innovations that greatly reduce the costs, delays, and hassle of commuter bus service[63] so as to increase ridership. Both U.S. and European progress with trolleys, minivans, and subways is also encouraging. Even with standard (and usually overengineered) U.S. techniques, Robert Watson has calculated that fuller practical use of mass transit could add an extra 2.0 billion barrels by 2020 (3.2 risked mean ANWRs) to the mpg-standards net savings of 16.8 bbl described above.[64]

Other Transportation Efficiency Options

Surprising technical innovations are rapidly becoming available for noncar road vehicles too. The average U.S. heavy truck improved from 8.4 to 10.3 mpg during 1974–1984, largely through aerodynamic cowlings, slightly better engines, and fuller use of radial tires, whose share among heavy-heavy trucks increased from 22 to 44 percent during 1977–1982.[65] Unit trucks during 1974–1984 reduced their energy use per vehicle-mile by 22 percent while combination trucks increased it by 6 percent. Far greater heavy-truck energy savings—upward of 40 percent—are now available from turbocharged and adiabatic (uncooled) low-friction engines, improved controls and transmissions, better tires and aerodynamics, exhaust heat recovery, regenerative braking, and the like. Improved payloads and reduced empty back hauls (return trips) through better shipping management can also make important contributions. Together, these approaches can save about 60 percent of heavy-truck energy.[66] Furthermore, for regular shipments between defined areas such as particular factory clusters, GM's commercially available "Roadrailer," convertible in seconds from a heavy truck trailer to a railcar or vice versa, saves about 75 percent of 18-wheelers' energy, and more than pays for itself just by faster (100+ mph) and surer delivery of undamaged contents.

What of nonroad vehicles? Domestic waterborne commerce has already reduced its energy intensity per ton-mile by nearly half during 1973–1983. In marine transport, improved propellers, engines, hull defouling, and other innovations are saving ~25 percent, and high-tech sails and heat recovery have raised the saving to 50+ percent in some tests. Train efficiencies can be substantially boosted too, to say nothing of fuel substitution—electricity for dense corridors, fluidized-bed coal or alternative liquid fuels for low-density ones.

The 757/767/DC9-80 generation of commercial airliners is twice as efficient as the fleet it replaces, getting 45 passenger-miles per gallon, compared with 17.5 for the 1973 fleet, and—due to operational as well as technical improvements—~33 for the 1988 fleet. Still newer aircraft now in flight testing, some using modern airscrews attached to turbofans, will save another ~40 percent. More experimentally, maneuverable lighter-than-air craft continue to show promise for door-to-door containerized freight delivery.

In sum, one could do even better with today's transportation technologies than the Solar Energy Research Institute's (SERI's) remarkable team effort concluded in 1981.[67] SERI assumed a U.S. transportation system that in the year 2000 (compared with 1977) moves 17 percent more Americans, increases per capita personal travel by 30–70 percent in cars and 60–90 percent in planes, and raises freight ton-miles by 80 percent in trucks and 300 percent in planes. Nonetheless, transportation energy would fall from 19.5 q in 1977 to 12.6–16.5 q in 2000 (or to as little as 11.8–16.0 q of fuel with aggressive electrification, using an additional 0.75–1.15 primary q of electricity). Of this fuel requirement, the team estimated that as much as 5.5 q could be cost-effectively supplied by renewables (chiefly biomass methanol) in 2000, leaving as little as 6.3 q of transportation oil demand. And that calculation was based on projected technological improvements—to 60 mpg for cars, by 30 percent for planes, and so on—which have *already* been far surpassed. One begins to see, in light of this finding, how Royal Dutch/Shell planners can reportedly regard as plausible an unpublished recent scenario in which the United States, in the year 2000, has reduced its oil imports to zero.

Light-Vehicle Efficiency: Economics and Policy

As of 1984, only about a fifth of the total cost of owning and operating a car (~19–22 percent, depending on size) was its gasoline cost, when that averaged $1.20 a gallon (1984 $). Any factor cost whose fraction of total cost is so small clearly provides a weak price signal for buying an efficient car. Indeed, many analysts have remarked that over a range of perhaps about 20 to 50 or 60 mpg, the total cost of owning and operating an otherwise unchanged car is essentially flat: The more efficient car costs about as much more to buy as it costs less to run. Though such early-1980s projections badly need to be updated—both fuel and efficiency now look cheaper than was commonly assumed a few years ago—there is still certainly some range over which the conclusion holds. Within that range, normal price signals provide virtually no incentive for purchasing a more efficient car. This was empirically demonstrated in the early 1980s, when gasoline prices went to $1.35 a gallon, yet it is very doubtful that domestic carmakers would have offered far more efficient cars were they not forced to do so by law.[68]

Worse, at efficiencies above ~30–40 mpg (250–333 gal/y @ 10,000 mi/y), extremely large increases in fuel prices would be needed to provide a significant signal because so little fuel would be burned; yet there would still be room for a further approximately two-to-three-times efficiency gain with major benefits to the nation. This suggests that perhaps in the short run, and certainly in the long run, policy instruments should emphasize influencing the car-buying decision *directly* rather than via fuel prices. This is true regardless of whether one considers the inability of low-income people to afford any replacements for the inefficient cars that they tend to own (if they own any).

It is therefore worth comparing the cost of signals that *would* provide a direct incentive for car efficiency with the cost of competing supply-side investments. Although such an analysis is beyond the scope of this chapter, we did point out in the late 1970s that rather than building synfuel plants, the United States would save more oil, faster and cheaper,[69] by:

- Giving away a free 40+-mpg car in return for scrapping an old Brontomobile or

- Paying a $300+ cash bonus for each mpg[70] by which a new car improves on an old Petropig which is scrapped—or a corresponding bounty for scrapping an inefficient car that is *not* replaced

Unfortunately, despite a decade's sporadic effort, we have been unable to get anyone, including DOE and the carmakers,[71] to do a *serious* analysis of accelerated scrappage of gas-guzzlers as a cheap source of oil. (DOE did sponsor one analysis of scrappage, but under such artificially restrictive assumptions that virtually no benefit could result.[72]) None of DOE's voluminous analyses of oil-saving policy options mentions it. In fact, when we injected these two comparisons into a discussion at the 1986 meeting of the International Association of Energy Economists, many economists in the audience asked the previous speakers (who had called for massive synfuel investments) whether there was something wrong with our numbers. No, they agreed; the back-of-the-envelope arithmetic was impeccable.[73] So why, the audience persisted, were the speakers pushing synfuels? Because, they replied, it is inconceivable that Congress would do anything that is economically rational, so one must *start* with the second- or nth-best solution. This flippant reply reflects a real problem: a national preoccupation with "moon-shot"- or Manhattan-project-style big "solutions" such as the synfuels program and a corresponding mistrust of bottom-up, market-driven solutions.

The cynical economists might also have recalled that the Carter administration proposed rebating gas-guzzler taxes to buyers of efficient cars but dropped that interesting idea because at that time the only efficient models available were Japanese. Today, however, with efficient U.S.-made cars available and with empirical proof (provided by the manufacturers themselves) that car buyers respond substantially to rebates, what Bleviss called the "'gas-sipper' rebate" is ripe for revisiting. Without federal action and hence preemption, as she pointed out, states could also set their own efficiency standards (as California did with appliances, ultimately taking the country with it), or could make their annual car-ownership taxes large and progressive. For example, Sweden, which has only the population of Los Angeles County, has a progressive weight-based car excise tax that strongly influences the fleet's weight distribution[74] (weight is the single most important determinant of car efficiency). Several state governments in the Northeast, plus California, have expressed interest in state or regional standard tax rebate packages to fill the expanding federal regulatory void and try to correct market failures in car purchases.

We also noted in 1981 that if the U.S. auto industry, which planned to spend $100 billion on retooling during 1985–1995, spent twice that much (probably at least five times more than it would actually cost) on marginal retooling to convert production directly to a 60-mpg average, and then spread that probably overstated cost over the next new fleet of cars and light trucks, the average cost per vehicle would rise by less than $800, and at the 1981 gasoline price, buyers would receive a fourteen-*month* payback.

In view of this potentially large return to consumers and society, it is long past time for entrepreneurs—especially those in the oil industry now drilling against ever greater odds—to give careful thought to how they can capture the rent from car efficiency. For example, might wildcatters and oil majors (antitrust questions aside) invest in the carmakers' efficiency retooling, or in purchasers' marginal investments? Can one imagine an oil company–sponsored car credit company that invests in costlier but more efficient cars on a shared-savings basis?[75] Once oil companies find that it is cheaper to buy each other (hence reserves in the ground) than to drill, is it such a large step to start buying the even cheaper negabarrels in not-yet-purchased automobile gas tanks?

On early-1980s data, it could be said that in the lower-48 states are two supergiant oilfields, each bigger than the Ghawar field, the largest in Saudi Arabia; each able to product sustainably (not just to extract once) over 5 million barrels per day for less than $7 a barrel; each largely untapped; and each capable of *eliminating* the level of U.S. oil imports then prevailing (5.4 MMB/D), before a synfuel plant or power plant or frontier oilfield ordered at once could produce any energy whatever, and at about a tenth of its cost. These two oilfields were, of course, the "accelerated-scrappage-of-gas-guzzlers oilfield" under Detroit[76] and the "weatherization oilfield" (including saved gas fungible for oil) in the nation's attics. Today, both those oilfields are still there, roughly 80 percent untapped; indeed, improved technology has expanded their reserves and reduced their finding and lifting costs. If you went to the ends of the earth to drill for very expensive oil, which might not even be there, while someone else found all that cheap oil under Detroit, would you not feel a twinge of embarrassment? By investing in frontier drilling instead of modernizing the U.S. car industry, do U.S. decision-makers not simultaneously make boomtowns in the Arctic and ghost towns in the industrial heartland?

Of course it is true, as a managing director of Royal Dutch/Shell once remarked, that once you sell a man a "negabarrel," he has it, and you can't sell it to him again. But it is equally true, as we replied, that once you sell him a barrel of oil, you don't have *it* any more, so you can't sell it to him again either. The issue should be, which kind of investment and sale will lead to the maximization of profit and the minimization of regret? Light vehicles are certainly the most promising new oil province to start exploring.

Saving Oil in Buildings

Oil burning in U.S. buildings fell by 41 percent during 1973–1986, leaving only 2.57 q/y of residual consumption. Nearly all of that is for space heating, two-thirds of it in the Northeast. Although relatively small—only 8 percent of U.S. oil use in 1986—oil use in buildings cannot be considered in isolation from the far larger use of natural gas in buildings for similar purposes (6.97 q in 1986, or 42 *percent* of that year's total gas use).[77] These two fuels are interchangeable in a wide variety of uses, particularly in industry. They can be significantly substituted even in transportation.[78] Options for saving them in the buildings sector therefore are worth considering together, so as to expand options for substitution in both transport and industry. Furthermore, gas can be widely substituted for oil *within* buildings (especially with the help of cheap new distribution-pipe and -installation technologies). Whether saved through efficiency or substitution, the 2.57 q of oil burned in U.S. buildings in 1986 is equivalent to one and a third times the nation's 1986 imports from the Gulf.[79] Over a decade, it is also equivalent to some 4.4 billion barrels of crude oil, or 1.33 times the risked mean reserve that might exist under unexplored parts of onshore Alaska, or nearly seven times the risked mean reserve claimed for ANWR.

The Department of Energy has developed a "market" scenario for weatherization in households, which account for about 82 percent of all the oil used in buildings. This scenario assumes, somewhat optimistically in view of recent budget cuts, that 20 million homes will be retrofitted by 1998 so as to save ~32 percent of their current oil use. Robert Watson calculated that a more widespread program, using better technologies more fully to save ~55 percent in 53.5 million single-family homes over the same period, would yield incremental savings of ~1.7 billion barrels of oil, or ~7.6 billion barrels of oil, gas, and LPG, by 2020. (Utilities and public agencies have cost-effectively demonstrated such savings in many parts of the United States.) The lower figure is about 2.4 times the risked mean oil reserve for which Secretary of the Interior Donald Hodel wanted more drilling off the Atlantic Coast.

That potential saving, however, arises only from reducing heat flow through the buildings' shells. Additional, and synergistic, savings are available from improved space- and water-heating appliances. Watson's retrofit case modestly assumes converting furnaces from an average Annual Fuel Utilization Efficiency (AFUE) of 0.68 to 0.90, converting water heaters from a recovery efficiency of 0.75 to 0.90 and a standby loss of 4.9 percent/h to 2.0 percent/h, and changing showerheads from 5.0 to 2.5 gallons per minute (gpm). All these assumptions fall well short of economically attractive options now on the market, including furnaces up to AFUE-0.97 and high-performance showerheads down to 1.2–1.5 gpm. Nonetheless, the cumulative saving by 2020 from using these modestly efficient appliances in all existing oil- and gas-burning homes would be 4.5 billion barrels–equivalent—about two-fifths more than the risked mean reserves hoped for under onshore Alaska. Similar improvements in the new homes built over the next few decades would add another 0.8 billion barrels' savings, and those new homes' shell improvements, another 1.0 billion barrels' worth of space-heating.[80] Counting multifamily dwellings would further increase these savings.

The SERI analysis cited earlier found, by empirically based supply-curve analyses done in previously unprecedented detail, a practical potential to save during 1977–2000 some 7.7 q/y of fuel (essentially all oil and gas) in buildings still standing by 2000. (Achieving that saving linearly would imply an average saving of 2.68 q/y; the actual saving during 1977–1985 was 2.04 q/y, somewhat behind schedule, but was achieved by generally less thorough retrofits than the SERI/LBL [Lawrence Berkeley Laboratories] group assumed.) The team assumed increases during 1977–2000 of 17 percent in population, 10 percent in the average floor space of new homes, 59 percent in commercial floor space, and 33 percent, 56 percent, 39 percent, and 59 percent in the saturation of central air conditioners, dishwashers, freezers, and swimming pools respectively. Yet they found a cost-effective potential to save by 2000 some 58 percent of fuel, and 33 percent of total energy, used annually in U.S. buildings.

Just standard weatherization techniques—insulation, weatherstripping, caulking, furnace tuneups, better showerheads, and the like—can save oil and fungible gas equivalent to upward of half of the 5.0 million bbl-equivalents-per-day (9.54 q/y) used in U.S. buildings in 1986. The SERI/LBL analysts found, for example, a practical potential to save in existing homes (using circa 1979 technologies and a 3 percent/y real discount rate) half of all space-heating fuel at 1986-$ costs of $17/bbl marginal or $10/bbl average. A 75 percent saving, they found, would cost about $66/bbl marginal but only $20/bbl average, with the average cost of the incremental savings from 50 to 75 percent being about $28.6/bbl. (Many empirical program costs have since proved to be substantially lower than these.) In contrast, in 1985 and 1986 respectively, the average retail barrel of #2 heating oil was priced at $45.00 and $35.00; the average barrel-equivalent of residential natural gas, at $34.50 and $33.00. Thus the average cost of the 50 percent to 75 percent space-heating fuel savings would be about two to three times less than 1986 average retail fuel costs, let alone the far higher marginal costs of frontier hydrocarbons or synfuels.

A 50 percent saving in 1986 residential oil and gas use would be equivalent to two-and-a-half times the 1986 U.S. imports from the Gulf. The savings' average cost would be under $10/bbl: three-fourths of all residential oil and gas use is for space heating, and it is generally even cheaper to save water-heating and appliance energy than space-heating energy. Thus spending *one year's* budget for the Rapid Deployment Force[81] (meant to seize Middle Eastern oilfields) on good weatherization programs could more than eliminate U.S. oil imports from the Middle East.[82]

New technologies offer even larger savings. For example, whereas the hot-water-system improvements assumed by Watson reduce input fuel by only ~42 percent, a fuller retrofit package[83] would save ~65 percent (~0.4 MMB/D of oil and gas nationwide) and cost less than $2 per barrel-equivalent saved. Similarly, in building-shell retrofits, "superwindows" now on the market offer insulating values in the R-10 to R-12 range[84]—better insulated than most people's walls. They achieve this performance by various mixtures of spectrally selective coatings or suspended films and heavy-gas fillings. In most U.S. climates, windows better than ~R-5 can yield a net winter heat gain even facing due north. Spectrally selective windows also reject summer heat, reducing cooling loads, and greatly increase comfort year-round. They look like double glazing, weigh about the same, and cost so little extra that their marginal cost is typically recovered in about two years. When used throughout the United States, they will save at least as much oil and gas energy as Alaska now provides. Over a shorter than likely twenty-year lifetime, they save frostbelt heating energy at a cost equivalent to about $2–3 per barrel. Since normal weatherization does not include reglazing, nearly all of that saving is in addition to the weatherization savings projected above.

Industrial Oil Savings

Less is known about saving oil in industry than in vehicles or buildings, because the sector is so heterogeneous. Moreover, of the 7.9 q of petroleum used by industry in 1986, 42 percent, or 3.33 q, was used not as a fuel but as a raw material feedstock.[85] In addition, 0.47 q, or 2.8 percent, of natural gas was used as a feedstock, chiefly for plastics and nitrogen fertilizers. Nonfuel use of oil and gas has fallen steadily, by a total of 19 percent and 22 percent respectively, since 1980, largely through more-efficient production processes and uses: For example, very efficient processes for making high-density polymers permit plastic bags to be made stronger *and* severalfold thinner, needing less hydrocarbon input per bag. Potential future savings of feedstocks are more complex and possibly larger than in fuel uses, since they embrace not only continued process improvements but also reduced end-use of the product itself: fewer road repairs resulting from lighter (more efficient) vehicles,[86] less plastic packaging, recyclable polymers, and innovations from materials science.

Of the 4.57 q of oil and 5.90 q of gas used as fuel in industry in 1986, most is fungible between these two fuels[87] and a substantial fraction can be saved through both conventional and innovative technologies.[88] While data on which to base a sound estimate of the untapped savings potential are sparse, SERI's analysis *A New Prosperity* suggested that a 1977–2000 primary-energy intensity reduction of ~30 percent[89] could be readily and cost-effectively achieved. Many analysts scoffed at this supposedly oversanguine projection. In fact, however, that 30 percent reduction *was actually achieved by 1985.*[90] Yet most U.S. industrial energy managers say they are still far from exhausting savings that pay back in two to three years—far shorter than any frontier oil venture.

Further encouragement can be drawn from a detailed demonstration that Swedish industry—the world's most fuel efficient[91] to start with—could cost-effectively save ~50 percent of its 1975 fuel use per unit output by using the best available 1980 technologies, or ~60–65 percent by using more advanced technologies now entering the market.[92] It therefore appears conservative to expect *another* 20 percent intensity reduction in U.S. industry by 2000. If the 1977–1985 rate of U.S. industrial savings were simply sustained, that 20 percent additional saving would be achieved by about 1993.

Utility Oil Savings

The recently merged U.S. Committee for Energy Awareness/Atomic Industrial Forum and allied lobbying efforts have been spending more than $25 million per year trying to blur the distinction between electricity and oil, and between past oil savings and the potential to repeat them, so as to imply that building more coal or nuclear power stations is vital to displacing imported oil in the future. As was shown earlier, however, building such plants has in fact made only a small contribution, at enormous cost,[93] to total U.S. supply expansion. Future oil-displacing potential is even more limited. During 1984–1986, an average of only 5.84 percent of U.S. electricity was made from oil, and only 4.06 percent of all the oil consumed made electricity (down from 10.1 percent and 16.9 percent respectively in 1973). Outside a few limited regions, oil and electricity therefore have almost nothing to do with each other. Indeed, since such a small part of national utility fuel is oil, and only

26 percent of the average 1985 retail electric bill was for fuel (the remainder being for fixed costs, nonfuel operations and maintenance [O & M], and grid losses), doubling the oil price would directly increase the average U.S. retail rate[94] by only ~0.1¢/kwh, or ~1.5 percent.

More power plants would therefore be virtually irrelevant to the oil problem—except that their vast cost would *slow down* investments in effective oil savings. Every dollar spent on power plants cannot be spent on other measures (such as more-efficient cars) that would save more oil, faster, cheaper. In terms of opportunity cost, power plant investments thus retard oil displacement. A great deal of that retardation has already occurred as a direct result of the 1970's ~$270 billion investment in unneeded electric capacity and its ~$30 billion in annual federal subsidies. Had policymakers resisted the siren song of the power plant builders and allocated a fraction as much money to fast, cheap oil savings, the United States would probably not be importing oil in 1988. Indeed, so extravagant was the misdirected power plant–building rush that at least 27 percent of the nuclear plants built since 1973 have displaced not oil but coal, the most abundant fuel in the United States.

Without the 1973–1986 coal and nuclear expansion, 1986 oil imports, being nearly offset by oil savings elsewhere, would have risen by at most 5 percent (generously assuming that the nine-tenths of the savings that were in the form of residual oil would in fact have been replaced by new oil imports). This is not to denigrate the substantial oil savings achieved by this substitution—only to say that it would have been achieved faster, at about 1 percent of the cost, by saving the oil-fired electricity instead, tapping only a fourth of electrical efficiency's 1973 potential.[95] Nonetheless, during 1984–1986, electric utilities did still burn an average of 1.2 q/y of oil (~93% heavy, mostly residual, oil) in steam-raising plants. Three major categories of oil-saving opportunities that do merit attention are available to reduce or eliminate this use.

First, it is often more efficient, both economically and thermodynamically, to burn fuel (of whatever kind) in cogeneration, yielding both electricity and useful heat, than in two separate boilers, one for process steam or heat and the other for electrical generation. Conversion to cogeneration can often more than double system efficiency, halving the consumption of fuel per unit of total work done. Such opportunities are now available and often attractive, not only in process industries, but also in commercial buildings ranging from hotels and restaurants to carwashes and laundromats. Packaged gas-fired cogeneration apparatus is available down to the tens-of-kw and even the kw range and is being increasingly applied even at the scale of single apartment buildings.

Second, on-site combined cycles, and new generating technologies such as steam-injected gas turbines and other advanced power cycles, now permit low capital cost, short lead time devices like combustion turbines to be so modified as to match or surpass the thermal efficiency of costly, elaborate supercritical steam plants. As such cycles are increasingly retrofitted into existing oil- and gas-burning apparatus, savings often approaching a factor of two can be achieved at very low cost.

Third, and most important, the modest amounts of oil and gas still burned in power plants—and, for that matter, most of the coal and all of the uranium too—can be cost-effectively displaced by new technologies that save electricity at the point of use, more cheaply than utilities can make it.[96] An astounding range of new technologies, many less than a year old, can wring several times as much work out of the electricity used in 1988, yet deliver unchanged or improved services. Superefficient lights, motors, appliances, and building components can together, if fully used in existing U.S. buildings and industries, save about three-fourths of all electricity now used, at an average cost far below that of just operating a typical coal-fired or nuclear power plant, even if building it cost nothing.[97] Since reduced demand normally causes utility dispatchers to back out first those plants that cost the most to run, and since those plants normally burn oil and gas,[98] it appears that capturing even a small fraction of the end-use electric efficiency potential would suffice to displace virtually all the oil- and gas-fired capacity now operating.[99]

A host of innovative, mainly market-oriented ways to finance and deliver the new hardware to customers is also being proven in practice. In fact, if the whole United States saved electricity as cheaply and quickly as Southern California Edison Company's customers have consistently done in recent years, the nation's long-term power needs would decline by at least 40 gw per year, equivalent to ~8.5 percent of present peak load per year. About four-and-a-half years' worth of such savings would back out all ~181 gigawatts (gw) of oil- and/or gas-fired capacity existing in 1987,[100] much of which is already idle anyway. The utilities' average cost of achieving those savings would be one- or two-tenths of a cent per kwh saved—roughly a hundredth the cost of electricity from a new central power station, and equivalent in heat content to about $2–3 a barrel.

Combined Oil-Saving Potential

The opportunities just described for each sector do not lend themselves to easy summary. In very round numbers, however, potential oil savings achievable by the year 2000 (by purely technical means, not counting gas savings or oil-gas substitutions, and assuming SERI's high levels of services to be provided) are on the order of:

- 3.5-7.5 q/y in transportation[101]
- 1.2 q/y by unambitious measures (Watson's assumptions) in buildings[102]
- Essentially all of utilities' present 1.2 q/y of thermal plant oil use
- At least 0.9 q/y in industrial fuel use
- Probably at least 0.8 q/y in feedstock use

This totals about 7.6–11.6 q/y. That is 24–36 percent of total 1986 oil use—a shrinkage of one-fourth to one-third in total oil use despite average real GNP growth of 2.65 percent/y for the rest of the century (slightly faster than the average of 2.51 percent for 1973–1986). This annual oil saving by 2000 would be equivalent to about thirteen to twenty times the average 1984–1986 U.S. annual imports from the Gulf. And it is well within DOE's often overlooked estimate[103] that 10–25 q/y of energy in all forms could be cost-effectively saved in 2000 by fully using current and expected technologies.

Even that enormous saving greatly understates the long-term potential once capital stocks are retrofitted or replaced, and once gas (or alternative renewable and nonrenewable fuels) is more fully substituted. An idea of just the long-term efficiency (not substitution) potential can be gained by asking how much oil would be saved once the technical improvements noted earlier have been fully applied: say, 80-mpg cars, 50-mpg light trucks (big enough for a lot of heavy hauling), 40 percent savings in heavy trucks, buses, and trains, 50 percent in ships and aircraft, another 20 percent in industrial fuel and feedstock use, ~100 percent in utility steam plant use, and 75 percent in buildings.[104] Based on 1986 use patterns, those savings would add up to 17.1 q/y, or 53 percent of total 1986 oil use—and that is before substitutions. Just displacing the remaining industrial and building use, initially by gas for convenience (using the gas separately saved by similar efficiency gains in industry and buildings—so far we have counted only their oil savings), would save an additional 7/0 q/y or 22 percent of 1986 gas use. This would reduce total U.S. oil use to 8/1 q, or 25 percent of its present level. All of these savings would be economically very attractive at 1987 fuel prices. None would require any technology not already demonstrated and commercially available or in advanced preproduction testing. And U.S. oil use reduced by three-fourths could be entirely provided by less than half of recent domestic output, without even using alternative liquid fuels at all.

Though these data hardly suffice to construct an elaborate "supply curve" of potential oil savings, the approximate costs indicated earlier can be mentioned as indicative:

- If Volvo's cost estimates for putting its LCP-2000 prototype into production are accurate (namely, a marginal cost of approximately zero), and if comparable cost and (correspondingly reduced to, say, 55 mpg) performance are transferable, as seems plausible, to light trucks, then the steady-state saving of such a fleet in the year 2000, namely[105] 4.43 q/y for cars + 1.84 q/y for light trucks = 6.27 q/y, would have a marginal cost of approximately zero. Saving a bit more might cost a bit more.
- Since airlines and trucking firms have been pursuing the efficiency gains described earlier as vigorously as their capital constraints permitted, under the range of oil prices prevalent from 1978 to 1988, it seems reasonable to suppose that the average cost of such measures is easily competitive with those empirical fuel prices, and probably under ~$10/bbl. More empirical data on this are needed.
- Since SERI showed that 1979 technologies could save 50 percent of fueled space-heating energy through building-shell improvements at an average cost of $10/bbl, Watson's comparable 55 percent savings including water-heating (where a ~65 percent saving can cost only about $2/bbl) can be reasonably assumed to fall within the same price range. In fact, many of Watson's measures, especially the more efficient replacement furnaces, have a simple payback less than five years at present fuel prices, meaning that their equivalent oil price is about $4/bbl (or $6/bbl discounted at 5 percent/y real rate) over a twenty-year life. These savings cost essentially the same for natural gas as for oil.
- We have already cited analyses showing in detail how to save about three times as much electricity as all oil- and gas-fired power plants now make (in 1986, 15 percent of total electric output), at zero net cost to society.
- It is commonly observed by industrial energy managers that the savings that they have achieved since 1973, and will continue to achieve for at least the decade of the 1990s as available capital permits, typically offer simple paybacks under three years. Conservatively assuming that incremental savings of oil or gas will instead yield only a four-year payback at average 1984 industrial energy prices ($6.3/10^6 Btu), but will last for the normal industrial-equipment lifetime of twenty years, a four-year payback corresponds to an equivalent cost of saved energy (discounting the value of future savings at 5 percent/y real) of about $2.0/10^6 Btu or $10.7/bbl. It seems very likely that the *average* cost of such measures will be substantially lower. The same appears to be true of industrial savings in feedstocks.

These costs range from roughly zero to roughly $10/bbl. Many probably fall within, often toward the low end of, the range in between. It seems mathematically inescapable that the weighted-average price of all the measures needed to add up to even the largest oil savings described above, including those achieved by saving gas and using the saved gas to displace oil, would probably be less than $10/bbl (1986 $)—to save about three-fourths of all oil now used.

What Do Such Big Oil Savings Mean?

However such efficiency potential is assessed, it is clear that capturing far less than all of it would stretch economically and environmentally acceptable domestic oil and gas resources for very many decades beyond the time horizon commonly assumed. If, in addition, some level of imports (safeguarded by suitable diversification and stockpiling such as have already occurred) were considered tolerable as a bridge to a sustainable liquid-fuel system, the domestic oil depletion, whether economic or geological, could be postponed indefinitely. The domestic petroleum era would then last not for a few more decades but for at least a few more *centuries.*

Moreover, reducing the sense of urgency in exploration and development of new oilfields could undoubtedly yield technologies that work better and cost less. Thus, by asking its engineers to minimize cost while accepting slower construction, rather than to minimize construction time with virtually no regard to cost, Shell recently cut the total development cost of its Kittiwake field in difficult North Sea conditions by an unexpected 40 percent—from $20 to $12 a barrel. How many other such opportunities have the energy industries missed by being in too much hurry? Better oil technologies do not just save money; they effectively shift the supply curve so as to expand the economically exploitable reserves, thus buying more time. But an even more critical, longer-term virtue of this approach is that it helps buy the time to put in place the infrastructure needed for life *beyond* oil.

This is not to explore the rich menu of renewable liquid-fuel options, particularly those based on sustainably grown biofuels that contribute no CO_2 to threaten the earth's climatic stability[106] nor acid gas to threaten its biological productivity. That menu already contains so many combinations of cultural practice, feedstock, conversion process, fuel product, and end-use device that most of the more interesting possibilities have not even been explored yet. Technologists need the time to do so thoughtfully, and probably, given the long logistical lead times of deployment, a set of incentives driven by a social rather than a market discount rate.

Efficient use of oil buys the time needed to choose and use a diverse range of renewable liquids for transport; to displace most if not all oil uses in other sectors; and to reduce transport fuels to levels probably not requiring fossil fuels or special fuel crops, and probably consistent, given careful management, with ecological sustainability. As we stated in the recent *Atlantic* article cited at the start of this chapter:

> The efficient use of oil can also buy time for the decades-long switch to the renewable sources which, one way or another, we'll adopt as oil becomes too costly. This transition won't be quick or cheap, but that's all the more reason for getting started now—before the cheap oil, and the cheap money made from it, are gone. Already, American oil is becoming costlier than others' oil; and the faster the oil is used, the sooner those other oil-supplying nations in their turn will find their oil becoming costlier than OPEC's huge reserves. The problem that we have now, others will have later, although Saudi Arabia (according to our present knowledge of petroleum geology) will have it last of all.
>
> The short-term oil savings and diversification in our sources of oil extraction that have resulted from the past two oil shocks now offer a unique opportunity: roughly a two-decade-long respite (longer if exploration of little-known areas is unexpectedly successful, shorter if federal policy continues to stifle gains in efficiency) from Middle Eastern dominance of global oil supply. If this interval is frittered away, it could end with the United States, its alternative options expired, needing Middle Eastern oil more than ever. If, instead, we increase our oil efficiency and make sensible use of diverse alternative fuels, this grace period could expire on a United States that no longer substantially depends on oil from the Middle East or anywhere else outside our borders. Without efficient cars, no liquid-fuel future makes sense for long. With efficient cars, alcohols and other liquid fuels made from natural gas and sustainably grown biofuels—abundant or even inexhaustible resources, whose use poses little or no risk to the world's climate—can do the job at reasonable cost.

The basic priorities for oil investment remain the same in general form as when we compared in 1983 five ways to invest $100,000 to save oil:[107]

- Catalyze a program of door-to-door citizen action to weatherize the worst buildings, as Fitchburg, Massachusetts, did in 1979, and as dozens of towns have done since. Experience shows that over the first ten years, the investment of $100,000 in such a program can save 170,000 barrels of crude oil, at about $0.60 a barrel.
- Pay the extra cost (at the highest published estimate) of making forty-four cars achieve 60 mpg. The first decade's savings: 5,800 barrels at about $17 a barrel.[108]

- Buy about 3,000 barrels of foreign oil, put it in a hole in the ground, and call it a "strategic petroleum reserve." After ten years, the oil may be available, but the storage and carrying charges—probably between $50 and $70 a barrel—will be unrecoverable.
- Buy a small piece of an oil-shale plant. After ten years, it will have produced nothing. After that, if it works, it will produce up to 9,000 barrels of synthetic oil per decade, probably retailing at between $70 and $120 a barrel, in 1982 dollars.
- Buy a tiny piece of the Clinch River Breeder Reactor. After ten years, it will still be under construction. After that, if it works, the $100,000 investment will yield up to 500 "barrels" of energy (as electricity) per decade, retailing at over $370 a barrel, in 1982 dollars, and probably uncompetitive even with roof-mounted photovoltaic cells.

The Clinch River Breeder was finally cancelled, but its successors live on in enormously costly civil and military fission and fusion programs that leave mere budgetary crumbs for efficiency R & D. To this day, the U.S. government, and too much of the private sector, continues its stampede to pursue energy options (preferably at taxpayers' expense) in precisely the reverse order: Worst buys first.

Today, however, it is becoming ever clearer that trying to buy more efficiency *and* more supply, because we cannot make up our minds, is a dangerous diversion. Strong efficiency gains are sufficient to stretch domestic reserves through the transition to the era after oil. They are so many times larger than what might be obtained from grandiose supply expansions (ANWR, currently unleased offshore continental shelf, et cetera) that the latter are trivial by comparison.

Moreover, not only does the United States not need both kinds of options, but it cannot afford both, and they compete for scarce resources. Every dollar spent drilling in frontier areas, with high risks of dry holes and with finding and lifting costs well above $10/bbl, is a dollar *not* spent on drilling in cars and attics, with zero dry-hole risks and with finding and lifting costs well below $10/bbl. These options are sometimes claimed not to be mutually exclusive or even competitive as alternative ways to allocate resources. Logically, of course, there is no *guarantee* that money not spent on supply will be spent instead on efficiency, but it is equally true that money spent on supply *cannot* be spent on efficiency. From a marginalist economic perspective, the two investment alternatives should and must be compared as if their costs were fungible. The past decade's rapid shift of investment from central power plants to efficiency and decentralized plants, to the tune of more than $100 billion in commitments during 1981–1984 alone, bespeaks the capital market's flexibility in doing just that. Indeed, a major lesson of the recent and unhappy boom-bust experience in most sectors of the energy industries is that trying to get both supply expansions *and* efficiency improvements risks getting neither—or, as lately, *succeeding* in getting both and hence bankrupting the supply enterprises, which *need* new demand to pay for new supply.

This is shown most clearly by the electric utility industry's recent behavior. Since 1973 the United States has spent some $200 billion (plus at least $100 billion in federal subsidies) building unneeded power plants. Today, many of the overbuilt utilities are mistakenly trying to recover their costs by ordering their efficiency staffs to market more electricity instead. The Electric Power Research Institute estimated that these "strategic marketing" programs will create by 2000 some 35 gw of new *on*-peak demand.[109] Thus, for many firms, supply investments did not merely divert resources from efficiency, but have now abandoned neutrality and become a positive enemy of efficiency. Nor is the damage confined to the electric sector: ~$300+ billion is so large an overinvestment, compared with the marginal cost of saving oil, that it is no exaggeration to say that the United States imports oil today *because* it bought needless power plants *instead* of oil efficiency.

Likewise for the oil sector itself, spending a lot of money on drilling in a largely drilled-out province can guarantee—by sunk costs if it fails and by skewed incentives to boost demand if it succeeds—that the efficiency potential will be realized too little and too late. For time is of the essence. *Promptly* becoming very efficient in using oil could reduce or (if desired) eliminate imports *and* fuel the decades-long transition to alternative transport fuels. But the domestic reserves that, if used so prudently, could bridge the country to beyond oil will instead be burned if the efficiency gains needed to preserve them are not achieved both strongly and quickly. The United States must pick what works and get on with it. This is the predicament and the peril. It is as if, crossing a wooden bridge over a chasm, we noticed its girders were catching on fire, and instead of damping down the flames and proceeding briskly across the bridge while it was still sound, we foolishly returned to the near bank (or lounged on the middle of the bridge itself) to warm ourselves by the bonfire—until the bridge crashed in ruins.

In this race against time, it is rapidly growing too late for dithering: Bad buys on the supply side are foreclosing good buys on the demand side. The opportunity cost of the bad buys is depleting domestic oil before its replacement is installed. If we did not know how to do any better, such failure might be a forgivable result of ignorance. Since we do know, it would be an unprecedented tragedy, a grave threat to U.S. security, and quite unnecessary.

Oil Efficiency: A Key to Real Security

The national security argument for drilling for more oil, or for projecting military force to induce others to part with their oil, has been made for so long that it seems to have become the last refuge of scoundrels. But it is too important an argument to be cheapened by being applied where it does not fit. "Energy security" means more than just an unbroken line of tankers bringing oil from halfway around the world. It embraces at least six goals:

- Maintaining reliable access to affordable energy for all nations' development
- Preventing conflict over fuel-rich regions like the Gulf
- Making domestic energy systems resilient against accidental or deliberate disruption
- Abating CO_2 emissions, which might threaten global climate
- Controlling acid-gas emissions, which can damage forests, lakes, and other resources
- Inhibiting the further spread of nuclear bombs

Different ways of seeking to enhance energy security can merely trade off these problems against each other or can help to solve all of them at once; can increase or decrease economic costs; and can worsen or lessen environmental and social impacts. It is often said that if one is not going to burn large amounts of Middle Eastern oil, then, because natural gas is quite limited, one must instead burn equally large amounts of coal or uranium. Since coal makes CO_2 and acid rain, whereas uranium makes bombs, this is a singularly nasty choice of evils. But efficient energy use—the "fifth fuel"—has already gone a long way toward solving all six energy/security problems simultaneously. And far from costing extra, it costs far *less* than burning the oil, coal, or uranium. The resulting "energy-security insurance policy" thus bears a negative premium.

Some of efficiency's contributions to real security are obvious enough. With reference to the first goal, for example, efficiency stretches world oil resources and softens price, leaving more oil for others at more affordable prices. Efficiency technologies are themselves more accessible to developing countries than are many supply technologies, though less assiduously promoted by vendors and aid agencies, because efficiency has relatively low capital cost, small scale, modularity, and high velocity of cash flow (owing to its short lead time and fast payback). If offered the opportunity, developing countries that are building their infrastructure from scratch could become energy efficient *faster* than we in the West, who have trillions of dollars' worth of obsolete capital stocks to replace or retrofit.

As for the second goal—avoiding conflict—efficiency is accessible to all, not restricted to occupants of mineral-rich territories. Efficiency, systematically harnessed by a few major countries, can go a long way toward making the Gulf's perilous concentration of oil resources simply *irrelevant* to human affairs.[110]

The third goal—making domestic energy systems resilient—is one of the most important and least understood.[111] It is not commonly realized, for example, that a handful of people could cut off three-quarters of the oil and gas supplies to the eastern United States, for upward of a year, in one evening's work, without even leaving Louisiana. (Electric grids are even more fragile than that.) In 1988 Secretary Hodel sought to drill for oil in the Arctic National Wildlife Refuge so as to prolong the life of the Trans-Alaska Pipeline System (TAPS). From a security perspective, that would be a very bad idea. TAPS runs for 798 miles through some of the roughest country in the world, yet is accessible for most of its length by road or floatplane. It has already been repeatedly, if incompetently, bombed and shot at by people who apparently sought theater, not real damage. The army has declared TAPS indefensible. In 1977, one of its pumping stations was blown up by a technician's mistake; had it been a northerly rather than the least important (most southerly) station, and in the winter, the nation could have been treated to the spectacle of 800 miles of hot oil slowly congealing into the world's largest Chapstick.

That frail lifeline is how the United States currently delivers in 1987 24 percent of all the crude oil it lifts and 15 percent of all its refinery inputs: 83 percent more oil than the United States imported in 1987 from the Gulf. There are many alternative routes for Gulf oil, but none for North Slope oil. Gulf oil has proven surprisingly hard to disrupt: Kharg Island continued to ship oil amid heavy air attacks. Yet TAPS's pumping stations, or the "Hollywood and Vine" manifold of large pipes at its north end, or certain terminal facilities at its south end, could be disabled for a year or more (the lead time to remake some of the pipe is several years) by a few kilos of well-placed *plastique*. Because of remoteness, weather, and specialized facilities, the damage could also be far harder to mend, and easier to repeat once mended, than damage to non-Arctic oil facilities. Continued dependence on TAPS, therefore, puts far more of U.S. oil supplies at risk to one simple, unattributable, and unstoppable act by a lone terrorist than could possibly be cut off by an all-out war in the Strait of Hormuz.

When TAPS was designed and built, its engineers apparently assumed a "technological paradise" in which everything worked according to the blueprints, and terrorism was the stuff of novels. If Americans ever lived in such a world, they do no longer. Drilling in the Arctic National Wildlife Refuge for still more oil, so as to prolong dependence on TAPS, would—on the less-than-19 percent chance it succeeded[112]—perpetuate one of the gravest *threats* to U.S. national security.

There is now abundant evidence that resilient energy systems, in which major failures of supply are no longer possible, cannot be achieved by hauling fuels from ever more remote places. True energy security comes from making supplies more diverse, dispersed, inherently uninterruptable, and very efficiently used. Efficient use lets alternative supplies meet a bigger fraction of needs and makes existing stockpiles last long enough to mend what is broken or to improvise new supplies. (Thus, a 60-mpg car fleet could run on its normal in-tank inventories, if the tanks were not downsized, for a month without refueling, and on the "pipeline inventory" of the oil-supply system for about a year. In contrast, a modern refinery deprived of its feed is often out of business in a few *days*.) Far from costing more, this approach actually *reduces* energy costs. It is also the direction in which the market is already taking us.

There is a growing consensus that a less contingent, more inevitable kind of security threat looms in the coming decades: serious and probably irreversible changes in the earth's climate, caused by the CO_2 released by burning fossil fuels. In an earlier analysis for the German Federal Environmental Agency,[113] we showed that very efficient use of energy is *the only practical, large-scale option* for averting this threat. Other authors have since come to similar conclusions.[114] Here again, efficiency's security benefits are better than free.

A similar "no losers" approach is available for the acid rain from power plants. Rather than raising electric rates to put diapers on dirty coal plants, utilities can employ a variety of proven methods to help customers use electricity far more efficiently. The utilities can then burn less coal and emit less sulfur (preferably backing out the dirtiest plants first), but mainly they will save a great deal of money, because efficiency costs less than coal. They can then use part of the money to clean up the remaining plants and the rest to lower their rates to more competitive levels. At least three states—Wisconsin, Minnesota, and New York—already officially recognize the validity of this approach. A recent analysis[115] for the Midwestern (ECAR) region, which is responsible for a third of power plant acid-gas emissions, assumed a potential to save only 26 percent of electricity now used—too low by perhaps threefold—and unrealistically high costs for those savings. Despite these strong conservatisms, the analysts found that using electric efficiency to finance a 55 percent acid-gas reduction would cut that reduction's present-valued cost (depending on the exact investments chosen) from \$3.6–8.4 billion to *minus* \$3.7–7.7 billion. Simultaneously abating much of the CO_2 emissions from the same plants would be a free bonus.

Another serious threat to national and global security is nuclear proliferation. We have shown elsewhere[116] that the main technical driving force behind the spread of nuclear bombs is "civilian" nuclear power programs. They provide the materials, skills, equipment, data, and above all the innocent "cover" for bomb programs. But in a world without nuclear commerce, all these ingredients, though obtainable on the black market, would be harder to get, more conspicuous to try to get, and politically far costlier to be caught trying to get—because for the first time the reason for wanting them would be *unambiguously military*. This would not make proliferation impossible, but would make it far more difficult: for most *n*th countries of concern, prohibitively difficult.

The global collapse of the nuclear enterprise, if recognized for what it is and capitalized on with programs to help developing countries meet their legitimate energy service needs, is thus a timely opportunity to inhibit proliferation. That collapse has no precedent in industrial history: Nuclear capacity in 2000 will be at most 6–8 percent in industrialized countries, and 2–3 percent in developing countries,[117] of the levels officially forecast in the early 1970s. That this double-edged venture is dying of an incurable attack of market forces is the best possible news for world peace, and incidentally (by the resources it frees up) good news for faster oil displacement too. Energy efficiency—by both saving electricity (which displaces reactors) and displacing directly used oil (a common argument for building reactors)—is the key to *un*spreading the bomb.

Changing the World

Listing some of the specific security benefits of energy efficiency is usefully concrete, but risks overlooking a far wider range and perhaps more important indirect benefits. It is sobering to reflect, therefore, on how *the whole world* could have been made more secure if the past decade's improvements in U.S. energy efficiency had instead been undertaken a generation earlier. In 1951, for example, President Harry Truman's Paley Commission called for a major effort on energy efficiency and renewables. Had its recommendations been followed:

- The United States would not then have entered the world oil market in the early 1970s as a major importer. OPEC would not have gained most of the market leverage that underpinned the 1973–1974 embargo and the accompanying price increases, global recession, and worldwide monetary inflation.

- Developing countries would have been less squeezed by the world oil market and would be better able to support themselves today.
- The enormous transfer of wealth to the Middle East would have been reduced by both the lower price and the reduced consumption of oil. The dangerous Middle East arms race, with its spillover into terrorism, might therefore have been drastically curtailed. The Iran-Iraq war, had it occurred, would have been nowhere near its actual level of violence. Israel would probably be more secure and would require correspondingly less U.S. assistance.
- It is questionable whether Islamic fundamentalism, accelerated by rapid and culturally insensitive industrialization, would have emerged in significant force at such speed; whether its threat on the flanks of the Soviet Union would have been seen to justify the invasion of Afghanistan; and, just conceivably, whether President Jimmy Carter, absent the Iranian hostage crisis, might not have been reelected, helping to avoid the voodoo-economics calamity.
- Oil choke points like the Horn of Africa and Strait of Hormuz would be seen as less vital U.S. interests, and the military missions associated with maintaining freedom of passage in such areas would be correspondingly downgraded.
- Much of the terrorism of the 1980s might have been curtailed, owing to reduced motivation, financial support, and weaponry.
- The recycling of petrodollars via Western banks' force-fed loans to developing countries would probably have been diminished, and with it, the Third World debt crisis, with its accompanying risks to the political stability of those countries and the financial stability of the world.
- The loans' invitations to large-scale corruption, militarization, and inappropriate forms of development by less developed country (LDC) governments would have been correspondingly reduced: The multibillion-dollar looting by Ferdinand Marcos and Sese Seko Mobutu would have been less likely to occur, leaving such nations as the Philippines and Zaire at least potentially fairly healthy.
- The Mexican economy would have had an opportunity to pursue a more resilient development strategy rather than one precariously perched on high oil prices. This would have had important implications for, say, U.S. immigration policy. In general, oil exporters would have gotten the benefits of steady, sustainable development without the costs of boom-and-bust instability. Houston would have enjoyed slower but steady growth, while frontier energy boomtowns would probably not have experienced their current economic crash because they would not have become overgrown in the first place.

Britain would have depleted its North Sea reserves far more slowly, providing a softer economic landing as oil output declined.

- U.S. competitiveness, balance of trade, net wealth, fiscal integrity, and energy security might have been markedly improved. The pervasive economic benefits of low real oil prices, which proved so valuable (outside the oil patch) in 1986, would probably have occurred *throughout* the 1974–1987 period, without the disruption which their exceptional occurrence brought *inside* the oil patch.
- Hundreds of billions of dollars' investments in uneconomic expansions of energy supply would have been avoided, along with their side effects at home and abroad, ranging from acid rain to nuclear proliferation to insolvent utilities.
- With fewer pressures to earn oil-buying dollars by exports, pressures on U.S. farm communities, topsoil, and groundwater could have been reduced, and the vast and destabilizing exports of advanced weaponry by the United States, France, and other countries, might have been more readily controlled.

Such speculation reinforces the decade-old joke that the best form of Middle Eastern arms control might be U.S. roof insulation. Of course, other, unforeseen, thoroughly disagreeable events might, in this alternative scenario, have replaced those avoided. No one can guarantee that on the whole the alternative outcomes would have been preferable to what has actually occurred. But the outcomes are clearly so *different* in their security implications that this thought experiment at least merits further pursuit (and implementation, lest we have to relearn these lessons the hard way over the *next* decade or two). The benefits of energy efficiency, pursued to their logical conclusions, may well prove to be far more pervasive and interactive than anyone has imagined.

Conclusions

For an oil company seeking to chart a course through the turbulence of the coming decades, these relationships by which energy efficiency fosters security are not theoretical niceties; they define the future business environment. And they do so in ways less trivial than merely saying one cannot sell oil to people who have been blown up. Both acid rain and CO_2 constitute serious long-term (and, in some places, not so long term) threats to customers' ability and willingness to continue to buy fossil fuels. Lack of affordable energy services stifles the sustainable global development on which energy companies' markets ultimately depend. International tensions over places like the Gulf threaten both the demand for and the supply of energy, and inject geopolitical uncertainties that defeat sound planning.

Economically, the energy industries have much housecleaning to do to ensure their own solvency and indeed their long-term survival. Those who claim to live by the market are often among the last to appreciate its verdicts. The emerging energy service marketplace—where oil and gas must compare not only with other fuels but also with more efficient provision of mobility, comfort, light, torque, and other desired services at least cost to the customer—has profound consequences, which have barely begun to sink into the consciousness of many chief executive officers (CEOs), and which demand difficult adaptations in corporate missions, career goals, and personal identities. Engineers and managers who have spent their lives building multibillion-dollar projects may feel less emotionally fulfilled by doing millions of small things instead. Many managers have gotten into the bad habit of looking at the top line instead of the bottom line, seeking bigger sales and revenues instead of seeking to cut costs more than to increase revenues. Further, a generation of industry leaders grew up in a fat era when cost discipline was lost, both upstream and downstream rents were plentiful, and sloppy habits would not predictably attract competitive penalties. Yet the competitive forces that have so lastingly softened demand for oil and gas have barely begun to express their full market potential. The energy savings that have turned the industry on its head have only started to scratch the surface of what is now available and cost effective.

Those energy companies that are first to internalize the full meaning of the competitive energy service marketplace will make more money at less risk by selling less energy, but more and cheaper energy services. In so doing, because sustainability is indivisible, they will contribute signally to both the world's security and their own.

Notes

1. The authors are grateful to the many reviewers of the draft of this chapter, both within and outside the oil industry, for their insightful criticisms and suggestions, but the authors are solely responsible for the data and opinions given here.

2. "Best buys" could be defined either in the narrowest terms of engineering costs and market prices, or more widely to include externalities. This chapter adopts the former convention but then qualitatively discusses the latter. The California Energy Commission and several public-interest groups hope to develop such an analysis during 1988–1989, ideally deriving a "supply curve" of all salient ways to save or get oil, arranged in order of increasing cost.

3. These are analyzed in A. B. and L. H. Lovins, "The Avoidable Oil Crisis," *Atlantic*, December 1987, pp. 22–30. See also subsequent correspondence, ibid., April 1988, pp. 10–11, and June 1988, pp. 10–11.

4. This term is due to David R. Brower.

5. A. B. and L. H. Lovins, *Atlantic*, op. cit. supra. Dr. Earl Ravenal, who provided the FY1985 analysis of Gulf military costs ($47 billion) used here, has not yet updated his results for the following two fiscal years but hopes to do so for FY1987 using the expenditure data released in January 1988. Per barrel, that cost will probably be somewhat lower than the FY1985 level, owing to higher imports from the Gulf, but still several hundred dollars per barrel. It may of course be objected that if U.S. forces were not in the Gulf, they would be somewhere else and still incurring comparable costs. The primary mission of Central Command, however, is Gulf intervention; and about one-fourth of all active army and marine divisions, aircraft carriers, and fighter wings have a first-priority commitment to Central Command. If the Gulf ceased to be militarily important, a major reassessment of force requirements would obviously be in order. See T. Sabonis-Chafee, "Projecting U.S. Military Power: Extent, Cost and Alternatives in the Gulf," September 1987 paper to Pugwash Conference (Gmunden, Austria), Rocky Mountain Institute Publication #87-23.

6. The extra cost, if any, of developing and making more efficient cars is probably far more than offset by the reduced costs of finding and providing their fuel, not to mention avoided military and environmental costs, the financing costs of associated trade and budget deficits, et cetera.

7. R. H. Williams, 31 July 1984 testimony to USHR Subcommittee on Energy and Power.

8. To their credit, many oil executives (such as Robert O. Anderson) who at the time pushed for an Energy Mobilization Board soon realized that the environmentalists who opposed it, on both substantive and procedural grounds, had thereby helped to save the industry from unprecedented disaster. See A. B. Lovins, "Is Red Tape a Code Word for Law?" *Washington Post*, 3 August 1979, op-ed.

9. It was aided, ironically, by some of the same individuals responsible for the earlier fiascos. Interior Secretary Hodel, for example, was widely regarded in the oil industry as sympathetic to its plight. His efforts to help the industry, however, might appear in a different light if it were recalled that he was trying to help the Northwest's utilities when he designed the mid-1970s policies that led directly to the $7 billion Washington Public Power Supply System (WPPSS) default in the Northwest (after it took only two years, 1980–1982, for his prophesied electric shortages to turn into a seemingly endless glut). His emphasis on supply rather than on demand seriously harmed the very utilities he sought to help. See A. B. Lovins, "Scraping the Bottom of the Barrel," *Wall Street Journal*, 1 May 1987, p. 21.

10. This term is analogous to the more popular and euphonious "negawatts," which originated as a typographic error in a Colorado Public Utilities Commission PUC document. Observing that a negawatt (saved electricity) is like a megawatt, only cheaper, we popularized the term, and it is now widely used by utilities.

With reference to oil, we try to avoid the economic term "produce," since it invites confusion between production and consumption. In physical terms, an oil company is not "producing" oil at all—ancient geological processes did that—but only digging it up and burning it.

11. Recent DOE analyses by H. R. Holt ("Boom and Bust: Chaos in Oil Prices, 1901–1987: A Statistical Analysis," draft, 8 March 1988) showed that real oil prices since 1987 satisfy every statistical test of randomness, with no significant autocorrelation beyond −2 y. The baseline is surprisingly flat, with a real 1972-$ increase averaging only 4¢/bbl/y (in two steps, −1¢/bbl/y during 1902–1972 and +25¢/y during 1973–1986): The real price in 1987 was 2¢/bbl below the real *1901* price. Price volatility, however, has increased fivefold since 1972 in mean deviation and eighteenfold in variance.

12. These and most other U.S. energy data, throughout this chapter, are from the Energy Information Administration's (EIA's) *Monthly Energy Review*, September 1987, DOE/EIA-0035(87/09). That issue introduced a revised car-efficiency data series differing significantly from early data for 1970–1986.

13. That is, "If the 1976 size class shares for autos were applied to the 1987 car class fuel economies, the resulting new car mpg would be 27.7 in 1987 (just 0.4 mpg lower than the actual value)." Phil Patterson, *Periodic Transportation Energy Report 1* (DOE CE-15, 202/586-9118) 16 November 1987. This occasional newsletter is the best current data source on U.S. transportation energy use. (Patterson's car finding, however, does not hold for light trucks: The same issue reported that 42 percent of the 5.3-mpg gain for new light trucks—a gain less than half the 10.9-mpg improvement in new cars—was due to a shift to smaller models.)

14. Marc Ross has pointed out that U.S. steel consumption per dollar of GNP is now below its *1870* level, and falling.

15. EIA's *Annual Energy Review 1986* showed 135.7 million passenger cars (apparently including personal light trucks and minivans) registered in 1986. At 18.32 average mpg in 1986 (*Monthly Energy Review*, op. cit.), then driving 9,625 miles per car in 1986 (ibid.) would have taken 1.85 million barrels per day (MMB/D) more at 1973's 13.10 mpg, or slightly more counting refinery/marketing/distribution losses. In fact, however, the saving was probably greater, because the number of registered cars includes personal light trucks and vans, which started as less efficient and had more to save. (The Department of Transportation's present standard for new light trucks is 19.5 mpg.) In 1986, Alaskan oil output was 1.87 MMB/D, while reported gross imports of Gulf crude and products totaled 0.91 MMB/D. ("Gulf" in this chapter refers to the Arab OPEC states, plus Iran, less Algeria and Libya: that is, to Saudi Arabia, Iran, Iraq, Kuwait, Qatar, and the United Arab Emirates. Over 2.0 MMB/D of their ~10 MMB/D oil exports are shipped overland, not through the Strait of Hormuz.)

16. This ratio was in excess of a hundred until the early 1980s, then fell as the relative share of renewable energy supply expansions (shown in the tables) significantly increased.

17. Strictly speaking, net busbar output of nuclear electricity converted back to steam-equivalent at the nuclear plants' heat rate, so energy consumed by in-plant machinery has been deducted.

18. Authors' analysis based on EIA data (*Monthly Energy Review*, March 1987).

19. Unpublished analysis by Charles Komanoff, summarized in *Science* 239:128 (1988). We are indebted to Komanoff also for the format of Tables 7.1 and 7.2. The comparison is actually with 1978, but reflects achievements in and after 1979, and is therefore described here (though not by Komanoff) as having occurred *during* 1979–1986 (inclusive).

20. Savings are reflected as a reduced ratio or primary energy consumption to real GNP; most of this results from technical-efficiency improvements. The savings shown in Table 7.2 are slightly different because, when "non-EIA" renewable supply is included for both the starting and the ending year of each comparison, the numerator of the energy-GNP ratio changes slightly from the original amount reported by EIA.

21. Following Komanoff (op. cit.), 1978 coal extraction is taken to be the average of 1977 and 1979 values. This smoothing avoids understating 1978 coal output as a result of that year's coal strike.

22. Nuclear power, like geothermal electricity and hydroelectric power, is stated in equivalent primary terms, based on EIA heat rates. That is, the contribution shown here is the increased output of nuclear *steam*, not electricity, which is only 31.6 percent as great, not counting grid losses.

23. "Other EIA supply" excludes wood and wood wastes, direct solar energy capture by anyone except major utilities, and several minor renewable sources: None of these is shown in the summary statistics at the front of EIA's *Annual* or *Monthly Energy Reviews*, although later sections show some for certain years (usually ending in 1984).

24. The total of these three contributions—savings, coal, and nuclear—exceeds 100 percent because of the balancing entry for declining oil and gas output.

25. Both EIA and other sources show hydroelectricity only as reported by utilities (for EIA, only large utilities), wholly or almost wholly generated by dams that they own. There is also, however, a considerable output from privately owned hydro dams, many of them small or low-head, but it is difficult to determine its magnitude without a risk of some double counting. DOE's *Energy Security* (March 1987), p. 206, reports "nearly 0.4" q of 1984 (primary) output from "low-head hydro," and 6.8 gw on line at the end of 1985, much of it new, but it is unclear how much of this, if any (the Gas Research Institute [GRI] says none), is included in EIA's utility-based statistics or how fully it represents private hydro output of electricity or of direct mechanical drive. As a conservatism, therefore, all non-EIA private-hydro and "small hydro" contributions are ignored here, although they might at least double the 1979–1986 hydroelectric growth shown here.

26. EIA actually showed 0.01 q/y of other renewable output in 1977, 1979, and 1984–1986; this consisted largely of wood and wood wastes burned *by electric utilities*. Nearly all of the wood consumption shown elsewhere by EIA,

in obscure, specialized publications (note 28 infra), was thus omitted from its widely cited summary statistics. This resulted in an understatement of ~3–4 percent in national energy use and supply—more energy than nuclear power delivers.

27. Smoothed to the average 1970–1986 capacity factor, to avoid distortion by annual runoff fluctuations. The smoothed primary outputs for 1973, 1979, and 1986, respectively 2.548, 3.062, and 3,295 q; the unsmoothed outputs used by EIA are respectively 2.86, 2.93, and 3.04 q.

28. Conservatively taken as equal in 1986 to the Gas Research Institute's estimate for *1985* (in GRI's 1986 base forecast), namely 2.653 q. That is consistent with EIA's last published estimate—2.633 q in 1984. For 1973 and 1979, EIA's corresponding estimates of wood use were 1.528 and 2.149 q (DOE/EIA-0341[82] and [83]). GRI also referred to a substantial amount—1.26 q in 1983, for example—of "nonwood wastes" including such nonrenewable terms as refinery offgas, coke-oven and blast-furnace gas, but also including partly or wholly renewable sewage and landfill gas. GRI believed that most or all of these waste gas streams were probably excluded by EIA too, and none was reflected here.

29. This figure is undoubtedly an underestimate. It is derived from EIA's last published estimate (0.251 q in 1984) for alcohol fuels and miscellaneous crop wastes (such as bagasse, rice hulls, cotton gin trash, pineapple waste, nut hulls, et cetera—*Annual Energy Review 1986*, p. 215) plus GRI's last published estimate for direct solar capture by nonutilities (0.040 q in 1985), less the 0.01 q counted by EIA as "other"—windpower/woodburning/photovoltaic/solar-thermal/waste-fired electric power plants owned by electric utilities. EIA provided no data on the much larger amounts of such capacity owned by others (such as the 1.4+ gw of private windfarms, which alone account for ~0.02 primary q/y), nor on nonelectric appliances of other renewable sources, such as geothermal direct heating (estimated in DOE's *Energy Security*, p. 203, at >0.0002 q). As a further conservatism, none of these figures counted any of the rapidly expanding energy recovery from municipal solid wastes, most of the energy content of which can be considered renewable.

30. Much the same is true abroad. In Japan, for example, Komanoff (personal communication, 31 March 1988) calculated that during 1978–1986, Japan's GNP grew 36 percent while primary energy consumption grew only 4 percent (compared with 19 percent and −5 percent for the United States; Japan, even though more efficient to start with, outpaced the United States by 4:3 in efficiency gains). Japanese nuclear output grew by 1.1 primary q/y, but Japanese savings grew by 5.5 q/y, a 1:5.2 ratio. Even in France, savings have outpaced nuclear expansion by severalfold; in Western Europe as a whole, by at least tenfold.

31. The ratio of annual savings gained during 1973–1986 to 1986 domestic crude oil extraction (18.35 q) is 1.43 counting only the renewables included in the EIA summary statistics; 1.37 including the fuller list of renewables; and 1.36 with hydropower smoothed. Please see note 20 supra.

32. Our effort to do so here is not particularly profound but strives for simplicity and transparency. No doubt a more detailed statistical analysis would turn up interesting new details, but at the risk of obscuring fundamentals.

33. All energy and GNP data in these and subsequent figures are from EIA's March and September 1987 *Monthly Energy Reviews* and *Annual Energy Review 1986*. Other data are from the *Statistical Abstract of the United States* and the Commerce Department's October 1987 "Economic Indicators."

34. They disingenuously claimed that this was the result of free market behavior, not their marketing strategy. Other manufacturers operating in the same market but with different sales goals seem to have had no trouble meeting the standards.

35. The official figure is apparently secret, but an estimate in excess of $1.2 billion has been prepared from the published data by the Center for Auto Safety in Washington, D.C.

36. This assumes ~117 million cars in 1986 driven 9,625 miles, ~38 million light trucks driven 11,016 miles (1985), on-road mileage 15 percent worse than EPA mileage (DOE methodology), and 1.88 bbl crude per bbl gasoline (1986), since marginal imports are driven by light-product demand. Some unknown fraction of the reduction in annual fleet-efficiency gains, however, may also be due to the administration's 70 percent reduction in the print run of the annual "Gas Mileage Guide," so that two-thirds of new-car buyers were unable to get a copy.

37. Calculated from EIA's *Monthly Energy Review*, March 1987, p. 16.

38. That is, 3.48 additional q of petroleum would have been needed to produce the 1986 GNP at the 1984 level of oil productivity (oil-consumption/real-GNP ratio).

39. The 1985 gain in oil productivity (3.05 percent) was nearly as fast as the average gain (3.21 percent) during 1982–1985—a relatively stable and representative period during which, however, the average real price of leaded regular gasoline *fell* by an average of 7.94 percent/y and the average real refiner acquisition cost *fell* by 10.48 percent/y.

40. The December 1987 *Monthly Energy Review*, published in March 1988, gives preliminary full-year 1987 data of 2.88 percent GNP growth, 1.56 percent oil-productivity growth (more than making up the 1986 decrease), and domestic oil output down 4.26 percent, yielding a 5.58 percent rise in imports, moderately close to the actual 6.03 percent.

41. DOE's 1984 estimates, from *FY1987 Energy Conservation Multi-Year Plan*, July 1985, p. 97. The numbers of vehicles are 1986 registration data from EIA's *Annual Energy Review 1986*, p. 61. DOE's March 1987 *Energy Security* gave slightly different values for an unstated year: 59 percent light vehicles, 17 percent heavy trucks, 9 percent ships and trains, 8 percent aircraft, and 7 percent "military and other." A detailed disaggregation, with comparative forecasts, was provided by M. Miller and A. Vyar, "Transportation Energy Demand from 1980 to 2010: The ANL-85N2 Forecast," Argonne National Laboratory #ANL/CNSV-TM-169, August 1985. The Oak Ridge National Laboratory *Transportation Energy Data Book: Edition 9*, ORNL-6325, April 1987, gave slightly different shares for 1984: 44 percent cars, 0.1 percent motorcycles, 0.7 percent buses, 12.3 percent light trucks, 15.8 percent heavy trucks, 3.6 percent off-highway heavy vehicles (construction, mining, and farming), 72.9 percent total highway; 8 percent aircraft,

6 percent watercraft, 4 percent pipelines, 2.5 percent railways, and 3.5 percent military operations. None of these discrepancies is important to our thesis here.

42. Light trucks are in the process of rising from a fifth to a fourth as numerous as cars, and tend to average at least 4 mpg less efficient. Light trucks thus use nearly a third as much fuel in total as do passenger cars. More work is needed to improve and perhaps partly to displace trucks, since otherwise, early in the twenty-first century, trucks may come to use as much fuel as cars. Phil Patterson (*Periodic Transportation Energy Report* 2, DOE, 23 December 1987) reported that although light trucks accounted for 30.6 percent of new light vehicles in model year 1987, they were driven 15 percent more miles, average 23 percent less efficient, and (as of 1983) lasted 37 percent longer. The combined effect would be that light trucks' share of lifetime fuel use by 1987-model-year light vehicles would be *48 percent.* Fortunately, about two-thirds of light trucks' gain in market share since 1983 is from minivans (ibid, at p. 9), which in engineering terms are more like cars than like utility trucks.

43. The absolute consumption cited for trains in 1984, 0.63 q, included nearly all of what EIA reported as 0.013 q of end-use electricity, implying that trains used ~0.62 q of direct fuel—98 percent of their total use. In contrast, Oak Ridge National Laboratory (ORNL) reported 0.52 q used by trains, of which only 92 percent was direct fuel.

44. This mode used an estimated 4.6 percent of the 1984 total end-use transportation energy (0.91 out of 19.68 q), but accounted for nearly all of the 0.52 q of natural gas used for 1984 transportation. Oil use by pipelines would be correspondingly less—about 0.4 q/y, or 2 percent of total transportation oil use.

45. EIA's *Annual Energy Review 1986*, p. 21, stated that in 1986, the Department of Defense used about 0.0236 q of motor gasoline, 0.273 of distillate and residual fuel oils (presumably including diesel fuel), and 0.708 of other petroleum products, chiefly aviation fuel. The total, 1.004 q, was 2.85 percent of national petroleum (including NGL) consumption. Arbitrarily assuming that all motor gasoline, half the distillate-and-resid category, and 90 percent of the "other" went to transportation would imply a DOD transportation fuel use of about 0.8 q, or 3.9 percent of national transportation fuel use. The 1984 "Other (incl. Military)" transportation fuel use estimated by DOE was 0.68 q.

46. T. Sabonis-Chafee, op. cit. supra (note 5). The Vietnam war was more land based than a Gulf war would probably be, and hence less fuel intensive, yet it used ~1 q/y of transportation fuels.

47. Phil Patterson, *Periodic Transportation Energy Report* 3, DOE, 12 February 1988.

48. These and later mpg ratings, unless otherwise stated, are "composite" EPA ratings weighted 55 percent city/45 percent highway. On-road mileage for gasoline-fueled cars is typically less by 10 percent city/20 percent highway. This correction is incorporated into the foreign-car mpg ratings given in this chapter. See D. L. Bleviss (Federation of American Scientists, Washington, D.C.), prepublication draft, *The New Oil Crisis and Fuel Economy Technologies: Preparing the Light Transportation Industry for the 1990's* (Westport, Conn.: Greenwood Press, 1988), Appendix.

49. Assuming that the average new car does not in fact do better than the reduced standard. In fact, in model year 1986 (1987), Ford achieved 27.0 (26.8) mpg and GM 26.6 (26.4), compared with Chrysler's 27.8 (27.6). The *average* car sold in the United States was rated at 28.2 (28.2), but only because Americans, despite restrictions on Japanese imports, bought a record 27.4 percent (29.2 percent) share of foreign cars averaging 31.6 (31.0) mpg, compared with domestic cars' 26.9 (26.7) mpg. Data from USDOT, National Highway Traffic Safety Administration (NHTSA), NEF-31, "Summary of Fuel Economy Performance . . . ," 1 February 1988; the NHTSA contact is George Entwistle, 202/366-5303.

50. The federal government's "conditional" mean estimates of economically recoverable (at high prices) undiscovered oil in these areas are respectively 3.2 and 3.8 billion barrels. ("Conditional" means *if* economically recoverable oil is found there at all; in ANWR the probability of finding such oil is said by the Interior Department, assuming *very* high prices, to be 19 percent, and by state of Alaska geologists, who also predict about half the quantity, to be 10 percent.) The annual mean output of such a mean discovery, if it occurred, would be roughly the mean recoverable reserve divided by the field life (officially stated to be at least thirty years). But in fact, development lead times and phasing considerations would limit mean-reserve ANWR output in 2000, according to Interior, to 0.147 MMB/D. By inference, output offshore California in that time frame would probably be comparable. But 2000 would be close to the *end* of the lifetime of the car fleet bought in model years 1986–1988 and thereafter. That fleet of >110 million automobiles, getting 26 instead of 27.5 mpg and driving ~10,000 miles per year, would use an extra >0.150 MMB/D—slightly more than either area's likely output (if any) in 2000, and considerably more than their mean output in earlier years when new 1986–1988 cars would still be operating. (A barrel of gasoline is again conservatively equated here with a barrel of crude oil, although not all of a barrel of crude can in fact be refined into gasoline.)

51. For example, in a fleet consisting of 80 percent cars getting 60 mpg and 20 percent getting 10 mpg, the average is not 50 mpg but 30 mpg. This becomes intuitively clearer when one remembers that, with equal miles driven, each 10-mpg car uses as much oil as *six* 60-mpg cars do.

52. Except, apparently, to inhibit market action by reducing the information available to consumers. DOE has also largely abdicated its research role, leaving much innovation (owing to the major U.S. carmakers' short time horizon) to foreign vendors (Bleviss, op. cit., Chapter 9). It is interesting, though, that General Motors believes (Al Sobey, personal communication, 6 June 1987) that average U.S. new car efficiency, influenced by competitive forces, will continue to increase by ~1–2 percent/y for at least the rest of the twentieth century without any government action. This implies year-2000 new car averages on the order of 31–36 mpg.

53. The oil savings calculations in this and the next paragraph are by Robert K. Watson, Natural Resources Defense Council, San Francisoc. They are purely technical, omitting potential savings of ~10 percent of car fuel by traffic

management, and do *not* count the (1986 U.S. average) requirement for 1.88 bbl of crude oil to make 1 bbl of gasoline. Since light-product demand drives imports, one should multiply all the given savings by ~1.88 to obtain crude oil savings, but this step is omitted here as a conservation except where specifically stated.

54. "Risked mean" reflects the Minerals Management Service's adjustment of how much economically recoverable oil *might* be in the ground (a computer-simulated mean of 6.9 billion bbl, including 3.2 in ANWR) for the service's estimate of the likelihood of finding *none.* The price assumed by Interior in assessing what is economically recoverable from ANWR, however, is $35/bbl (1986 $) in 2000, rising to $39–61/bbl depending on which of Interior's two cited sources one adopts, and possibly rising thereafter at an unspecified rate. Such levels are far above what the oil industry apparently expects, since it is not drilling now in far cheaper areas. The federal analysts have so far provided no sensitivity test on their price assumptions—surely the first people to assume a single price forecast since the oil-shale industry. Lower prices, however, would sharply increase the minimum recoverable field size and hence the risk of finding no such field. Moreover, Interior discounts projected benefits at a risk-free real rate of only about 1 percent/y. Yet even a slightly lower price trajectory or a more reasonable discount rate would make the claimed net benefits of ANWR oil strongly negative and the risked mean reserve virtually nil. See, e.g., W. T. Georald, *Materials and Society* 11(3):729–307 (1987) (effects of using state of Alaska's geological assumptions and post-1986 tax law). Furthermore, J. S. Young and W. S. Hauser (Bureau of Land Management [BLM] Alaska Office), "Economics of Oil and Gas Production from ANWR for the Determination of Minimum Economic Field Size," undated, ca. 1987, concluded that lowering the 1984-$ oil price from $40 to $22/bbl raises minimum economic field size in E (W) ANWR by 5.0- (4.2-) fold, from 0.41 (0.33) to 2.03 (1.39) million bbl. In contrast, Interior gave an aggregated estimate of 0.15 @ $40/bbl and 0.44 @ $33/bbl. Obviously, the steep rise in required field size at lower prices was unfavorable to Interior's case, since the probability of finding a minimum recoverable field falls sharply with its increasing size, so Interior presented no low-price option.

55. Taking all of Interior's data at face value, and risking the 3.23 billion bbl of claimed conditional reserves only with the 0.19 stated probability of finding any economically recoverable oil. On Interior's uncorrected data, however, the probability of finding at least the claimed mean amount (3.23 billion bbl) of economically recoverable oil is only $0.19 \times \sim 0.34 = 0.065$.

56. See, e.g., C. Gray and F. von Hippel, "The Fuel Economy of Light Vehicles," *Scientific American,* May 1981, pp. 48–59; TRW (McLean, Va.), "Appendix—Data Base on Automobile Energy Conservation Technology," 25 September 1979; Office of Technology Assessment, *Increased Automobile Fuel Efficiency and Synthetic Fuels: Alternatives for Reducing Oil Imports* (Washington, D.C., 1982); Bleviss, op. cit., 1987.

57. Bleviss, op. cit., offered an excellent summary of the 1984–1985 market status of these and other innovations. *Popular Science,* January 1988, p. 52, reviewed a typical one, the Fiat Uno minicar's continuously variable transmission.

58. R. K. Whitford, "Fuel-Efficient Autos: Progress and Prognosis," *Annual Review of Energy* 9:375–408 (1984).

59. Bleviss, op. cit., pp. 156ff.

60. *Auto Week*, 3 August 1987, p. 6. *Popular Science*, December 1987, described a slightly different test result—138 mpg at a steady 56 mph, while *Datafax*, October 1987, p. 12, mentioned 64 mpg city and 85 mpg at a steady but excessive 75 mph.

61. Ibid., p. 118.

62. *Statistical Abstract of the United States 1987* (Washington, D.C.: U.S. Bureau of the Census, December 1986), p. 590. The ORNL *Transportation Energy Data Book*, 6th ed. (Park Ridge, N.J.: Noyes Data Corp., 1982), showed for 1974–1984 an increase of energy intensity per passenger-mile by 45 percent for transit buses (largely reflecting reduced ridership), 32 percent for intercity buses, and a 4.5 percent intensity decline for school buses.

63. Personal communication, 6 June 1987, by Jaime Lerner, director, Rio de Janeiro Plan for the Year 2000 (Rua São Bento, 8. 6.° andar, CEP 20.090 Rio de Janeiro. RJ, Brasil). Lerner developed unsubsidized, U.S. 10¢/ride commuter-bus systems in Rio and Curiciba, some with one-minute intervals. His on-street "boarding pods" and special door designs nearly trebled density—to a staggering 12–18,000 passengers per hour per corridor.

64. This assumes that from 1988 onward, improved mass transit holds average number of cars per household constant, and average mileage driven per car-year constant at 10,000 (1 percent above the 1986 level). The saving would of course be larger in scenarios with less-efficient cars, since little fuel is saved by displacing a 60-mpg car. Still further savings, of course, are available from home occupation, mixed zoning, living nearer to where one wants to be, telecommunications, and other substitutes for physical mobility.

65. M. C. Holcomb et al., *Transportation Energy Data Book: Edition 9*, ORNL-6325, Oak Ridge National Laboratory, April 1987. During this five-year period, the use of "aerodynamic features," "variable fan drives," and "fuel economy engines" all more than doubled too, although their 1982 shares were only 8.3 percent, 27.5 percent, and 30.0 percent respectively.

66. A. and H. Lovins, F. Krause, and W. Bach, *Least-Cost Energy: Solving the CO_2 Problem* (Andover, Mass.: Brick House, 1982); G. Samuels, *Transportation Energy Requirements to the Year 2010*, ORNL-5745, 1981. Essentially identical technologies apply to buses.

67. SERI, *A New Prosperity: Building a Sustainable Energy Future* (Andover, Mass.: Brick House, 1981). This remains the most careful, complete, and knowledgeable federal efficiency analysis to date but was initially suppressed by the incoming Reagan administration, then published as a congressional committee print and by the private publisher Brick House. It was apparently placed on the administration's *Index Librorum Prohibitorum*, to be officially ignored and certainly not followed.

68. Evidence: During model years 1981–1987, the average efficiency of new cars (light trucks) rose 2.5 (2.1) mpg for domestic models seeking to avoid CAFE penalties and gas-guzzler taxes, but *fell* 0.5 (2.1) mpg for imports, which, though

selling to the same market, were almost all efficient enough to be untouched by the standards.

69. Compared with an assumed *retail* synfuel-product price of ~\$70/bbl (1981 \$), equivalent to \$1.67/gal. This seems realistic to low in view of actual performance: Those synfuel plants that work at all seem to be able to survive only with fixed-price purchase contracts and with upstream subsidies on the order of \$30–40/bbl. In late 1981, when we made the synfuels/scrappage comparison in many public forums, the estimated 1981-\$ plant-gate price of synfuels was estimated by such vendors as Exxon at ~\$45/bbl, but by early 1982, their estimates had soared to >\$100/bbl. These costs do not include the refining/marketing/distribution markup (normally ~\$12/bbl), nor kerogen's ~\$5/bbl refining premium.

70. Up to some rather high ceiling or subject to a sliding scale, as marginal savings diminish at high mpg.

71. We also approached the United Auto Workers, who in principle have long supported accelerated scrappage, but apparently the union's staff has not filled the analytic void either.

72. Energy and Environmental Analysis, Inc. (Arlington, Va.), "Energy Impacts of Accelerated Retirement of Less Efficient Passenger Cars," 17 October 1980 contract to USDOE Office of Policy Evaluation under contract #DE-AC01-79PE-70032.

73. Of course, it can use refinement, e.g., to take account of people's tendency to drive new cars more and old cars less.

74. L. Schipper and A. J. Lichtenberg, "Efficient Energy Use and Well-Being: The Swedish Example," *Science* 194:1001–13 at 1005 (1976).

75. And correspondingly in other sectors: E.g. financing, for an undercapitalized airline, the reengining of a low-bypass-engined 737 fleet on a shared-savings basis.

76. Yielding (ca. 1980) >4 MMB/D from cars and ~1.5 MMB/D more from light trucks, assuming an end-point fleet average of ~60 mpg. Efficiency gains since then have already captured ~1 MMB/D of that potential, but also permitted more ambitious end-point efficiencies at far lower marginal costs than were expected just a few years ago.

77. In addition, utilities in some regions, especially on the Gulf Coast, burn substantial amounts of natural gas to make electricity, especially to meet the peak loads arising from buildings' space-conditioning needs. The 1986 oil and gas use by U.S. electric utilities, prorated by the residential and commercial sectors' share of annual electric sales (a conservative procedure, since it neglects peaking requirements and peaking plants' lower heat rates), adds to the direct consumption an indirect consumption of 1.67 q of gas and 0.90 q of oil. The total use of gas and oil in buildings in 1986 was thus about 8.64 and 3.47 q respectively—a total of 12.11 q/y.

78. Many countries and some parts of the U.S. operate fleet vehicles on compressed natural gas; LPG operation is also common; methane can be shift-reacted to methanol using classical technology; and the Shell process to convert methane directly to gasoline shows promise of being able to be simplified to

one catalytic step, bringing its cost into an interesting range. By various methods, over varying scales of time and costs, therefore, conserving natural gas can considerably expand the range of oil-saving transportation options for direct vehicular-fuel substitution as well as for displacing oil from boiler fuel as a vehicular-fuel source.

79. Or one-and-four-fifths times the Gulf imports if indirect use by utilities is included.

80. For simplicity and conservatism, two additional kinds of savings—the free reduction in air-conditioning loads in the fueled buildings (through the shell improvements already paid for to save space heating) and the potential to save electric heating and cooling loads through similar improvements in all-electric buildings—are omitted here, though both can yield significant and quite cheap oil savings beyond those already discussed.

81. Renamed "Central Command" (USCENTCOMM) in 1983; see T. Sabonis-Chafee, op. cit. supra.

82. For illustration, Raventhal's authoritative estimate of the FY1985 cost of Gulf forces, which are only a small portion of those allocated to Central Command, is $47 billion per year (ibid.) or a fifth of the entire nonstrategic force budget for FY1985. A more reasonable estimate of Central Command's budget, with overheads allocated, might be about a quarter of nonnuclear forces, or about $59 billion in FY1985. Using the lower figure, and assuming LBL's generously high average 1986-$ cost of $10/bbl for saved energy (space heating only, 1979 technologies) and a 20-year nominal measure lifetime, $47 billion would buy ~0.64 MMB/D of savings. Since the $10/bbl average cost corresponds to a larger saving than necessary—1.4 MMB/D—to displace Gulf imports, we should actually use LBL's cost for saving only the first ~0.6 MMB/D of fuel (space heating only, 1979 technologies). That cost, $4.75/bbl, implies that $47 billion would buy not ~0.64 but ~1.36 MMB/D of savings. In contrast, Gulf imports during 1984–1986 averaged 0.57 MMB/D—less than half the savings available for one year's Gulf-force cost.

83. Full R-11 wrap, bottom board (rigid insulation under the tank), anticonvection loops or valves (or ~15′ pipe insulation near the heater), 120°F setback, 1.5-gpm showerheads, warm-wash/cool-rinse laundry, and faucet aerators with fingertip controls. Such retrofits, if well designed, provide service equivalent or superior to original performance. Additional savings are cheaply available from stack dampers and from electric (pilotless) ignition.

84. Alpen, Inc., of Boulder, Colorado, has commercially provided R-10 glazings and can provide ~R-12 on request. (Windows in that range use two heat mirror films, an optional low-emissivity coating on one of the panes of glass, and an advanced gas fill—either krypton or krypton/CO_2.) Rocky Mountain Institute's headquarters, in an 8700-F° -d/y climate with temperatures down to −47°F, is heated by the passive gain from older Alpen glazings rated at R-5.4 or, in a few cases, at ~R-6.7 or R-9.1.

85. Comprising 1.09 q for asphalt and road oil, 0.29 q as lubricant, 0.73 q as petrochemical feedstock, 0.82 q in the form of LPG as feedstock, 0.13 q as petroleum coke, the same as special naphtha (another feedstock), and 0.14 q

as wax and other miscellaneous products: EIA, *Annual Energy Review 1986*, p. 15.

86. And better understanding of asphalt. Although the United States spends more than a billion dollars a year on asphalt, so little is known of its composition and behavior that the reasons for the failure of certain batches, and acceptance testing techniques to avoid such failures, are still unknown. Such appalling ignorance of the basic properties of a basic economic material, accounting (with road oil) for 3.4 percent of total U.S. oil consumption, would surely not be tolerated in any area less institutionally backward than infrastructural technology.

87. The Gas Research Institute (Paul Holtberg, personal communication, 30 December 1987) estimated that as of 1985, all of the boiler fuel and ~40 percent of the process heaters can switch from residual oil to natural gas with a couple of years' lead time. (Short-term gas-to-resid-switchable capacity totaled ~1.5 q/y; total resid boiler fuel, half that.) It might be objected that the 0.75 q of residual oil used as boiler fuel cannot be displaced because it has no other use; but it can be cracked to lighter products, and over the long run, refinery modernization will greatly reduce its output. As one oil-major CEO remarked, "Why should we make it resid? It's like coal, and we already have more coal than we can sell." Curiously, the same people who argue that resid cannot be displaced in industry often assert that building more coal-fired and nuclear power plants can displace the oil still burned by electric utilities, even though 94 percent of that oil (as of 1986) is resid.

88. A modest fraction of those technologies involve substitution of electricity for fuel—for example, in ultraviolet or microwave paint drying and curing—but those additional uses of electricity seem likely to be far smaller than industrial electric *savings* through adjustable-speed motor drives and a host of other electricity-specific efficiency improvements. We estimate that ~13 classes of efficiency improvements to existing industrial drive systems can save roughly half of their input electricity, at average costs ~0.3–0.5¢/kwh.

89. Corresponding to a 3 percent increase in industrial primary energy use with a 48 percent increase in industrial value added.

90. The actual pattern was a 12.9 percent fall in industrial primary energy use with a 25.1 percent rise in real industrial output—i.e., a 30.4 percent decrease in energy intensity or a 43.6 percent increase in energy productivity.

91. Schipper and Lichtenberg (op. cit. supra) showed that in the mid-1970s it was about a third more energy efficient than U.S. industry, despite its greater share of the most energy-intensive products. Its efficiency has since improved by probably as much in percentage terms as has that of U.S. industry.

92. T. B. Johansson et al., *I Stället för Kärnkraft; Energi Ar 2000*, DsI 1983:18 (Stockholm, Industridepartementet), summarized in *Science* 219:355–361 (1983).

93. In correspondence currently in press at the *Atlantic*, Charles Ebinger and Mark Mills, *Atlantic*, June 1988, p. 10, claimed a $14 billion-a-year oil saving. Although this figure appears to be exaggerated, even taken at face value it is hardly a good buy, since the total cost of the electric capacity built to achieve that displacement exceeds $300 billion, not even counting its operating costs—which, for a typical (trouble-prone) U.S. nuclear plant, exceed those of an oil

plant, based on exhaustive empirical data from Komanoff Energy Associates in New York.

94. Of course, this sensitivity would vary by region, and it reflects only first-order sensitivity, not counting possible cross-effects on the prices of other fuels or of capital. Data used in this paragraph's calculations are from EIA's *Monthly Energy Review,* March 1987, and Edison Electric Institute's (EEI's) *1986 Statistical Yearbook* (Washington, D.C.).

95. EEI construction expenditures (excluding the allowance for funds used during construction—AFUDC) for investor-owned utilities (IOUs), divided by 0.8 (IOUs' sales share) as a rough surrogate for including corresponding investments by public utilities.

96. As of FY1984. H. R. Heede and A. B. Lovins, "Hiding the True Cost of Energy Sources, *Wall Street Journal,* 17 September 1985, p. 28. Heede found that in FY1984, electrical technologies received about $30 billion (b) in direct Federal subsidies—65 percent of the >$46b/y total—even though they supplied only 13 percent of the delivered energy. Electricity, per Btu supplied, was about 11 times as heavily subsidized as were directly used fossil fuels. A dollar of subsidy to nuclear power (which got nearly $16b in subsidies—about equal to the annual retail revenues of all nuclear plants then operating) yielded about 1/80 as much energy as a dollar of subsidy to efficiency and to nonhydro renewables. It is of course these two latter classes of technologies that had their subsidies virtually abolished and nuclear power that had its subsidies largely maintained or increased.

97. Specifically, the average cost is certainly below 1¢/kwh and probably nearer .5¢/kwh (1986 $ @ 5 percent/y real discount rate). The latter cost is equivalent in its heat content—not in terms of the price of oil that would have to be burned to make the same amount of electricity—to electricity at ~$8.6/bbl. However, the average cost of saving half of the present total electrical use is approximately zero—because the first ~120 gw of savings (in lighting and its associated net heating, ventilation, and air conditioning [HVAC] energy) has a strongly negative cost, due to maintenance savings that more than pay for the measures themselves. That negative cost counterbalances small positive costs for a roughly equal increment of nonlighting measures. All these opportunities, and practical ways to implement them with high saturation, speed, and confidence, are exhaustively documented by Rocky Mountain Institute's COMPETITEK℠ quarterly update service. A semitechnical summary of salient options is in A. B. Lovins's August 1987 testimony to and for the District of Columbia Public Service Commission (RMI Publication #87-6), which ordered a major efficiency program begun in spring 1988. A technical analysis of how to save ~75–80 percent of the electricity used in existing Austin buildings, at average costs <0.9¢/kwh, is *Advanced Electricity-Saving Technologies and the South Texas Project,* 1986 (RMI Publication #87-7).

98. Accounting for all avoidable operating costs, however—including all O & M (not just its short-term variable component) and net capital additions—reveals that the typical U.S. nuclear plant has levelized operating costs, all avoidable by shutdown, in the vicinity of 5¢/kwh. That is generally more than for coal-fired and often more than even for oil- or gas-fired plants, so in principle,

many nuclear plants, on strict economic-dispatch grounds, might be backed out even before many oil plants.

99. At first it might appear that for operational reasons, much of this small- and intermediate-load-factor capacity would in fact continue to operate, since large solid-fueled plants often exhibit poor load following and slow ramp rates. In practice, however, electric end-use efficiency and load management, along with better integration of hydropower and cogeneration resources, can largely if not wholly obviate this concern.

100. North American Electric Reliability Council (Princeton, N.J.), *1987 Electricity Supply & Demand,* p. 25.

101. This relies on the technically conservative SERI analysis. Watson's extended light-vehicle CAFE standards, reaching only 48 mpg for new cars and 33 for new light trucks by 2000, would yield a net saving (subtracting DOE's "market"-case projection) of 1.8 q/y. Far larger light-vehicle savings could be achieved by 2000 through any combination of higher efficiency levels and (more importantly) accelerated scrappage. The 1:88:1 crude:gasoline ratio is assumed here to be 1:1.

102. Applying SERI's projected 58 percent fuel savings in all buildings to 1986 oil use in buildings yields 1.08 q/y in oil savings, but in practice there would probably be more incentive to save oil than gas.

103. *Energy Security,* March 1987, p. 94.

104. This could be achieved just by LBL's space-heating savings in fueled buildings (costing an average of $20/bbl with 1979 technologies), to say nothing of savings in water heating and in all-electric buildings.

105. Assuming the ANL-85N2 stock forecast (134.8 million cars and 54.5 million personal light trucks) in 2000, 1,543 and 303 billion vehicle-miles per year respectively, and base-case efficiencies of 27 and 15 mpg respectively.

106. For an introduction, see our summaries in *Brittle Power: Energy Strategy for National Security* (Andover, Mass.: Brick House, 1981), pp. 358–363; in *Energy Unbound: A Fable for America's Future* (with Seth Zuckerman) (San Francisco: Sierra Club/Random House, 1986), pp. 124ff.; and with Marty Bender in W. Jackson et al., ed., *Meeting the Expectations of the Land* (San Francisco: North Point Press, 1984), pp. 68–86.

107. A. B. and L. H. Lovins, "The Fragility of Domestic Energy," *Atlantic,* November 1983, at p. 126.

108. Cost estimates at the time ranged up to at least tenfold lower than this. More recent estimates suggested that the average costs of such efficiency gains (as opposed to the marginal cost of the last increment of savings) probably fall into the range $0–10/bbl—more consonant with the costs of eliminating most of the heat-flows through building shells.

109. EM-4815-SR, 1986.

110. In *Least-Cost Energy* (op. cit. supra), for example, we showed how full use of 1980 efficiency-and-renewables technologies, cost effective at 1980 prices, could support a world of eight billion people with five times today's total economic activity (a tenfold increase in developing countries), yet eliminate dependence on Middle Eastern oil and on most other fuel resources. Goldemberg et al., op. cit. infra, have convincingly extended this work.

111. Extensive details and some 1,200 references can be found in our Pentagon analysis *Brittle Power,* op. cit. supra, summarized in *Atlantic,* November 1983, pp. 118–126.

112. See A. B. Lovins, *Wall Street Journal,* 1 May 1987, op. cit. supra; "Comments on the Draft *Arctic National Wildlife Refuge, Alaska, Coastal Plain Resource Assessment,*" RMI Publication #87-2; and response to AIP Critique #020, RMI Publication #88-5.

113. *Least-Cost Energy,* op. cit. supra, summarized in *Climatic Change* 4:217–220 (1982).

114. D. J. Rose et al., *Technology Review,* May/June 1984, pp. 49–58; J. Goldemberg et al., *Energy for a Sustainable World* (Washington, D.C.: World Resources Institute, 1987). RMI researchers W. N. Keepin and G. Kats will shortly publish an analysis showing that nuclear power, contrary to widely held assumptions, cannot in principle be of much help with the CO_2 problem and indeed makes it worse by diverting investment from cheaper, faster efficiency improvements.

115. H. Geller et al., *Acid Rain and Electricity Conservation* (Washington, D.C.: American Council for an Energy-Efficient Economy, 1987).

116. In *Energy/War: Breaking the Nuclear Link* (Friends of the Earth, 1980) summarized (with Leonard Rose) in *Foreign Affairs* 58(5):1137–77 (Summer 1980); with Patrick O'Heffernan (senior author) in *The First Nuclear World War* (New York: Norton, 1983); and in numerous technical papers cited in those works.

117. A. B. Lovins, *Development Forum* (Geneva: United Nations, September 1986), p. 4.

8

The Oil Market and Production Control

Alirio A. Parra

The international oil industry is still passing through the aftermath of recent turbulence. Oil markets everywhere are in a state of transition characterized by accelerated structural change and determined moves by the producers to integrate downstream. At the same time, doubts are being raised as to whether OPEC can adapt to the new market circumstances and effectively implement strategies that are valid both for short-run stability and for longer-run growth.

Perhaps the meeting in Vienna in April 1988 between OPEC and a group of independent oil producers was the first concrete sign of a move toward a realignment of responsibilities among the world's oil producers. It is within the framework of recent market developments that the evolving strategies of OPEC can be better understood. The extent to which they may allow the oil industry to operate in a more stable environment in the next few years will depend on their acceptance by all producers at large. In the longer run, reintegration should add strength to the process of stabilization and reestablish the internal control mechanisms of the industry itself.

The events surrounding the collapse of world oil prices in 1986 have had a significant impact on our thinking today. For many, it was a year in which the world seemed to turn upside down. The oil industry went through a period of tremendous turbulence and unprecedented change. Price volatility in the markets made planning and investment decisions even more difficult than usual and led to the postponement or slowing of many new exploration and production ventures. By the end of 1986, it was obvious that this violent upheaval had benefited no one, not even the consumers. More importantly, it dramatized the fundamental situation of the oil industry as one of massive cyclical imbalances between potential supplies and real consumption requirements, imbalances that may take a period of years to work themselves out. Indeed excess capacity exists in nearly all segments of the business, from production to refining to distribution. With hindsight of course, it should have been evident that the price collapse was inevitable. The previous OPEC pricing regime had been rigid and inflexible and quite inappropriate in times of sharply falling demand. Rigid prices gave impetus to the role of OPEC as a marginal producer with consequences that went far beyond the policies that had motivated this stance.

The fixed-pricing regime was intended to provide stability, but in fact it had a number of negative consequences with quite the opposite effect. By holding prices up in an unresponsive way, it dissociated producers from market realities. Demand was dampened excessively and the development of new and quite often high-cost production was encouraged in non-OPEC countries. Long-term price elasticities were effectively ignored. The combination of declining demand and growing non-OPEC supplies led to the loss of market share for the organization, equivalent to some 13 million barrels per day compared to ten years before. As market size shrank, internal tensions within OPEC and external downside pressures were aggravated by the overhang of potential production and the rising availability of non-OPEC supplies, which were assured a market under the OPEC umbrella. These past policies progressively eroded the ability of the organization to maintain stable industry conditions. To someone looking back, it is most surprising that market cause and effect were ignored for so long and change in the system was not instituted earlier. What OPEC had failed to do was to understand change and to shift from the approach of fixing and defending prices at levels impossible to defend except over the briefest periods of time to a more flexible and market-oriented system.

In late 1985, in an overreaction to a further dwindling of the market, controls on supply were suddenly relaxed, as member countries sought to regain outlets for their oil by competing for markets. The "fair share" that OPEC wished to regain was never defined clearly in terms of either volume or timing. Few members had any real concept of what market share was being sought. What should have been a longer-term strategy was compressed into a few months, with unwelcome effects for just about every market participant. Additional production came onto the market without an adequate corresponding increase in demand. Prices declined by two-thirds and volatility reached undreamt of proportions. For OPEC, it meant that revenues had declined not only through loss of markets but also because of the plummeting of prices. For other producers, the situation was equally serious, as the economic basis for new exploration was undermined, whereas for the consumers, global energy policies were endangered.

The events of 1986 only served to emphasize what was already known, that fundamental change in the energy markets is a long-term phenomenon. For example, substantial changes in prices do not produce changes in consumption immediately, and individual producers are not pressured to cut back production as prices decline because the producers' behavior is dictated by high initial capital costs and relatively low operating costs. Incremental production is cheap, thus encouraging "excess" output. It soon became clear, even to those who thought otherwise, that there are no automatic correctives, even painful ones, to imbalances in supply and demand. As with many industrial structures, for competition to produce benefits as opposed to upheaval, the "rules of the game" must be spelled out. Without some form of restraint on output in an oversupply situation, prices tend to drop toward the marginal cost of production.

The brief flirtation with a totally free market did not work. In effect, the market came to realize that the only practical way of bringing a significant degree of stability to prices, given surplus producing capacity within and outside OPEC, is supply management in its broadest sense, that is, the effective "proration" or limitation of worldwide supplies to bring them more closely in line with requirements. Historically, stability in the oil market has only been achieved in periods when supply has been administered. In this respect, there is a growing and perhaps reluctant acceptance that without OPEC, the possibility of a stable and secure environment is remote indeed. The immediate impact of the price crash in the summer of 1986 was unfortunate in many ways because consumption did not respond significantly and non-OPEC supplies were only reduced briefly. It did, however, set in motion changes in the fundamental parameters and in the positioning of OPEC for the future, changes that may ultimately be to the benefit of us all. New directions and fresh perceptions were becoming evident.

As a result of lower prices, the opportunity for growth in demand opened up once again. The conventional wisdom points to a demand curve that is disappointingly almost flat. Estimates indicate that oil use will increase at best by about 1–1.5 percent per year up to 1995. This comes to about one-quarter to one-half of the rate of growth of economic activity. However, in my opinion, global demand is hampered by the price rises of 1979–1980. The apparent resurgence of consumption in 1988 may represent the initial stages of the longer-run response to lower prices as some of the conservation measures work themselves out and the application of new energy efficient technologies is postponed. If this turns out to be true, it points the way to growth rates for oil of 1.5 percent or more. Under such conditions, a market size for OPEC oil of about 22 million barrels per day could be within reach, in say, five years. Such a scenario definitely eases the pressure on prices, but by no means does it eliminate it. Even under optimistic scenarios, demand cannot soak up the extensive shut-in potential and at the same time accommodate probable increases in production outside the OPEC area. In the light of this discussion the need for a measured approach to market management is necessary, at least for a period of years.

Until quite recently, many of us believed that production outside the OPEC area was flattening out. This may now not be the case. Since the late 1970s, some thirty-seven non-OPEC producers either expanded output or saw their first commercial production. The international oil industry is more diverse: There are more companies and more traders and, what is more important, more exporting nations. Over the four years 1985–1988, excluding the UK and United States, output is estimated to have increased by almost 1.5 million barrels per day. The main characteristics of these new producers include high initial investment costs; rapid pace of oil field development and in many cases an assured market within the integrated networks of the majors. Output may well continue to increase beyond the beginning of the next decade. In effect, these producers may now be the key variable influencing future price behavior.

It is within this framework that we must view OPEC's former actions relating to prices and supplies. In the past, as we have seen, OPEC has functioned somewhat imperfectly and often indecisively by switching back and forth between emphasis on fixed prices and reliance on production controls. This has hampered its role as a market regulator. To protect member country income, OPEC insisted on high per barrel revenue, to the exclusion of all other considerations. Then, for one brief period, all restraints were relaxed, and blind faith was placed on incremental revenues. To say the least, the results were disappointing. Apart from other policy considerations, until quite recently the OPEC stance encouraged major industrial consumers to move away from dependence on oil from member countries. Conversely, producers outside the OPEC area were encouraged to maximize output at prices well above those they would have received if the umbrella had been withdrawn.

In my view, all this is now changing, albeit very slowly, toward a more sophisticated approach to volume management. This would require realism and flexibility in OPEC's attitudes and the active participation of other producers. Together they would wish to promote the stabilization of oil markets at reasonably remunerative price levels. Fixed prices are important both in policy terms and because of market psychology. However, it has been next to impossible for the organization to agree upon one fixed price for any length of time and then to modify this price as required. In view of this, and perhaps because it approximates more closely market realities, a pricing band or range may be appropriate to accommodate the normal short-term fluctuations of supply and demand. The pricing band should only be seen as a supporting mechanism underpinning the essential commitment to a target price, which is presently U.S. $18 per barrel, but which would vary in the future. However, without a "trigger" mechanism on the downside, it is quite possible that the producers would find themselves selling the same amount of oil at lower and lower prices.

In actual practice, the present OPEC agreement—applicable for 1987–1988—already places a strong emphasis on volume as the main regulator of the system. Unfortunately, the essential approach to volume management, the feature that would have given the system the flexibility and sophistication to meet today's changing requirements, has apparently been abandoned. The recognition of seasonal factors is vital, if price fluctuations are to be reduced. The agreement incorporated an official selling price for a basket of crudes that brought back the concept of "residualism" as the center of the OPEC approach to stability. As a residual producer, OPEC would continue to reflect and bear the full brunt of international energy uncertainties.

It now seems that prices have moved away from OSPs to a concept of a "floating price" along with a pricing band; thus OPEC has moved away from being the swing producer for the world's energy markets. For the most part contracts are now made on the basis of this so-called floating price, in reality a market-related one. Nevertheless, U.S. $18 per barrel remains very much the target price. The question of market share is not being discussed, at least officially, but the concept is not by any means dead. In practical terms, quotas set for a given period can be viewed as the market share that OPEC wishes to maintain.

The basic problem confronting the producers' meeting in Vienna was the continuing erosion of prices and the reluctance of OPEC to act alone again. In addition, in spite of the so-called floating prices, member countries have still been losing market share to the non-OPEC producers. This clearly demonstrates that in order to move toward U.S. $18, it is now necessary for the non-OPEC producers to assist in supporting the market. As we now know, the task of managing the world oil market by volume controls cannot be carried out by OPEC alone. Quite succinctly, there are a number of very fundamental reasons for this:

- Present production quotas still leave little room for maneuver, so that small temporary changes in demand can have a magnified effect on prices.
- New inflexibilities in the OPEC system point to a minimum production level of around 18 million barrels per day. Production quotas below that level would be unstable and impossible to fully implement.

- Neither the ability nor the desire to swing to accommodate variations in demand or increases in supply outside OPEC is present anymore.

In this sense the future behavior of non-OPEC producers is critical to the market, to OPEC, and to themselves. Their weight is increasing, total production is now higher than that for the OPEC area, and finally, export volumes are similar to OPEC's. These producers can no longer afford to hold disparate policies in a market in which they exercise considerable influence.

The question should be asked: Can we achieve a more positive oil environment in the face of structurally weak market fundamentals? That will depend on the internal cohesion of the organization, which is suffering from severe strains caused by technical factors concerning the size and distribution of the quota, differences in pricing philosophy, and the effect of political tensions. It also rests on the willingness of non-OPEC producers to recognize their common interest in a system that could provide stability at a cost well below that of any other option. More than anything, the system needs time because of the slow response of demand to price changes.

It is within this context that we should see the recent historic meeting between OPEC and the independent oil producers represented by Angola, China, Colombia, Egypt, Malaysia, and Oman. It represented an explicit recognition that all producers have a common interest and that it is only possible to balance supply with perceived demand if there is an effective and cooperative effort. In other words, the independent oil producers now acknowledge that they are an integral part of the "supply package." They understand that whatever happens to OPEC also affects them. The success of this package will depend to a significant extent on the degree of cooperation that the independent oil-producing countries believe they can afford. Nothing could be more relevant for stability until 1990.

Although the offer by the independent producers to cut 5 percent of their current exports, equivalent to 183,000 barrels per day, has not been acted upon by OPEC, without doubt we are entering the first phase of a longer-term cooperation between all producing countries. The economic foundations for these moves are evident. In a soft market, the cost of depletion constraints may well be considerably lower than allowing the capital stock to drain away from their exploration and production activities. It would appear that we may be moving toward the creation of a small, strategic, shut-in production potential of a short-term nature in some of the independent oil-producing countries.

The immediate considerations as they related to the independent oil producers are basically tied to the volatility of prices, but over a longer period it is essential for them to look at production policies. Countries in the early stages of oil development should take a longer view of investments and lengthen rather than shorten the cycle so as to avoid the bunching of new production. Many of the new producers, when developing their own reserves, would benefit if they took a leaf from the Mexican and Norwegian experience.

In the longer run, a greater degree of reintegration appears to be desirable if a limit is to be placed on the more volatile aspects of market forces over any term. The scope for internal adjustments has been reduced, whereas previously the integrated system of the majors had infinite opportunities to correct imbalances. The flow of crude oil throughout the system was tightly coordinated, with the net result being a sophisticated mechanism of internal controls that sought to balance, to the extent possible, demand requirements with supply availability. At this time, the possibility of mismatching between supply and demand is permanently present.

One trend in the right direction that should be mentioned here is the move by a number of producers into downstream operations in the consuming countries. Although integration by a few producers does not provide the full answer to price stability, it does give an assurance as to market size for the competing firms. In addition, it should give back the structural strength to the chain of activities that normally constitute the oil industry. A more fully integrated industry would still have to operate in a competitive environment but, at the same time, would give a greater guarantee of permanence in the main consuming areas, thereby reducing the dangers of extreme volatility by continuous adjustment to market factors. I feel sure that there is no conflict between horizontal integration, which essentially provides linkages between producers, and vertical integration, which gives firms a stable place in the market. Each complements the other. Reintegration, as it proceeds further, would tend to be characterized by fewer participants and, what is more important, by a smaller trading sector, which would assume its traditional clearinghouse role. By tying producing companies into the main markets, the interests of producers and consumers would become permanently linked together. In a sense the energy security concerns of the past would become less visible in future.

In this respect, the consuming countries will play a critical role in the evolution of energy markets. In fact, a continuous process of interaction between producers and consumers may be just as important in the longer term as restraint and cooperative efforts among producers in the short term. From a positive perspective, I hope that would help to eliminate the present bias regarding oil from the energy policies of the industrial countries and perhaps lead to some rethinking of the concept of energy security. It is necessary to restore an environment of mutual confidence that will encourage consumers not to switch further away from oil and that will dampen the misallocation of resources in high-cost alternatives. The sharp increase in world proven reserves during the past decade and their diverse geographical nature should certainly lead to some new and positive thinking in this direction. Consumers would place much greater reliance on abundant and varied supplies that were not subject to the volatility of recent years. What is needed is a new framework of understanding.

In closing, I would like again to pose the question: Is a more orderly oil and energy environment achievable or are we condemned to move along the path of uncertainty and volatility? Much depends on the convergence of views among all market participants. Broad-based supply management can bring with it a sense of less uncertainty and give the industry and the consumer a perception of stability. There are some formidable barriers to overcome if we are to achieve far-reaching solutions. The political will to restore and maintain order in the markets would be further reaffirmed as more independent oil producers firmly identify their common interest with OPEC and the organization confronts its internal divisions. If any of us have doubts, I am hopeful that the events witnessed in summer 1986 will continue to be a powerful incentive for greater interaction and integration among OPEC, the independent oil producers, and the consumers, an incentive for an ordered market for oil that can be the foundation for growth and prosperity.

9

The Future of Independent Oil Refiners in the United States

Robert G. Reed III

The demise of the independent oil refiner[1] has gone largely unnoticed amid the clamor over energy security, oil prices, the search for new sources of crude, Middle East political crises, and the larger issues facing the world. The tremendous decline in the number of independent oil refineries has been ignored in the midst of plentiful oil supplies and abundant quantities of petroleum products. The absence of the independent refiner from the oil scene has not been missed by those who have stepped in to fill the void. The names of once-proud, now-troubled independent refiners fill the pages of business and industry journals. Bankruptcy proceedings or buyouts nowadays seem to be the terms most associated with the independent refiner. As the independent disappears from the oil industry, those who remain can only ask why.

The failure of any business enterprise can be blamed on many factors—management, the inability to compete effectively, or a lack of capital. For the independent refiner, these factors hold true, and so do many more. Whereas all sectors of the oil industry have been adversely affected at some time by the volatility of the oil market, the independent refiner perhaps has been most subject to the unpredictability of the marketplace and most unprepared to adequately cope with the situation.

According to the U.S. Department of Energy, 24 refineries throughout the nation closed in 1985, marking the fourth straight year of net declines in operable refineries. Between 1981 and 1985, a total of 101 refineries closed their doors (see Table 9.1). Ironically, these closures came on the heels of a remarkable expansion in refining capacity, which began in 1974 and added 56 units to the number of operable refineries in the United States. At the peak of the expansion in 1981, the number of refineries totaled 324, the highest number since the Korean War.

TABLE 9.1
Refinery Capacity and Utilization, 1949–1984 (MMB/D, Except as Noted)

	Operable Refineries Number[a]	Operable Refineries Capacity[b]	Gross Input to Distillation Units	Utilization[c] (percent)
1949	336	6.23	5.56	89.2
1950	320	6.22	5.98	92.5
1951	325	6.70	6.76	97.5
1952	327	7.16	6.93	93.8
1953	315	7.62	7.26	93.1
1954	308	7.98	7.27	88.8
1955	296	8.39	7.82	92.2
1956	317	8.58	8.25	93.5
1957	317	9.07	8.22	89.2
1958	315	9.36	8.02	83.9
1959	313	9.76	8.36	85.2
1960	309	9.84	8.44	85.1
1961	309	10.00	8.57	85.7
1962	309	10.01	8.83	88.2
1963	304	10.01	9.14	90.0
1964	298	10.31	9.28	89.6
1965	293	10.42	9.56	91.8
1966	280	10.39	9.99	94.9
1967	276	10.66	10.39	94.4
1968	282	11.35	10.89	94.5
1969	279	11.70	11.25	94.8
1970	276	12.02	11.52	92.6
1971	272	12.86	11.88	90.9
1972	274	13.29	12.43	92.3
1973	268	13.64	13.15	93.9
1974	273	14.36	12.69	86.6
1975	279	14.96	12.90	85.5
1976	276	15.24	13.88	87.8
1977	282	16.40	14.98	89.6
1978	296	17.05	15.07	87.4
1979	308	17.44	14.96	84.4
1980	319	17.99	13.80	75.4
1981	324	18.62	12.75	68.6
1982	301	17.89	12.17	69.9
1983	258	16.86	11.95	71.7
1984	247	16.14	12.22	76.2
1985[d]	223	15.66	12.18	77.6

[a]Prior to 1956, the number of refineries includes only those in operation on January 1. For 1957 and forward, the number of refineries includes all operable refineries on January 1.

[b]Capacity in million barrels per calendar day on January 1.

[c]For 1919 through 1980, utilization is derived by dividing gross input to distillation units by one half of the current year January 1 capacity and the following year January 1 capacity. Percentages were derived from unrounded numbers. For 1981 and forward, utilization is derived by averaging reported monthly utilization.

[d]Preliminary.

Note: Data are for refineries in the United States, excluding the Hawaiian Foreign Trade Zone.

Source: Energy Information Administration, *Annual Energy Review 1985* (Washington, D.C.: Department of Energy, 1986), Table 53.

Although some of the closures were smaller units of the major oil companies, the majority were small, independent refiners, usually inflexible and unsophisticated in their operations. For these independents, a complex and highly competitive environment spelled almost certain doom. These closures certainly took their toll on the refinery employees, investors, and individuals or businesses associated with this sector of the industry. Yet while the numbers may be shocking, this shakeout has produced economic benefits that have ultimately streamlined the industry and helped the market. The shakeout has spelled an end to overcapacity in the refining sector and an end to the unsophisticated, inefficient refiners that are unable to meet the demands of an ever-changing world (see Figure 9.1).

Whatever the future of independent refiners, their demise can be attributed to many causes, chief among them being:

- The unintended consequences of the federal oil entitlements program
- The inability to gain access to competitively priced crude oil
- The simplicity of the independent refineries, their lack of downstream capabilities, and their lack of adequate capital to implement an aggressive expansion program
- The inability to meet stringent, highly costly environmental standards imposed by the federal and state governments
- Government-mandated changes in petroleum product specifications, primarily related to environmental concerns
- Strong competition from the major oil companies and the invasion of niche markets by competitors
- Chaotic conditions in the crude oil market

Entitlements Program

The former entitlements program, which was called the Old Oil Allocation or Entitlements Program, was created by the federal government to address perceived inequities in U.S. refiners' crude oil acquisition costs during the Arab oil embargo and postembargo period.

The program was a system of price and and allocation controls that sought to equalize U.S. refiners' crude oil acquisition costs by distributing the benefits of access to lower-priced domestic crude oil proportionately to all domestic refiners through a system of monetary rather than physical transfers. Crude costs were equalized by requiring refiners to buy or sell entitlements based on whether their access to domestic oil was higher or lower than the national average. Refiners with greater access were required to purchase entitlements; refiners using foreign crude had to sell the entitlements.

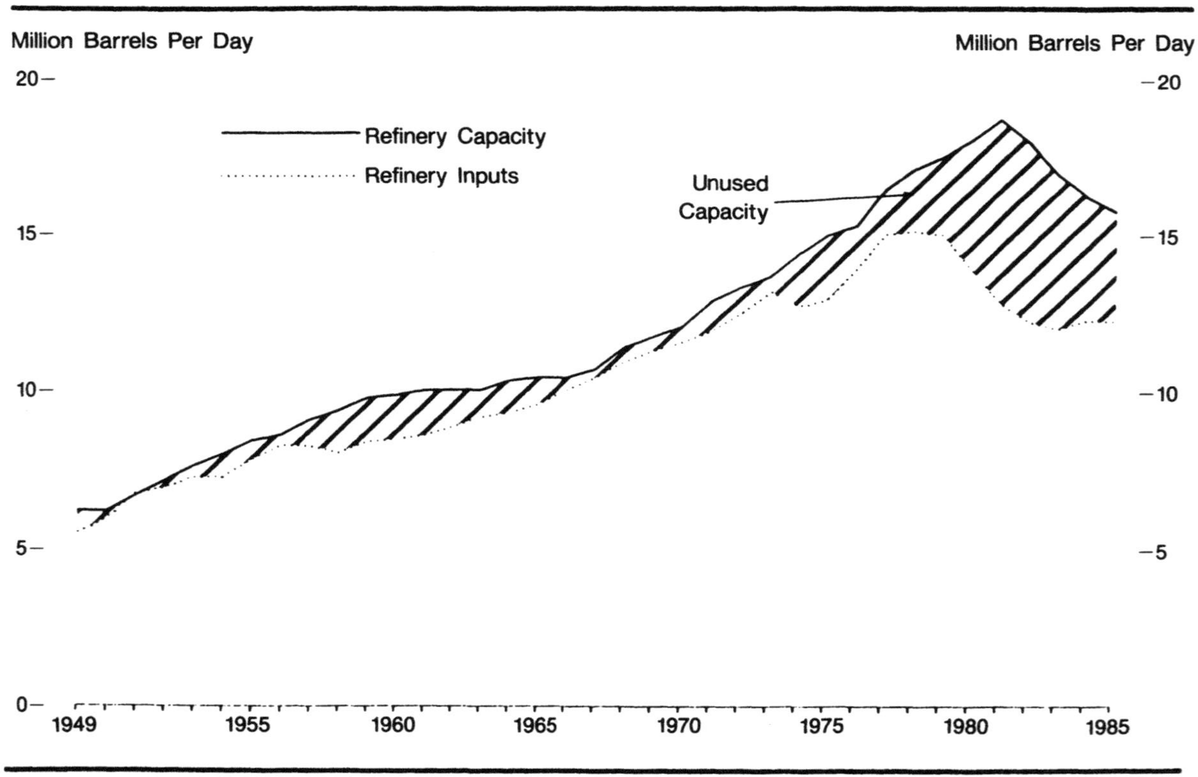

FIGURE 9.1 Refinery capacity and utilization, 1949–1985.
Source: Energy Information Administration, *Annual Energy Review 1985* (Washington, D.C.: Department of Energy, 1986), Figure 53.

A key element of this program was a "small refiner bias." This was compensation awarded to small refiners to offset their lack of economies of scale and higher operating and capital costs. It partially exempted small refiners—those under 175 MB/D capacity—from entitlements purchase requirements or awarded them additional entitlements to sell. The system awarded the greatest benefits to refiners running 10 MB/D or less.

The National Petroleum Council assessed the consequences of the small refiner bias this way:

> In the first two years after the small refiner bias program was implemented, 24 new refineries of less than 30 MB/D were built or reopened in the United States. During the seven years of U.S. price and allocation controls, more than 60 refineries of less than 30 MB/D were built, over two-thirds of which were under 10 MB/D. The bulk of these refineries were built only to take advantage of the subsidies available rather than to contribute to supplies of refined product.[2]

When the entitlements were eventually abolished, many of the small, independent refineries, no longer eligible for the subsidies, were unable to compete. The demise of these companies is reflected in the steady rise in refineries through 1981 and the rapid decline in the years since.

Access to Crude Oil

Many independent refiners have been unable to gain access to competitively priced crude oil, especially from foreign sources. The major oil companies are owners or partners in the exploration and production sectors of the industry, giving them a major advantage in the dependability, quality, and quantity of their crude supply. In most cases, the majors pay lower prices because they receive service fees (for example, from Saudi Arabia) or equity margins in consideration of their past capital investments (for example, from Indonesia, Nigeria, or Abu Dhabi). The independent refiner, meanwhile, depends in large part on the largesse of the major for its supply.

The majors, with their vast international or national networks, benefit from the economies of scale in importing and refining, an advantage unavailable to the small, independent refiner. Whereas the majors import and market in large quantities, the independent refiner makes small, periodic purchases of crude and is consequently left at the mercy of the majors for scheduling of deliveries and types of crude, key factors in determining the product slate and availability.

In addition, many of the independents operate in the shadow of the majors. The majors will dictate the price paid for crude, a price that must be matched by the independent refiner. The economies of scale of the independent refiner also make it necessary that crude be purchased from nearby sources to minimize transportation or pipeline costs. However, the limitations inherent in this method become evident as the refiner then is forced to use only one type of crude, often of lower quality, and is also unable to change the product slate to meet changing market demands. The result is the inability to be competitive.

Lack of Sophistication, Lack of Capital

The independent refineries that have closed lacked two important elements: sophisticated equipment that could accommodate a wide range of crudes and manufacture a wide range of products; and capital to upgrade their equipment and expand their downstream capabilities. The lack of sophistication of the independent refineries precluded them from processing different types of crude and refining them into products to meet market needs. In addition, without any downstream capability to market their products, these enterprises were left to find buyers for whatever they could produce, often at a less-than-competitive price. Lacking the capacity and the market, they were unable to prove themselves worthy of investment. Refineries cost millions to construct, whereas existing ones constantly need improvements and expansion. The search for capital is a never-ending one.

Independent producers obtain funds by selling oil rights and forming drilling partnerships. The major integrated independents and majors, meanwhile, can raise capital by selling more stock, turning to the capital markets, or forming joint ventures. The larger companies have well-established relationships with those institutions that can provide the needed capital.

By contrast, the typical independent refiner has neither the size nor the equity to be able to go to the financial markets for money. Refinery size, revenues and profits, and other factors all make the independent refiner a risky proposition for most bankers and lenders, many of whom are still feeling the effects of energy loans that turned sour just a few years ago.

Costly Environmental Regulations

The oil industry must obey major environmental regulations that have added and will continue to add tremendous costs to refining. Quite simply, it is a no-win situation for the independent refiner, who is faced with the dilemma of paying more for low-polluting, higher-priced crudes or buying expensive new equipment that will permit the processing of dirtier but more economical crudes.

Many of the environmental regulations govern air emissions. The Environmental Protection Agency (EPA) and local environmental regulators maintain strict standards on the amount and kind of emissions discharged by refineries. Refineries are required to install the "best available control technology" equipment to reduce pollutants. This has meant, for example, that compressors have had to be equipped with water injections to reduce nitrous oxide emissions. (The water injection cools the flame; the lower temperatures reduce the emissions.) However, the water must be very pure in order for the equipment to work properly, adding a water purifying expense to the cost of the water injection system.

In other areas, tanks holding products with vapor pressures above a specified government standard must be equipped with floating roofs. Companies are being held responsible for leaks from underground storage tanks, and gasoline stations may soon be required to be equipped with vapor recovery systems.

Disposing of the hazardous wastes generated by the refining process will also be a financial burden. If there is no nearby disposal site, as is the case in Hawaii, for example, refineries will be forced to ship their wastes to sites on the U.S. mainland—at great expense.

These examples provide just a sampling of the expensive environmental requirements facing not only the independent but also the entire industry. Added to various pollution taxes imposed on refiners, the ever-increasing cost of environmental compliance places a heavy burden on all sectors, especially those least able to afford them: the independent refiners.

Government Product Standards

On another major environment-related issue, the federal government has imposed and proposed stringent regulations on the content of petroleum products that can be sold in the United States. The phase-out of lead content in gasoline has added a significant cost to refiners. And in two more developments, the National Petroleum Council has estimated that a government-proposed reduction in motor gasoline vapor pressure of one pound per square inch would reduce gasoline manufacturing capability about 200 MB/D and increase operating costs by $1 billion. Likewise, reducing the benzene content could require investments of $4 billion.

The EPA's proposed reduction in the sulfur content of diesel fuel could cost the petroleum industry as much as $6 billion in compliance costs, according to a preliminary estimate by the National Petroleum Refiners Association. The gasoline vapor pressure standard would pose an especially difficult problem for the independent refiner. Removing these light ends from gasoline will mean that the refiner must sell these products separately and at a lower price that it would have obtained had those products been permitted to remain in the gasoline. The result: reduced profitability. Clearly, the under-capitalized independent refiner may be unable to make the plant modifications needed to meet government product standards.

Competition from Major Oil Companies

It is no revelation that the international majors (such as Exxon, Shell, British Petroleum, Mobil), the international integrateds (Unocal, Arco), and the government-owned foreign firms have the resources to effectively compete in any marketplace. They have the money and manpower to build new refineries or start up closed ones, to make needed capital improvements, to price their products competitively, and to bring these forces to bear on their competitors. Not so the independent refiner. The independent refiner is finding it difficult, if not impossible, to effectively compete against these Goliaths.

The Uncertainty of Supply

In this backdrop of uncertainty, independent refiners will also face growing uncertainty over their traditional supply of crude oil, the domestic producer. Lacking the upstream capacity of the majors, lacking the long-term supply relationships with the foreign producers, the independent refiner can only hope to cultivate new relationships that will ensure its survival.

Chaotic Market Conditions

The crude oil market has been in turmoil since the Arab oil embargo of 1973 and the Iranian crisis in 1979. Prices seem to rise and fall with each economic report and forecast, with reports of political turmoil in the Middle East, or after each OPEC meeting (see Table 9.2 and Figure 9.2).

Until the Arab oil embargo, prices were effectively controlled by the major oil firms. From 1973 to 1982, the market was subject to the OPEC government–controlled official selling prices. Since 1983, the market has determined the prices of crude and products. Dramatic changes, upheavals,

TABLE 9.2
Refiner Acquisition Cost of Crude Oil, 1968–1985 (Dollars per Barrel)

	Domestic[a]		Imported[a]		Composite[a]	
	Current	Constant[b]	Current	Constant[b]	Current	Constant[b]
1968	3.21	8.51	2.90	7.69	3.17	8.41
1969	3.37	8.47	2.80	7.04	3.29	8.27
1970	3.46	8.24	2.96	7.05	3.40	8.10
1971	3.68	8.29	3.17	7.14	3.60	8.11
1972	3.67	7.89	3.22	6.92	3.58	7.70
1973	4.17	8.42	4.08	8.24	4.15	8.38
1974	7.18	13.30	12.52	23.19	9.07	16.80
1975	8.39	14.15	13.93	23.49	10.38	17.50
1976	8.84	14.01	13.48	21.36	10.89	17.26
1977	9.55	14.19	14.53	21.59	11.96	17.77
1978	10.61	14.70	14.57	20.18	12.46	17.26
1979	14.27	18.16	21.67	27.57	17.72	22.54
1980	24.23	28.27	33.89	39.54	28.07	32.75
1981	34.33	36.52	37.05	39.41	35.24	37.49
1982	31.22	31.22	33.55	33.55	31.87	31.87
1983	28.87	27.79	29.30	28.20	28.99	27.90
1984	28.53	26.39	28.88	26.72	28.63	26.48
1985[c]	26.65	23.86	27.04	24.21	26.76	23.96

Note: Refiner acquisition cost of crude oil for each category and for the composite is derived by dividing the sum of the total purchasing (acquisition) costs of all refiners by the total volume of all refiners' purchases.

[a]Data 1968 through 1973 are estimated.

[b]Constant 1982 dollars calculated using GNP price deflators, 1982 = 100.

[c]Preliminary.

Source: Energy Information Administration, *Annual Energy Review 1985* (Washington, D.C.: Department of Energy, 1986), Table 62.

and reversals in the oil industry with respect to pricing, refining, and trading methods continue to this day.

Major oil companies with their combination of upstream and downstream sectors have had to quickly switch their corporate focus from one operation to the other in response to the prevailing price structure. Smaller, independent upstream firms have at times enjoyed profitable periods, as independent refiner/marketers were suffering losses. Similarly, as the pricing mechanism turned to favor refining, the upstream independents and sectors of integrated firms faced less profitable times.

This is the tumultuous business environment in which the independent refiner has had to operate, and will continue to operate in the foreseeable future. Clearly, those refiners unable to compete in the market will face lean, hard times.

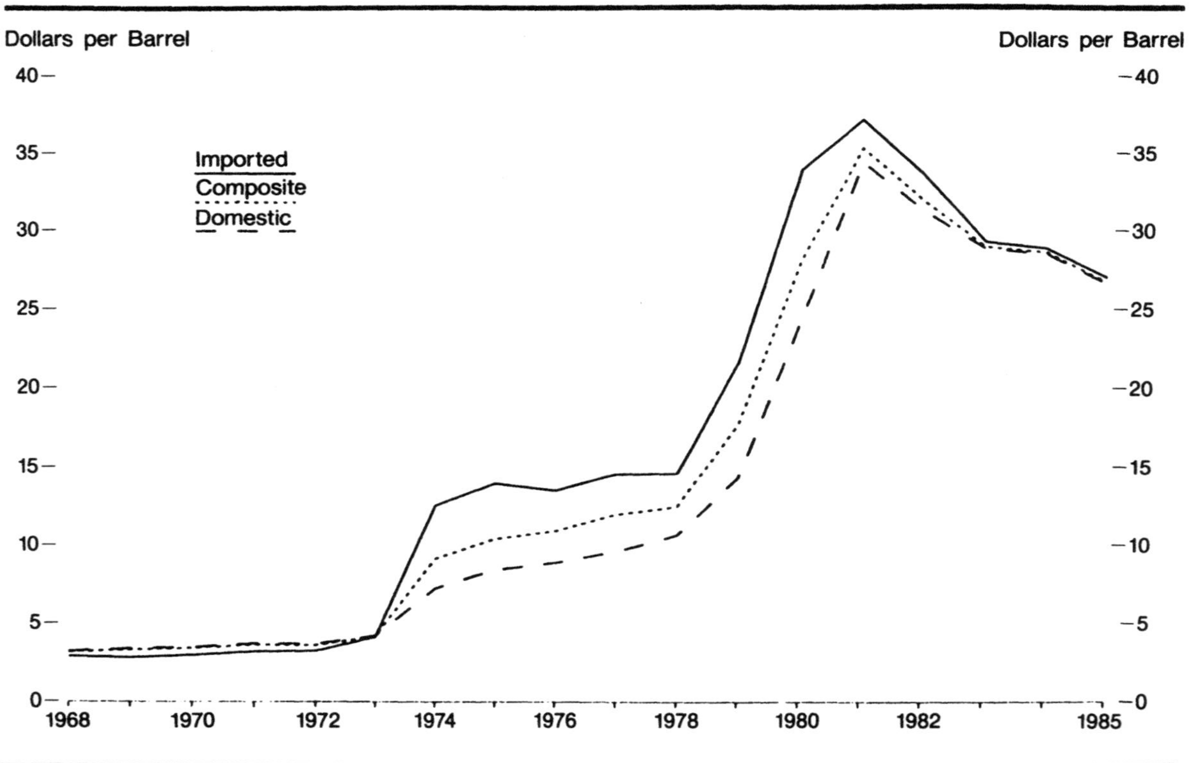

FIGURE 9.2 Refinery acquisition cost of crude oil, 1968–1985.
Source: Energy Information Administration, *Annual Energy Review 1985* (Washington, D.C.: Department of Energy, 1986), Figure 62.

Future

Given these conditions, one could speculate that the future of the independent refiner is a bleak one. But for the innovative, creative independent, that fear is unfounded. In fact, these conditions have forced the independent refiner to seek new ways to survive—and to prosper.

The experiences of Pacific Resources, Inc. (PRI) serve as an example of how an independent refiner has adapted to the changing conditions of the industry. PRI operates a modern 67,900-barrel per day refinery in Hawaii with major reforming and hydrocracking capacity. The refinery was originally built in 1972 to refine light, sweet crudes from Southeast Asia. Over the years, it has been modified and upgraded to allow the processing of lower American Petroleum Institute (API) gravity, higher-sulfur crudes from different parts of the world, thus enabling it to deliver competitively priced products into the Pacific region. PRI thus has the flexibility to obtain crudes from a variety of domestic and foreign sources, an option unavailable to refiners who failed to upgrade their plants during more prosperous times.

PRI supplies a full range of products throughout the Hawaiian Islands, including gasoline, diesel, jet fuel, and bunker fuel to a cross section of customers, including the U.S. military. The company also exports products to Korea, the Philippines, Australia, the many island nations of the South Pacific, and Japan.

PRI's refinery operates in a foreign trade zone, an area designated by the U.S. government in which goods can be imported, processed, and subsequently exported without incurring any customs duties or other taxes. This advantage has enabled PRI to be competitive in international trade. It is unlikely that any other single refinery in the world serves as many countries in as large a geographic area as does PRI. The refinery's marketing area literally exceeds 50 million square miles.

Creating Market Niches

Succeeding in this region has required that PRI create market niches—as opposed to geographic niches. As a general rule, independents face a difficult challenge in penetrating the Asia-Pacific market. Fortunately, a few market niches remain, ignored by the majors because returns are not considered to be significant to their overall systems. Identifying the niche opportunities available in the region requires the independent refiner to be market responsive. It has to be open to new ideas to adjust to the extreme volatility of the crude and product markets.

For PRI, this has meant expanding its sale of products in its home base of Hawaii. The expansion has resulted in the establishment of a network of retail gasoline stations, increased sales of bunker fuel to ships calling on Hawaii, and steady jet fuel sales for the scores of international and domestic carriers flying to Hawaii, to name the most prominent.

PRI has made a significant impact on the region by remainaing innovative and flexible. PRI processed the first exported cargo of Gippsland crude from Australia. The company was the first to sell gasoline to Japan in 1985 after the Japanese government opened its trade doors to imports. PRI also completed a sale of Indonesian crude oil to the People's Republic of China, perhaps a U.S. first. Like PRI, the independent refiner will have to be market driven to compete and survive in the years to come.

Operational Flexibility

The independent refiner will also have to be fast and flexible in its operations, to change quickly as the market changes. As mentioned earlier, PRI has made major improvements to its refinery so it can accommodate a variety of crudes. This has given the company the flexibility to change its product slate to obtain competitively priced crude from different domestic and foreign sources, while meeting the demands of the market. A prime example is its construction of a cogeneration plant, which generates electricity and steam for the refinery, thereby reducing operating costs.

PRI has also developed innovative pricing mechanisms that have kept it competitive with the majors. During the era of netback deals, for example, PRI and others without such contracts (the contracts essentially were for the majors and a few large independents) often had to rely on creative pricing to secure inexpensive crude. Crude pricing at the time of arrival helped reduce the risk of price fluctuations during voyage time. Linking long-haul crude prices to spot prices of regional crudes was another method that was not technically a netback, but that nevertheless resulted in more advantageous pricing. Still another approach involved partial netbacks where crude was valued as a percentage of the spot crude price and some percentage of one or more primary products yielded from the purchaser's refinery. The key has been imaginative approaches to a volatile market and being flexible enough to shift quickly as the market demands.

Strong Management

The success of any organization depends in large part on the individuals who lead it. PRI has adopted innovative and flexible compensation programs to attract strong managers with the experience and knowledge needed for the company to prosper. Companies unable or unwilling to adequately compensate their employees will find their most knowledgeable and talented individuals drawn away by other organizations.

Industry Relationships

The survival of independent refiners may depend in large part on their relationships with the majors and producers. Thus far, these relationships have included buyouts of independents by the majors, partnerships, and the development of long-term relationships with larger firms.

The most significant development has been the entry of OPEC producers into the refining sector: Venezuela, an OPEC member, purchased 50 percent of Champlin Petroleum Company (now Union Pacific) and 50 percent of Citgo. Kuwait owns most of Gulf Oil's facilities in Europe and recently purchased a 20 percent interest in British Petroleum. Saudi Arabia and Nigeria have been exploring business ties with Texaco.

This trend is likely to continue as producers logically seek to garner more control over their downstream capabilities. Conversely, this entry of the OPEC producers could mean the salvation of troubled independent refiners badly in need of capital and stable sources of crude. A number of independent refiners have already established joint ventures or been bought outright by the majors. The processing arrangement developed by Arco and Tosco, an independent, is an example of the employment of this particular survival strategy.

Another potential development involves the reintegration of the industry, with exploration, refining, and marketing companies forming competitive entities to take on the majors. The previously cited integration of OPEC producer Venezuela with Champlin and Citgo is a prime example. Venezuela has committed 500 MB/D to these type of deals and recently announced its intention of expanding to 700 MB/D, a formidable challenge to all competitors. Likewise, a relationship between the Saudis or Nigerians and Texaco could create an organization that would link all elements of the petroleum business and introduce yet another major force in the industry. For PRI, this stiffened competition will require that the company seek and develop long-term relationships with producers, as well as with larger firms that have the oil resources and capital to help the company compete.

Expanding Beyond Hawaii

The evolution of the industry will also mean that PRI will need to expand beyond the shores of its island home. PRI has already moved into a number of South Pacific markets and established trading and marketing operations throughout the U.S. mainland and Asia.

PRI's efforts to expand its sales in Hawaii were dealt a severe blow when the Federal Trade Commission (FTC) blocked the company's planned purchase of Shell Oil Company's Hawaii assets, which included a network of retail gasoline stations, terminal facilities, and other property. The FTC's decision will have a chilling effect on any oil company's efforts to expand in a given market. The government's opposition to PRI's local expansion will accelerate the company's search for new markets for its products.

Conclusion

The turmoil and volatility of the marketplace and the oil industry have placed tremendous burdens on the independent refiner. Most of these burdens are beyond the ability of the refiner to control. The extreme volatility of the crude oil market is expected to continue until OPEC production increases to a level that permits OPEC members to generate the income necessary to fulfill their national goals at an average price of about $18 a barrel.

At that price, new supplies will be limited, and demand increases likewise limited, so prices can be stabilized when OPEC reaches a production level sufficient to satisfy its members. Using a combination of decreases in crude production and a small annual increase in demand, OPEC should then be able to realize steady increases in production during the next several years. By 1991–1993, demand for OPEC oil could be between 21 and 22 million barrels per day, a satisfactory level for the members' income needs. Until then, the market should retain its volatility; after that, the market should stabilize and the producers of crude oil should be able to raise their prices at will.

The adroit refiner will have an opportunity to profit from the volatility, but at great risk. And once stability returns to the marketplace, the crude producers will probably extract a large tax from the refining sector, keeping the refiners' margins lean. The result will be the reintegration of the oil industry—and the likely demise of independents in all sectors of the industry during the next ten years. For Pacific Resources, Inc., and others like it, the years ahead pose new challenges, but challenges that can and will be met by creativity, flexibility, and the determination to succeed.

Notes

1. For our purposes, in independent refiner shall be defined as a refining company that is not government owned, not owned by a major oil company, does not have its own production, or does not conduct its own exploration activities.

2. "Factors Affecting U.S. Oil and Gas Outlook," Washington, D.C.: National Petroleum Council, February 1987, p. 47.

Bibliography

Anderson, Robert O., *Fundamentals of the Petroleum Industry,* Norman, Oklahoma: University of Oklahoma Press, 1984.

Energy Information Administration, "Annual Energy Review 1985," Washington, D.C.: U.S. Department of Energy, May 1986.

________, "Petroleum Supply Annual 1986," Washington, D.C.: U.S. Department of Energy, June 1987.

"Energy Security: A Report to the President of the United States," Washington, D.C.: U.S. Department of Energy, March 1987.

"Factors Affecting U.S. Oil and Gas Outlook," Washington, D.C.: National Petroleum Council, February 1987.

Platt's Oilgram News.

National Petroleum News: 1987 Fact Book, June 1987 (annual special issue).

10

Oil Trading: Yesterday, Today, and Tomorrow

M. Silvan Robinson

Traders often get an inflated idea of their own importance. Their trade, after all, is the price of oil, and that is what is news. Not just the trade press, but the great newspapers, and the government leaders of the world, quite rightly opine and guess what will be the price of Brent and Arab Light and what this will do to world economic growth rates. Traders, for whom these prices are their daily bread, can be forgiven for thinking that the transactions they carry out and the role they fill are of some importance. They delude themselves. Traders are mere journeymen in the great game, a function of the changing structure of the oil business rather than a dominant force.

This is not of course how they are seen by some producing governments or by the chief executives of exploration and production (E & P) functions in oil companies—or for that matter by some of their chairmen who as often as not have grown up in the E & P function. To such people, oil trading is an unwelcome and disruptive influence, contaminating the wholesome, straightforward business that is their birthright. Oil, they think, has a historic right to a reasonable profit and a stable environment. The technical skills involved in discovering oil deep in some filthy swamp or waterless desert and the engineering effort that brings the oil to the refinery should be rewarded. And refineries, too, carry out an ever more complex technical job servicing a public need.

The trader, though, offers nothing. The lust for a quick buck made by sitting in front of a screen playing complex paper games just like any discredited Wall Street junk bond salesperson both is alien to the practical base of the business and creates an instability that makes it impossible to plan anything rationally anymore. Billions of dollars are at risk of being poured down the drain because the industry has been taken over by electronic whiz kids who have never seen a real barrel of oil and have no idea how it is produced. Traders are not popular, but somehow or other they cannot be wished away.

This attitude is like the old-fashioned habit of shooting the messenger bearing bad tidings. The trader is no more responsible for the present instability of the oil business than is the messenger for the bad news he carries. The trader is merely the transmitter and perhaps the amplifier of signals, the product of a changed corporate environment, not the instigator of it. The trader is a skilled middleman taking advantage of an increasingly disrupted industry structure and of imperfect markets. The trader is also quite a new phenomenon. I can remember highly confidential telexes passing my desk in the early 1960s expressing managing directors' shock and horror that Caltex had "broken ranks" and was offering to supply the industry refinery in Karachi at a price of, I think, $1.61 per barrel in place of the norm of $1.63, on the excuse that it would supply Arab Light not Iranian crude. A movement of a few cents brought seismic industry reactions. Today $.02 is all in the rounding up. Then industry structure was dominated by the integrated majors. OPEC to be sure existed and had created a system of tax reference prices. But supply and demand were balanced within the big company systems. We had supply departments, not trading departments. There were small units dealing in exchanges so as to balance supply and demand at the margin and improve logistics; but the main emphasis was on a centralized system distributing in as rational a manner as possible supplies from the company's own production or (for example in the case of Shell) brought in under long-term contracts. To help in rationalizing supply packages, so that the right crudes were taken to the right refineries, "supply values" were calculated, based on theoretical refinery yields, and refineries around the world were told by the parent organization what they were to process. The "center" would arrange shipping. It was not a particularly efficient way of allocating resources, but in a blunt sort of way it worked.

This orderly, benevolently authoritarian structure gave little responsibility to operating companies and little influence over production levels to host governments. But it can be argued that it was the most stable system of international oil administration that has existed.

It was broken open by pressures of competition and geopolitical imperatives. The initial competitive pressures came from the independents (Occidental, Hess, Hunt, et cetera) that struck oil in Libya. This new oil disrupted the carefully balanced supply structures of the majors. But the fundamental political change was the nationalization of the major concessions in the wake of the 1973 supply crisis. The most important effect of this change was not loss of upstream profitability by the concession holders (they found other ways of making money) but the shift in responsibility for production levels and programs. No longer could a careful balance of interests be worked out between the interlocking concession holders of Aramco, the Iraq Petroleum Company (IPC) group, and the Iranian consortium, allocating the development of resources in the key Middle Eastern areas. Instead, national oil companies signed long-term contracts, often with the ex-concession holders, but increasingly with a diversified portfolio of trading partners. And each country was responsible for its own development plans and production levels.

People often forget that OPEC quota control, as opposed to price control, started only in 1982. For most of the postconcession period, OPEC was held together by Saudi Arabia's accepting the role of swing producer, with production rising to 10 million barrels per day in 1979–1980 and falling below 3 million at times in 1985. The need for quota control was a function of Saudi Arabia's growing unwillingness to shoulder the burden.

This background is relevant to an understanding of the development of trading. So long as the majors ran integrated supply systems that balanced world supply and demand, there was no need, or room, for trading except in the most peripheral sense. But the breakup of the concession system and specifically the shortages of the two oil crises of 1973–1974 and 1979–1980 provided just the conditions for the development of trading—and enabled fortunes to be made by the lucky or the brave—and of the new breed of midstream trader. Regulations always have loopholes, and the clever manipulation of loopholes, often in the gray area of the law, is what gets the cash registers ringing. Within the United States the price gap between the administered prices for "old oil" and "new oil" offered temptations that proved irresistible. Overseas, in supply crisis time, anybody lucky enough to get a term contract at official prices—say in Nigeria in 1979—could make $5–8 per barrel profit by reselling the crude in the open market. "Bag men" stalked the ministries of the producing world, offering appropriate inducements, and did not always come away empty-handed. Mathematically, an 80,000-barrels-per-day contract worth $5 per barrel profit would earn $1.5 billion in a year. Not bad for starters. Since then some of the trading groups that made money this way have followed the old maxim of certain English manufacturing barons: "To get on, to get honour, to get honest . . ."

Incidentally, as a historical footnote, it was not just trading companies that became rich. Kuwait Petroleum Corporation (KPC), operating as a profit center separate from the Oil Ministry, managed to reallocate its crude portfolio ("national necessity, force majeure, et cetera") and charge $5 per barrel (or more) premiums to their unfortunate customers. It was this little windfall that enabled Kuwait to go downstream and buy Gulf's European assets.

Since 1979 the international trading environment has never been the same. The process was hastened by the curious behavior of Saudi Arabia in the crisis—although it increased production to help cover shortages, it misallocated the oil—selling, not to "have not" companies like Shell and British Petroleum, but to the Aramco partners, which had lost very little in Iran, and to some consumer governments, which often did not know what to do with the oil. The consequence was a terrific scramble in the spot market. Downstream affiliates and other customers that had lost their traditional sources were let loose to find supplies for themselves, and middlemen traders found an easy market. Japanese refiners were particularly hard hit, and this opened the door for the ever-resourceful Japanese trading houses to take a leading position.

With the ending of shortages and the arrival of surplus, things did not revert to "normal." Spot crude became cheaper than term; fears of supply security gave way to a determination always to get the cheapest barrel. The drive came from the intensely competitive and fractionated downstream refining and marketing sector, both from affiliates of majors and independents; and traders had to respond. Refinery capacity remained obstinately in surplus, margins were terrible, and the market unforgiving. High-cost supplies could not be passed on to the customer; survival depended on a good acquisition strategy, and good meant cheap. An internal affiliate trader with secure term supplies but high prices and inflexible techniques would find itself with a rapidly shrinking customer base.

That brings us to the present day. These environmental changes have caused quite dramatic transformations in trading methods. There is steadily growing acceptance within major oil companies that they must cease to operate internalized supply systems, and instead accept an open market approach. In-house trading is being stripped of special privileges. Shell probably led the way, but the logic of events is drawing even the most centralized campanies like Exxon in the same, or parallel, directions. This means importing new and specialized skills into the very bosom of the staid environment of central offices—a fascinating process of culture change, of which more later.

The second revolution is the advent of the Wall Street traders, chastened perhaps by the events of Black October (1987), but with an undiminished lust for seizing opportunities to use money-market techniques in immature and imperfect markets. Imperfect, that is, in the economic sense of the term. Whereas in the "fungible" money markets minimal imperfections are available for the alert to seize on and arbitrage, oil, still largely conducted as a physical trade with few organizations having the size and financial strength to cover all the markets, can still offer surprisingly wide opportunities—forward paper markets out of line with physical carrying costs; Singapore out of line with Rotterdam; gas oil not in a sensible relationship to gasoline; Brent, Dubai, and West Texas Intermediate (WTI) all over the place. The urge to seize on these imperfections, hedge them in, write options, delta hedge, gamma hedge (there is a whole new vocabulary) with the expectation of making a few cents on a lot of barrels proves quite irresistible.

It is not of course always that easy, not least because oil still is a physical, not a proper, trade. Positions can get very illiquid; products are *not* fungible. Those who think only paper and not about the traditional oil-trading skills can get their fingers very badly burnt. This is leading the new traders increasingly into the wet oil as well as the paper business. But, as one adept Wall Streeter put it, "What we are witnessing is not the commoditization of oil, but the financialization of oil." A barrel of oil is just money. And like deposits in a bank, a physical barrel can be multiplied many times over. WTI and related New York Mercantile Exchange (NYMEX) products are transacted at the level of world consumption. A barrel of Brent can trade ten to twenty times over. Dubai is acquiring some of the same characteristics. Why is it happening and where will it end?

The why is easier to answer than the where. The concept of hedging, or risk management as it should more properly be called, is increasingly being seen as the correct approach. This is quite a revolution in thinking for the standard oilman. In 1985 there would have been boardroom consternation if a trading manager asked authority to take positions on the NYMEX. (Brent tended to slip through because it *looked* like normal oil trading, never mind that forward Brent contracts were, and still are, more risky and unsecured than equivalent transactions on the NYMEX.) Futures though looked like, let us say, *gambling*. Doctors, dentists, speculators and all that. Are you not getting outside the business you know and understand? Have not traders lost millions of dollars overnight as uncontrolled fever grips them? Most trading managers have gone through this sort of inquisition.

The answer is yes, of course, this sort of trading requires new skills for oilmen; it needs different sorts of people; and of course it is risky. But to do nothing in today's world is far more risky than to learn new trades. There are now virtually no companies integrated from source rock to pump as in the old days. All buy a large proportion of their supplies, and most are set up with free standing organizations at each business phase—profit responsible marketers, refiners, and traders. And whether integrated or not, all companies are operating in an environment where the variation of a dollar or more a day in the oil price is quite unexceptional; $.50 is almost the norm. If you buy a cargo in the Gulf, it will take seven weeks to get it to the United States or Northwest Europe. And in that time, heaven or the Ayatollah alone knows what may happen to the price. There is no more dreadful experience that buying a cargo in what turns out to be a falling market and watching the price sink daily— all eyes on you, every refinery leaving the cargo to get more and more distressed. Do this once and you will never want to leave a cargo unmanaged again.

The logical response, therefore, is to play safe, and only lift a cargo in the Gulf if you can be reasonably sure that its price plus freight broadly corresponds to the forward price of Brent or WTI; and when the opportunity arises, sell Brent forward. Over the ensuing month or so before you actually sell your cargo of Middle East crude, you may decide to move in and out of the forward market, improving (one hopes) on your original position; but the basic thrust of your policy will probably be to keep a reasonably balanced portfolio, so that if there is an unexpected market crash or surge you will not be too badly caught. After all, no science can predict when the next Middle East war crisis will develop or whether OPEC will suddenly get its act together. The example of "hedging" outlined above is rather simplistic. One cannot rely on the hedge working well—there could for example be a squeeze on Brent at the time you try to close out your position, thus upsetting your calculation; or the Gulf and Brent markets could move irrationally apart. Most hedging is much more complicated. To simulate the Mexican isthmus pricing formula for Europe would require an ability to take counter positions not only in Brent but in high- and low-sulphur fuel oil and probably in gas oil as well—and there are no developed forward markets in some of these products, either formal or informal.

So portfolio management becomes a pretty complicated affair. First, you have to have a really good understanding of your own supply position—not just physically, but economically. The big mental revolution is to think in terms of price timing, not volume timing—to understand that the most important thing is what happens to your profitability if the market goes up or down. Is your oil "priced" early (for example, two weeks before loading date) or late (for example, based on product values on date of arrival)? Have you sold before your acquisition is priced or vice versa? To have a good understanding of a large portfolio requires complex on-line computer programs, with a hierarchy of detail, so that individual traders can understand *and manage* their individual portfolios while the senior management tracks the overall trends and risks of the business. This structure is vital. Modern trading is far too complicated to be administered by orders from the top. Desk traders must be trusted to run their businesses, but the system must enable their actions to be monitored so that the overall policy of the trading group is maintained. As Aristotle might have said, it is a synthesis of the deductive and inductive process, and the binding thread is a common on-line information system.

Although price prediction may be a gamble, traders cannot be expected to fly blind. There are three main sorts of analysis that can at least help to improve on uneducated judgment: first, views on absolute prices; second, analysis of relative volatility; third, views on relative prices/discontinuities. Of course you can just give up. There are chartist systems based on the geometry of the great pyramids. Chartism is valuable only because some people may believe in the charts, and they may take actions that move markets because of it. My own experience is that the most useful indicators to watch are, on the physical side, the extent to which stocks vary from the desired levels and, on the financial side, the extent to which forward markets are overbought or oversold compared with the norm. And volatility is important. To take an obvious case, Brent is much more volatile than Dubai. There are good reasons for this, but you can make money out of it. You can apply volatility analysis to a whole range of products and aim to simulate or vary the volatility of your portfolio. But perhaps most important is the study of differences. There are logical relationships between markets and crudes and products, and these often get out of line for a time. You can make money by spotting the discontinuities. Of course you may have missed some change in the fundamentals, which justifies the change in relationship, so by betting the other way you lose money. But that is all in the luck of the game.

These sketchy illustrations give some idea of what a modern trader is thinking about. It is obvious that the modern trader is a quite different sort of person from the traditional oilman. He needs to know his oil. Nothing can take the place of understanding both what can be done with the product he is trading and the technicalities of the trading process—contracts, demurrage clauses, lay-time provisions, shipping requirements, legal jurisdication issues. But nowadays superimposed on that is a modern understanding of computer technology, software programs, the fundamentals of operations research, and option theory—all that the modern finance-house expert requires, and more. Oddly enough it is not difficult to find able recruits to fit the profile. The job has challenge and excitement and responsibility. It is much more difficult, certainly in a big organization, to pay such people properly, and even more difficult to fit them into a conventional career structure, plodding up through the ranks to achieve some minor general management by the age of fifty. Luckily I no longer have to worry about that.

When lecturing to courses filled with the more conventional sort of oil people, one is often asked about the ethics of modern trading—not the bagmen question, but the economic justification of the activity, the implication being, as I said earlier, that trading adds nothing and damages much. I do not think it is correct that trading adds nothing. One has to start with the premise that our business has become fractionated, unstable, and full of discontinuities. The downstream is highly competitive, the upstream pseudo-oligopolistic. Integration (apart from a few groping attempts by Kuwait and Venezuela) is out. The trading function is needed to keep the flows going. And it adds value in two ways. First, it reduces supply costs: through freight optimization, back hauls, and exchanges and by relentlessly searching out particular markets that can make the most of a particular crude or blend of crudes or by meeting specifications by blending two off-specification products. The market and trading are a more efficient mechanism for doing this than central supply allocation, with its calculated-value structures. Second, trading adds value by price arbitrage, by perfecting markets. It is a good thing for the world for there to be a single market defined by price competition across the geographical frontiers. Japan is better off if it can get gasoline from surplus capacity in the U.S. Gulf, not just from Singapore. Brent should be in line with WTI. Markets may fluctuate, but they should also equilibrate. This improves the sum of human economic well-being. It is the basis of free trade philosophy, and traders are needed to see that it happens. So traders should not be embarrassed by their role. In an odd sort of way even the unscrupulous traders who made money out of two-tier trading in the United States were helping to arbitrage markets and did less economic damage than the bureaucrats who invented and administered the two-tier system.

This is not to say that present-day trading methods do not cause disruption. The financialization of markets has much the same effect on oil as it has on stocks, shares, and currencies. Program trading exaggerates trends and causes adjustments to overshoot. The money comes pouring in or dries up completely. In the "free fall" of January 1986 no buyers were anywhere to be seen. Liquidity evaporated. The multiplication of barrels on the NYMEX does not, as some theorists would have us believe, broaden markets and make them more representative and stable. The use of those markets by individual oil traders to reduce their individual risks is a perfectly sensible thing to do; yet paradoxically the greater the individual use, the greater the overall instability. But so long as the fundamentals of the business are unstable, the protection of futures markets and quasi-futures markets will be sought. And the techniques will go on being extended.

So where will it go? I believe a number of things are probable. Most obviously, the risk-management instruments, which are at the moment concentrated in New York and to a lesser extent in London, will become universalized. Although NYMEX is actively traded by Japanese firms attempting to cover positions in Eastern markets, the basic risks are unnecessarily great. It just surely be logical that futures markets will be developed in some form in the Far East, particularly as domestic trade is becoming increasingly liberalized in Japan, Australia, and New Zealand. It is proving a slow process because people are finding that all the conditions needed for a successful futures market do not easily come together. But some global interconnection of forward markets is bound to happen, and disparities between markets will steadily be arbitraged away.

And there will be further important considerations for downstream operations. Alert, smaller companies already try to protect refinery margins and stock values by clever use of forward markets. The use of these techniques will grow—though whether the futures markets will ever be big enough to cope with stock management by some of the really large players is doubtful. But the process is irreversible and will have lasting effects on the downstream business.

I suspect that this financialization of refinery margins will *always* have a depressive effect on refinery profitability. Prices are set by marginal transactions, and someone somewhere will always have some cheap product or access to some cheap source of crude. Modern telecommunication techniques will transmit these signals around the globe. The temptation to dig themselves out of a hole is endemic to refiners—an incremental investment or catalyst change here, or making a step change to a new upgrading technique there—and seems irresistible. It may also be self-defeating. Who was it who said, "If you find yourself in a hole, stop digging"? My guess is that refining is going to be poor business for years to come. The process of arbitrage—expressed in the relationship between spot crude and Platt's or NYMEX product prices—will put a continuous damper on margins.

But Platt's, and the commodity market, end at the refinery fence, and there will still be money to be made from marketing. This is not good news for old-fashioned conventional middle-sized companies. The future will lie with three sorts of operation: with the really big companies with a wide spread of activities, financial clout, and technical resources to handle the high risks entailed (but only if such companies learn to accept modern trading techniques); with modern medium-sized opportunistic refiner/trader operations, where trading management predominates over refining management; and with niche players who have some special market or special access to supplies. The waves of creative destruction will go on breaking over the downstream, and modern trading techniques will go on eroding protective barriers. It is not a comfortable message.

As for trading companies themselves, there are also some messages. Big financial resources are needed, not for hardware, but because the risks are so huge. There may be some niches, but serious trading needs financial backing. Access to physical products on a global scale is a great advantage both because arbitraging world markets is the name of the game, but also because critical mass in a relatively illiquid market helps the application of risk-management techniques enormously. Some connection with downstream markets, either through product outlets or refining capacity, is increasingly necessary for a trader who does not want always to be left at the mercy of bear squeezes. Office representation in the main markets so as to trade a twenty-four-hour book is also pretty well essential. Good or backup computer services are inescapable. And overheads *have* to be kept down against a rainy day (it will come). To do all this at once is pretty hard.

Perhaps, after all, the modern trader is a bit more than a messenger of bad tidings. To try to ignore him is to ignore the need for change, so he might as well be used and used well. Trading needs above all two resources: modern computer information systems and skilled people. A good trader can earn millions with surprisingly little physical capital behind him. He works hard and under great stress. He deserves his reward.

11

Stabilizing World Oil Prices (SWOP): A Security Strategy

Ralph W. Snyder, Jr.

On a hot Sunday evening in mid-July 1979, the president of the United States told a nationwide television audience, "This nation will never use more foreign oil than we did in 1977, never." He told the nation that it was at a turning point in its energy history. He declared his intention to use his presidential authority to set import quotas forbidding entry into this country of "one drop of foreign oil more than his goals would allow." President Jimmy Carter further told the nation that its dependence on foreign oil would be stopped dead in its tracks right then.

The president's "battlefield" strategies for energy security included a request for this nation's most massive peacetime commitment of funds and resources to develop its own alternative sources of fuel. One stated goal was to decontrol U.S. crude oil prices, which had been under government regulations in one form or another since 1971. Another was to allow U.S. prices to rise to world levels, thus encouraging domestic development and conservation. Producers' revenue, which would increase because of decontrol, was to be taxed by the federal government; the tax, in turn, was slated to go into a proposed Energy Security Corporation (ESC), a government agency aimed at boosting production of synthetic fuel by guaranteeing loans and other agreements with private industry. A variety of other programs in the environmental and conservation fields were designed to help boost energy supplies.

The petroleum industry, in general, concurred with Carter's crude oil–price decontrol as a right step. But it criticized the excise tax as a deterrent to all-out discovery and development of new reserves. The industry faulted the heavy reliance on synthetic fuels, which required new technology and exceptionally long lead times for development.

Industry critics said that synfuels would not be able to fill the supply/demand gap as conventional production decreased while overall demand increased. Industry expressed its fears that President Carter's energy program gambled too much on synthetics without giving enough attention to the more dependable prospects of oil, natural gas, coal, and nuclear power. Generally, the industry showed concern for increased access to federal lands both on shore and offshore. In 1979, domestic production of crude oil and natural gas liquids was a little more than 10 MMB/D. Imports of 6 MMB/D of crude oil and 1.6 MMB/D of products made up the difference between domestic supply and total consumption of about 17.7 MMB/D.

Following President Carter's opening salvo in his crusade for energy self-reliance, total demand for crude oil and products decreased during 1980 through 1983, hitting a ten-year low at about 15 MMB/D. Domestic crude oil output reached a five-year high in 1985 as crude oil prices reached the highest point ever, following the dictates of the world oil cartel, the Organization of Petroleum Exporting Companies (OPEC). During this same period, crude oil and product imports plummeted to a seven-year low in 1983, 1984, and 1985. It was here that OPEC learned a belated lesson.

Some, but not all, members of OPEC are very sensitive to any increase in crude oil prices when market conditions will not support an increase. They are quite aware that higher oil prices only encourage consuming countries both to further conserve and also to switch to such alternative energy sources as coal and nuclear power. When OPEC imports into the United States dropped to 60 percent of 1973 levels and to 25 percent of 1977 levels, OPEC merely increased production, far exceeding its established goals. The result: World oil prices plummeted from $40 a barrel to $10 a barrel in the early part of 1986. Ironically, things apparently were going so well on the energy-economic front that the Reagan administration did not follow through on Carter's promise of using his presidential quota authority to limit quantitatively imports from foreign sources. Sure enough, the expected eventually happened. Imports began to rise again and domestic production began its long downhill slide. U.S. producers and oil service companies were forced out of business as domestic prices plummeted.

On December 27, 1987, the *Washington Post* reported that 200,000 homes were vacant in Houston, Texas, about twice the average for most cities of comparable size. The stockpile of repossessed property in Houston—with its oil-based economy—created a recession-fueled chain reaction. The cycle reportedly is being played out in many other areas, from Denver to Peoria to Miami. But nowhere is the problem more acute than in Dallas, Houston, Austin, San Antonio, and other Texas cities. They are burdened with the biggest real estate glut since the 1929 depression. No one disputes the severity of the problem. No one disputes that an economic upswing is the long-term remedy even though the recovery will rise and fall with oil prices. What is disputed, however, is how the U.S. government should sell the burgeoning surplus of property it is inheriting from debtors, failed banks, and bankrupt savings and loan associations. The list includes hundreds of thousands of repossessed homes, condominiums, shopping centers, and business complexes. No one knows the exact number because no one in the government is keeping a daily box score. But the harder the government pushes to unload this inventory, the lower the prices will go, and the less the original lenders will recover.

Investors from all around the country poured money into the state during the go-go years in the early and mid-1980s. Now, they can only watch anxiously, knowing the size of their losses depends on the outcome of the debate and its overall effect on the Texas economy. Record foreclosures have turned half a dozen federal agencies into landlords, each with a separate, sometimes conflicting, policy for selling off or renting tens of thousands of properties. According to a Houston joke, the Federal Home Loan Bank Board ought to vote on the city council because the agency has become the city's biggest landlord.

In September 1986, prompted by congressional concern about the economic consequences posed by the failing oil industry and the administration's concern about impact of the situation on national security, President Reagan ordered a high-level review of energy policy and national security. The administration made clear its twin concerns: the national security implications of oil imports and their effect on oil prices. The long-awaited study by the committee, headed by the secretary of the Department of Energy, was released in March 1987. It predictably warned that the United States should be deeply concerned about the shrinkage of the domestic oil and gas industry and its increasing reliance on imported oil.

Numerous proposals were forwarded to the cabinet's Domestic Policy Council for discussion before recommendations were readied for Congress. However, the secretary of energy staunchly opposed one proposal, charging that the study showed that an oil-import fee designed to curb oil imports "does not make sense from a fiscal standpoint." The analysis examined the effect of $5 per barrel and $10 per barrel import fees. It estimated a $10 fee would increase domestic production 500 MB/D by 1995 and would prompt 1 MMB/D in conservation, lowering imports 1.5 MMB/D overall. The study went on to say that the resulting higher energy prices would reduce economic growth, increase inflation, and hurt U.S. competitors in domestic and foreign markets. The report said that Congress, however, no doubt would likely exempt crude oil–import fees from some friendly countries and perhaps exempt users of particular products. It said a fee would discourage production from secure foreign sources by lowering world oil prices, thus discouraging expansion of production outside the Middle East.

Industry groups and companies pushing for an import fee blasted the report. One group seeking an import fee called the report a "whitewash" and criticized its prediction that the United States would be importing half of its oil in the mid-1990s. This group said that the predicted import level would come five years earlier than that. Chairman Bennett Johnson (D-La.), of the Senate Energy Committee said, "The mystery is why it took 300 pages and such delay. There is absolutely nothing new." Senator Pete V. Domenici (R-N.M.) said the report "poisons the well even more against an import fee" in Congress.

The OPEC cartel, by limiting its overall production during 1986 and the greater part of 1987, caused world oil prices to rise from the $10 low in 1985 to around $20 a barrel in fall 1987. But on December 15, 1987, oil prices tumbled in the wake of OPEC's inability to curb oil production.

The United Press International reported that on the last day of 1987 oil prices declined on U.S. markets and held steady overseas, ending the year down as much as $1.40/barrel from levels at the close of 1986. The price of oil traded on world markets dropped by more than $2/barrel since OPEC failed to take measures to curb runaway production and halt discounting at its winter meeting, which ended December 14. The thirteen-nation cartel simply extended its current production quotas and an $18/barrel benchmark price through June 1988.

On the New York Merchantile Exchange, West Texas Intermediate—the principle U.S. crude for immediate delivery—lost $.19 to $16.70/barrel. On the final trading day of 1986 West Texas Intermediate ended at $17.94/barrel in a prolonged rally triggered by OPEC's mid-December agreement to reduce production in order to drive up world prices to the official $18/barrel target.

West Texas Intermediate hit a high for the year of $22.75/barrel in mid-July 1987 and then began to weaken as OPEC greatly exceeded its production ceiling. On the U.S. Gulf Coast spot markets, where oil is sold to the highest bidder, West Texas Intermediate dropped by $.50 to $16.70/barrel and was $.80 below the close of $17.50 at the end of 1986. Britain's North Sea Brent crude for February deliveries showed no change at $17/barrel but was down $.75 from $17.75/barrel on the last trading session of 1986.

Fears have been mounting again that the United States is heading for an energy disaster because of its heavy dependency on imported oil. The *Oil and Gas Journal* estimated that combined imports of crude oil and products, excluding crude oil for the strategic petroleum reserve (SPR), will rise to 6.38 MMB/D in 1987 from 6.175 MMB/D in 1986 and all of the increase will be in crude oil. Reliance on imports will creep up to 38.97 percent of total supply from 37.93 percent in 1986. Reliance sank to a little more than 31 percent in 1983 and 1985.

Although the Reagan administration is seemingly committed equally to free trade and cheap energy, Secretary of the Interior Don Hodel, a former energy secretary, has sounded the alarm on imports several times. "We are headed toward a period in which we will be sitting in gasoline lines again—anytime in the next 2–5 years," Hodel predicted in 1987.

In the *Oil and Gas Journal* of July 6, 1987, Washington editor Patrick Crow wrote an article entitled "Rising U.S. Oil Imports Get Attention But No Action." Crow reported that in June 1987, while explaining to a House committee why Congress should approve his 5-year offshore drilling and Arctic National Wildlife Refuge (ANWR) exploration proposals, Secretary Hodel repeated the warning:

> We should not sit back and entrust our national destiny to an organization (the Organization of Petroleum Exporting Countries) dedicated to the use of oil in a way that whipsaws our economy and undermines our national policies.
>
> In my judgment, OPEC may be having a more serious impact today than some of its members had in 1973 when tight supply/demand market conditions existed, and they used an embargo and coordinated production cuts to escalate prices in an attempt to blackmail the U.S. on foreign policy issues.
>
> The Iranian revolution of 1978 led to further price increases, which OPEC sought to sustain. That OPEC strategy backfired because they drove prices so high so quickly they touched off an oil development rush and increased conservation in non-OPEC countries.
>
> Now, whether by accident or design, the whipsawing of prices undercuts potential competitive oil production from non-OPEC nations. As a consequence, along with oil, they have the ability to export economic instability. OPEC's ability to threaten actions can be as effective as the actions themselves.
>
> The psychological effects of this new twist may prove even more detrimental to the U.S.'s long term security than the earlier embargo.
>
> Like a person on an addictive drug—in this instance, temporarily cheap oil—we are in danger of losing our will to provide our own future. We may be putting ourselves at the mercy of a supplier who eventually will exact a very high price for a substance we must have to survive. Put in such a bind, I fear we might take drastic and unreasonable actions.

The Reagan administration's Energy Security Study found that increasing oil imports were in fact a threat to U.S. security. In March 1987 Energy Secretary John Herrington said:

> The crisis in the domestic petroleum industry, an industry that is critical to our energy security, is taking an enormous toll and is creating serious problems for the future.
>
> We cannot afford to be complacent. Energy security is a vital part of the foundation on which our foreign and domestic policies—and our economy—rests. As a nation we must recognize the warning signs and take thoughtful and prudent action that meets our responsibility to consumers, industry, and the nation alike.

The action the administration eventually took was widely criticized as being too little. It lowered the minimum bid for offshore leases to $25/acre from $150 and pledged to support a 100 MB/D fill rate for the strategic petroleum reserve if Congress could find the additional money.

Critics generally object to the administration's alleged do-nothing policy because the administration continues to strongly oppose a crude import fee or floor price. Senator Don Nickles (R-Okla.) endorsed a $20/barrel floor price for U.S. oil because he believed it would cause little or no harm to the economy but would provide a significant amount of security for the energy industry. Senator James McClure (R-Idaho) said: "It appears that part of the problem in developing a long term energy security policy has been the attitude of the Administration which seems to be that the free market will automatically take care of any problem." He went on to say: "I don't know of anyone outside the Administration who would agree with that."

A study by the conservative Heritage Foundation in spring 1988 warned of "a security catastrophe" if the administration did not change its policy "to avoid the incipient energy crisis by removing the market uncertainties that government action has fostered." The study further stated that the administration's only truly significant success with regard to oil and gas policy was to speed decontrol of oil prices initiated by President Carter in mid-1979.

It is incredible to me that the U.S. government allows its national security strategy to be dictated by the OPEC cartel. Yet, so many times in the past few years OPEC has called a meeting to announce new production limits and artificially high prices. The cartel scattered for home with their "quotas" in hand, began cheating on each other, and the prices started to slide. One confidant of former Saudi Arabian Oil Minister Yamani predicted oil prices dropping to $5/barrel after the

Iran-Iraq war was settled and the oil glut turned into a flood. Worse, a continued slide in oil prices would be nothing less than the final knockout blow to the economy of the Southwest. Anyone believing that OPEC, through "voluntary" production controls, will eventually stabilize world oil prices has a short and convenient memory.

In the early 1930s, overproduction of U.S. crude oil glutted the market and prices fell to $.10/barrel. It was then that the system of prorationing was born. It grew, in effect, from efforts to limit production by "voluntary" control. Producers cheated and Congress had to step in, enacting the Connolly Hot Oil Act that made it a federal offense for any producer to ship crude oil interstate that was produced in excess of the producer's quota.

In 1952, the world had acquired a surplus producing capacity, and free world markets were tending to be disrupted. A severe disruption would have occurred in the United States, except for cutbacks under the conservation programs of various state regulatory bodies. In July 1954, President Dwight Eisenhower established an advisory committee to study U.S. energy supplies and resources policy "with the aim of strengthening the national defense, providing orderly growth and assuring supplies for our expanding national economy and for any future emergencies." In February 1955, the committee reported that

> if the imports of crude oil should exceed significantly the respective proportions that these imports of oil bore to the production of domestic crude oil in 1954, the domestic fuel situation could be so impaired as to endanger the orderly industrial growth which assures the military and civilian supplies and reserves that are necessary to the national defense.

The committee concluded that in the interest of national defense imports should be kept in the balance that it had recommended and said that "it is highly desirable that this be done by voluntary individual action of those who are importing or those who become importers of crude oil."

On June 21, 1955, Section 7 of the Trade Agreement Extension Act of 1955 became law. This statutory provision required the director of the Office of Defense Mobilization to advise the president whenever the director had "reasons to believe that any article is being imported into the United States in such quantities as to threaten to impair the national security." Following the receipt of such advice, the president was authorized to make an investigation. If he found an article was being imported in such quantities as to threaten our security, he was authorized to adjust the imports of such articles to a level that would obviate the threat.

In April 1957, the president was advised by the director of the Office of Defense Mobilization that crude oil was being imported into the United States in such quantities as to threaten the national security. The president concurred and asked the director to investigate the possibilities of limiting crude oil imports by individual, voluntary action. Two months later, a special committee advised the president that the limitation was necessary and recommended a plan for the voluntary limitation of crude oil imports east of the Rockies (Petroleum Administration for Defense—PAD Districts I-IV). The committee's recommendations were approved by the president, and the Department of the Interior was chosen to administer the Voluntary Oil Import Program. To encourage compliance, the Buy American Act was incorporated into the program by Executive Order 10761, dated March 27, 1958. As a result of this action, companies that failed to comply with the program were ineligible to obtain government contracts for petroleum products. Notwithstanding these sanctions, the *voluntary* oil program failed. In the closing days of 1958, several companies had elected to cheat on their allocations and actually imported considerably more oil than their allocations allowed for. The fact must be faced: If voluntary production and import controls did not work in the United States, how could anyone think they can work in a thirteen-country cartel such as OPEC?

Following the failure of the voluntary oil program, President Eisenhower on March 10, 1959, issued Proclamation 3279, which set forth a system of mandatory controls. The mandatory oil-import program continued for some thirteen or fourteen years.

There are many who believe that had it not been for these mandatory controls and the economic climate that the controls provided, the Alaska North Slope oil would never have been discovered, developed, and produced. Presently, Alaska North Slope crude oil constitutes a most significant percentage of feedstocks to at least six West Coast refineries.

The Iran-Iraq war, with its potential of disrupting Gulf oil shipments, focused renewed attention on the U.S. strategic petroleum reserves. Taking a lesson from the 1973–1974 supply interruption, Congress authorized the SPR in the Energy Policy and Conservation Act of 1975. There seems to be little doubt in many policymakers' minds that the SPR will be used in the future. The question is when? Future oil-supply disruptions are considered highly probable in view of the Gulf turmoil. Even if a crude oil shortfall did not hurt the United States directly, the nation might have to share crude oil under the International Energy Agency (IEA) agreement that could be activated if the group or any of its members had a shortage of 7 percent or more. If the United States were required to share oil, it is likely that foreign crude oil bound for the United States would be diverted to other IEA countries and then offset with crude from the SPR.

The Department of Energy has in place an auction system to draw down the SPR. The primary method of SPR oil sales would be through open-price bidding, for which the energy secretary could establish a minimum price. Reliable sources state that the SPRs could be drawn down at a rate of approximately 3.5 MMB/D, with an added draw-down capability up to 4.5 MMB/D in the next year or so.

On December 23, 1987, the U.S. Department of Commerce agreed to institute a new study to see if the high level of oil imports threatened U.S. national security. Import oil's share of U.S. oil consumption had risen to 40 percent from 31 percent in 1985, when world oil prices began to fall. A comprehensive review such as that being conducted by the Department of Commerce must take into account that the governing statute authorizes government intervention in support of domestic price and production for the compelling purpose of protecting the national security.

In light of the foregoing historical facts and my own assessment of the present out-of-control situation, I propose a plan that would stabilize world oil prices for the United States. This plan, entitled Stabilizing World Oil Prices, would be tabbed as the SWOP Plan. The SWOP, a variation of *SWAP,* Plan would do just that. As designed, the plan would enable the Department of Energy to swap or exchange its higher-priced crude oil in the SPR for lower-priced imported oil as replacement. The president, under his existing authority, would issue a proclamation prohibiting any further offshore imports of crude oil for U.S. consumption when the world price dropped to $20/barrel or less. The Department of Energy (DOE) would immediately begin auctioning off oil at a minimum price from the SPR, replacing the intended oil imports. Concurrently, DOE would buy the cheaper foreign oil to replace the withdrawn oil from the SPR. The economic rent that would be derived from such a transaction would be pocketed by the government, thus reducing its national debt. Having such a plan in place, which would be automatically triggered when world prices fell below the established floor price, would assure domestic energy investors that they would not again be forced into bankruptcy by OPEC.

Other positive derivations from this proposed plan would be implemented by regulations. This would include issuing an import permit for direct imports, bypassing the reserves, and avoiding a physical swap when appropriate. The SPR, which is headed by the DOE assistant secretary for fossil fuels, would, in effect, be a clearinghouse for imported crude oil. The fossil fuels secretary could be assisted by executive reservists in the industry who are experts in crude oil procurement, transportation, and distribution. Regulations could be drawn that would fine-tune the operation, including provisions for a drawback on exports of crude oil derivatives, historical imports of unfinished oils, finished products, and residual fuel oil used as fuel. The psychological effect of having this easily implemented new program in place to be activated when necessary would neutralize OPEC's ability to dictate the U.S. domestic oil prices.

Under this plan the U.S. strategic petroleum reserve would be truly used to strategically safeguard its energy security. The program would provide a stable economic atmosphere for the domestic energy industry to work and produce and, as a positive side effect, create a market for the government to dispose of its properties that it has inherited from debtors, failed banks, and bankrupt savings and loan associations.

12

The Future of "Futures"

John Elting Treat and Barbara Laflin Treat

Futures Past

The emergence of oil futures markets and their remarkable growth were a natural, indeed inevitable, consequence of three concurrent but only partly interrelated trends in oil, financial, and commodity markets. By far the most important determinant was the structural change in oil markets themselves. The nationalization of production by OPEC and non-OPEC governments alike—and the subsequent pressures to eliminate large third-party crude resales—resulted in a "disintegration" of the oil market, which had been highly integrated since the days of J. D. Rockefeller. In the ten years following the 1973 Arab oil embargo, the crude oil available to the major companies fell by nearly 50 percent, from about 30 MMB/D to just over 15 MMB/D. Equity oil available to the majors fell even more sharply, by some 75 percent. The net result was a drop in the major's share of internationally traded oil from 62 percent to just 37 percent.

In addition to the newly created national oil companies, a host of oil-trading firms and "independent" refineries entered the picture. The links that had traditionally tied upstream and downstream (vertical integration) were weakened to the breaking point, while the reduction of horizontal integration (as large third-party crude sales were curtailed and joint venture production nationalized) further eroded the ability of the larger oil companies to exercise control over markets. Simply put, there were now too many actors with divergent commercial and political interests to guarantee market stability. The consequences were not long in coming.

After a decade of (virtually) universal confidence that oil prices would rise, prices began to weaken and fluctuate over an ever-wider range, climaxing in the dramatic events of 1986, when prices fell from nearly \$30 per barrel to less than \$10 in a period of only nine months (see

TABLE 12.1
Crude Oil-Price Trends and Volatility (average annual price, in current $ per barrel)

1950	2.51	1974	6.74
1960	2.88	1975	7.56
1961	2.89	1976	12.17
1962	2.90	1977	13.24
1963	2.89	1978	13.30
1964	2.88	1979	20.19
1965	2.86	1980	32.27
1966	2.88	1981	35.10
1967	2.92	1982	32.11
1968	2.94	1983	27.73
1969	3.09	1984	27.44
1970	3.18	1985	25.83
1971	3.39	1986	12.52
1972	3.39	1987	17.00
1973	3.89		

Note: Prices shown for 1950–1975 are "U.S. Wellhead." After 1975, series is "FOB Cost of Imports" into the United States.

Sources: Energy Information Administration, *Petroleum Marketing Monthly* (various issues).

Table 12.1). Although many feel stability returned in 1987, it is interesting to note that prices oscillated between $15 and $22 between September and December of that year alone. The fact is that stability has yet to rear its honored head in current-day oil markets.

Along with the structural change that was reshaping oil markets during the decade following 1973, a second important trend was emerging from the financial markets. High interest rates (along with high oil prices) at the beginning of this decade were making inventory maintenance very expensive, causing oil company managements to rethink traditional approaches to inventory and risk management (see Table 12.2). Also, hedging of financial risks was increasingly becoming a fact of life in foreign currency and interest rate markets. These trends ensured that oil companies were increasingly receptive to the hedging potential of the fledging oil-future market.

Finally, the third important factor that set the stage for energy futures' ultimate success was the general growth and diversification of futures contracts in a wide variety of new markets, and the growing sophistication with which they were being used and modified to offer an ever-wider range of hedging tools. For almost one hundred years, futures markets (then commonly called commodity markets) were pretty much confined to the traditional agricultural products (especially grains). From the mid-1960s on, however, there has been an explosion in the variety of products served by these markets. The first waves of expansion brought in new

TABLE 12.2
Interest Rates, Inventory Holding Costs, and Private Oil Company Stock Levels

	Interest Rate %[a]	Crude Oil Price/Bbl[b]	Monthly Holding Cost $/bbl	Oil Company Inventories[c]
1976	6.1	$13.48	.07	391
1977	6.4	14.53	.08	398
1978	9.2	14.57	.11	432
1979	12.2	21.67	.22	387
1980	14.0	33.39	.39	414
1981	16.7	36.69	.51	431
1982	13.6	33.38	.38	395
1983	9.9	29.19	.24	367
1984	11.3	28.60	.27	333
1985	8.6	26.78	.19	331
1986	6.2	15.01	.08	313

[a]Average annual London Interbank Borrowing Rate (LIBOR) 6-mo. rate.
[b]Landed-price of crude in the United States.
[c]Total OECD crude and product stocks at Jan. 1 of each year, in millions of metric tonnes.

Sources: Interest rates compiled from International Monetary Fund, *International Financial Statistics*, Washington (various issues). Crude oil prices compiled from Energy Information Administration, *Petroleum Marketing Monthly*, Washington (various issues). Holding cost and inventory levels compiled from Organisation for Economic Co-operation and Development, *Annual Report*, Paris (various issues.)

agricultural contracts, especially meats, and precious metals. The second phase, starting in 1970s, saw the introduction of financial instruments including currency, interest rate, and stock index contracts. A third phase brought in oil and a number of other industrial products. The fourth stage, which continues to evolve today, saw the introduction and rapid acceptance of options on futures contracts.

The introduction and success of oil futures was a product of these three trends. The growing volatility and loss of confidence in the future stability of oil prices demanded the emergence of new market structures and institutions. One obvious sign of the change was the rapid growth of spot markets and the trading companies that thrived on price volatility. Prior to 1979, only some 1–3 percent of internationally traded crude moved at "spot" prices and outside of term supply contract arrangements. By the end of 1985, virtually all crude moved at some sort of market-related pricing, and experts estimated that oil companies were acquiring anywhere from 30 to 50 percent of all supplies on a spot, noncontract basis (see Table 12.3).

The trading companies, independent refineries, and increasingly, the larger companies developed trading techniques to cope with the growing

TABLE 12.3
Growth of Spot and Forward Crude Oil Markets (Survey of Physical and Forward Cargo Transactions)

	Physical Cargoes	Forward Cargoes	Total
1973	54	0	54
1974	96	0	96
1975	154	0	154
1976	330	0	330
1977	327	0	327
1978	291	0	291
1979	315	0	315
1980	290	0	290
1981	405	0	405
1982	573	122	695
1983	1,014	806	1,820
1984	3,149	2,254	5,403
1985	5,628	3,058	8,686
1986	5,850	2,292	8,142
1987 (est.)	n/a	n/a	10,000

Note: "Physical" refers to where actual delivery of the cargo is taken.
Source: Philip Verleger, Jr., "The Role and Impact of Commodity Market Institutions in the Determination of Oil Prices," *Annual Review of Energy,* vol. 13 (Palo Alto: Annual Reviews Inc., 1988). Reproduced with permission. The data was compiled by Verleger from the *Petroleum Argus* data base, which, although only a partial listing of spot transactions, is the most comprehensive record available.

price volatility of these markets. The first response was to create informal, forward markets—at first only thirty days out, then sixty days and, more recently, ninety days out. A second response was an explosive growth in the demand for rapid, often "real time," pricing and other market information. Against this backdrop, futures became inevitable: a time-proven and efficient technique for coping with broad market instability.[1]

Futures markets, basically spot markets for standardized forward contracts, serve three functions:

Price discovery: giving an instantaneous reading of marginal price movements.

Risk management: allowing companies to hedge their price risks for limited periods of time. The hedging opportunity rarely extends more than six months forward, however, due to market illiquidity in the more distant months.

Speculative opportunity: attracting additional risk capital to the market from outside the oil industry. Low margin requirements—lower than in equity markets—enhance the attraction of futures as a vehicle for speculation.

By the mid-1980s, the commercial realities of the international oil industry had changed to the point where oil futures served a need for the industry and provided a simplified method for a broad range of investors to jump on the speculative bandwagon.

Futures Present

In 1988, after the smoke had settled from various attempts by exchanges in New York, Chicago, and London, there were four healthy futures markets (crude, heating oil, and unleaded gasoline in New York, and gas oil in London), one fledgling market (propane in New York) and three traded options markets (crude and heating oil in New York and gas oil in London).

When first introduced in late 1978, heating oil futures attracted smaller, independent marketers and refiners, who turned to the New York Mercantile Exchange ("Merc") as an alternative source of supply. Physical deliveries were initially quite high, as these smaller firms sought alternatives in a marketplace dominated by the larger companies. These initial participants were quickly joined by the spot oil traders and by a growing number of pure speculators on and off the trading floor, drawn from other financial and commodity markets. This phase lasted until well into 1983.

Then, with the introduction of crude oil futures and the increasing instability of prices, the larger refiners and integrated companies reluctantly entered the market. By 1984 over 80 percent of the fifty largest companies were using futures. Larger end-users, such as airlines and other major energy consumers, also appeared. In addition, a far wider range of speculators entered the scene, as trading volume and open interest rose high enough to meet the minimum liquidity requirements of the commodity funds (see Table 12.4).

Finally, another phase, dating from 1986, brought in almost all the remaining holdouts among the larger U.S. companies, more foreign participation, and a new group of traders—the "Wall Street Refiners"—companies like Morgan Stanley and Bear Stearns, which were attracted by the rising volatility of oil prices and the speculative opportunities presented by that price instability (particularly relative to other markets). As one Wall Street trader put it, "plywood was dead, so we looked around for some better action and found it in oil." The low internal cost of capital for margin maintenance and a built-in trading infrastructure made these new entrants formidable competitors for the older oil trading and supply companies.

However, even today, participation by independent producers and smaller end-users remains limited—the former by the lack of liquidity

TABLE 12.4
Growth in NYMEX Energy Futures and Options Trading (Daily Average Volume of Contracts Traded)

Contract[a]	1982	1983	1984	1985	1986	1987
Futures						
Crude Oil[b]		1,692	7,361	15,923	33,254	58,326
Heating Oil	6,927	7,414	8,366	8,831	13,100	17,174
Lead Gasoline[c]	413	1,614	2,614	2,669	3,319	
Unleaded Gasoline[d]				530	1,758	8,213
Propane[e]						168
Options						
Crude Oil[f]					4,509	12,468
Heating Oil[g]						1,330

[a]Each contract equals 1,000 barrels
[b]Introduced 3/30/83
[c]Terminated 10/31/86
[d]Introduced 12/3/84
[e]Introduced 8/21/87. Prior to that time, a contract had traded with mixed success on the Cotton Exchange
[f]Introduced 1/14/86
[g]Introduced 6/26/87

Source: Unpublished data provided by the New York Mercantile Exchange.

in the more distant months, the latter by ignorance of how the markets operate, the high management cost of setting up a futures trading department, and, for a number of domestic as well as international companies, a very real basic risk problem.

Futures trading has thus survived adolescence and entered a period of youthful maturity. But growth in the coming years will have to come from an expansion of futures trading opportunities in the form of new contracts, rather than from bringing in new participants. In other words, to continue to grow, the exchanges will have to offer a bigger and more diverse menu, not just put more seats around the table. The recent success of options would seem to confirm this point of view.

Futures Future

There has been much speculation about whether we have recently seen another turning point in the evolution of the oil market, signaling a return to greater integration of the industry.[2] The proponents of this "reintegration" theory cite the overseas downstream moves of a number of large producers as evidence of a turnaround. Certainly, a growing throng of producer governments including Venezuela, Kuwait, Abu Dhabi, Saudi Arabia, Mexico, Libya, Norway, and possibly even Nigeria have already purchased or are preparing to acquire substantial downstream shares in both Europe and, to a lesser extent, the United States.

Yet, although we agree that the "disintegration" since the late 1970s appears to have been halted, we doubt that conditions will soon return to the highly integrated conditions of the 1950s or 1960s. Even the substantial actions by Kuwait and Venezuela barely offset the continued emergence of new producers (the two Yemens, Colombia, Papua New Guinea, to name a few), the asset spin-offs by the majors, and privatization moves in several countries. Supported by the work of a number of experts, our view is that current moves toward reintegration are unlikely to recover much of the lost ground.[3] And only reintegration, both vertical and horizontal, offers the prospect of restoring stability, or at least predictability, to oil markets and prices. In the current environment, we see no credible combination of commercial and/or political interests that could impose the necessary degree of market control to achieve these goals. We therefore expect oil markets will remain volatile and difficult to predict, although the cycles of instability may become better understood. In such markets, futures will continue to play an important role.

The success rate of new futures contracts, whether in energy, finance, or agriculture, impells a certain humility in predicting future developments, however. In spite of voluminous contract justification requirements imposed by the Commodities Futures Trading Commission, and extensive independent research by exchanges, only one out of every five new contracts launched survives. Thus, any look forward must be viewed as highly speculative.

In general, our expectation is that only a handful of new futures contracts will finally be successfully launched over the next few years, despite considerable enthusiasm for starting trading in a number of new areas. The reason is that the criteria for a successful futures contract are simply too stringent, with too few physical markets that can actually meet those criteria. In assessing the suitability of any commodity market for futures trading, a fair number of the following conditions need to be present in the market:

- Price volatility or uncertainty
- Uncertain supply and demand
- Sufficient deliverable supplies
- Product homogeneity and perishability
- Market concentration
- Available price information
- A unique trading opportunity[4]

TABLE 12.5
Growth of Brent and Dubai Spot Markets (Survey of Physical and Forward Cargo Transactions)

	Survey of Spot Market Trade MB/D Volume[a]	Specific Crudes as a Percent of Spot Trade		
		Arab Lt.	Brent	Dubai
1973	74	28	0	0
1974	131	32	0	0
1975	211	23	0	0
1976	452	16	0	0
1977	448	14	0	0
1978	399	12	0	0
1979	431	19	0	0
1980	397	17	0	8
1981	555	28	5	3
1982	952	17	20	7
1983	2,493	6	33	6
1984	7,401	9	49	4
1985	11,898	3	58	8
1986	11,153	0	65	12
1987(est.)	13,700	0	60	15

Note: "Physical" refers to where actual delivery of cargo is taken.
[a]Estimated volume of both physical and forward spot transactions, in thousands of barrels per day.

Source: Adapted from data in Table 12.3.

But although we expect only a few new futures contracts to flourish, we do expect to see a proliferation of new forward markets, which can operate under much looser terms than formal futures contract. Those new forward markets will be started whenever participants in a particular market believe that a forward contract would be useful and will disappear whenever that is no longer the case.

Despite the difficulty in predicting the successful launch of new futures contract, the editors of this volume—like the bloodthirsty crowds in Rome's Coliseum—demanded that we enter this dangerous arena, in spite of our only modest chances of emerging with our reputations intact. We offer up, therefore, our predictions on how oil futures contracts can be expected to evolve in "the future."

Crude Oil. There is a need for at least one internationally traded crude oil contract. Brent and Dubai are the leading candidates, with each of contracts having developed a commanding position in overall spot and forward cargo trading (see Table 12.5).

But each of these faces serious obstacles. The failure of two Brent contacts at London's International Petroleum Exchange (IPE) and the relatively small size of the physical market for Dubai make it more difficult for another crude contract to survive. In fact, declining production of West Texas Intermediate may pose difficulties even for the existing NYMEX contact. The best bet, however, would be for the trading of the new (third) Brent contract by the IPE (and perhaps eventually a Dubai in Singapore as well).

However, the latest developments suggest a clear lack of enthusiasm in New York for international cross trading. This reluctance stems in part from concerns over the lack of liquidity for such markets overseas, but also from the parochial interests of the New York floor traders who dominate the NYMEX Board of Directors and see little direct benefit from such an arrangement. Our prediction is that at least one international crude contract will succeed.

Residual Fuel Oil. The third major product group—after heating oil and gasoline—is not yet covered by a futures contract. The fragmentation of the resid market, both in terms of quality and geography, poses serious problems. There are poor price correlations between high- and low-sulfur grades, making it difficult to find a common ground. In addition the major role played by highly regulated or government-owned utilities constitutes a formidable obstacle. Although utilities are not as conservative as they once were, the failure of earlier attempts at resid trading in New York and the recent failure of the Rotterdam and IPE resid contracts suggest a healthy skepticism on the part of end-users. Once a contract is up and running successfully, the problems posed by lack of quality homogeneity can likely be overcome, but initially establishing a close link between the way the physical and paper markets work is important.

Nevertheless, the high sulfur resid/bunker contract with Singapore delivery that Simex plans to launch has a chance, particularly if it is developed (and traded) jointly by New York and Singapore (and perhaps even the IPE). Achieving an adequate level of liquidity would of course be crucial. Such a contract could serve heavy crude oil producers, refiners, traders, marketers, and consumers in the Pacific Basin, including the U.S. West Coast, and the Middle East. A plan by the NYMEX to offer a 1 percent resid contract on the Gulf Coast—although logical—is a longer shot.

Propane. The propane contract was recently given a new lease on life at the New York Mercantile Exchange, after two lukewarm bookings at the New York Cotton Exchange. The new NYMEX contract, which substitutes physical delivery for the earlier unpopular warehouse receipt mechanism, has made a slow start. However, a final judgment should be reserved until the NYMEX natural gas contract is launched, since many observers believe arbitrage between those two contracts will provide a substantial boost to propane liquidity. But if propane does not achieve an open interest of 5,000 contracts within six months after introduction of the natural gas contract, forget it.

Natural Gas. We predict that this will be the next (and perhaps the last) big success story in energy futures. The time is overdue for such a market, which the New York Merc plans to launch in 1988, with Houston delivery. The contract has in fact been on the Merc drawing board for over four years.

Options. Nothing will probably ever match the breathtaking launch of crude oil options, but natural gas options should prove quite popular, particularly with the highly regulated local distribution companies, for which an option will be far easier to explain to regulators than the more complex world of futures margining. We do not expect gasoline options will have much more success than the modestly traded futures contract. A resid option is an eventual possibility, but only if the underlying futures contract proves successful.

Overall our expectation is that trading volume in the energy futures contracts will grow, but at a slower rate than the 75 percent increase of 1987. We anticipate that the growth rate will gradually decline as the markets mature, and as fewer new contracts are introduced. Our prediction is for a growth rate averaging 25 percent per annum from 1988 to 1992. Open interest will grow even more slowly than the trading volume itself.

The one other new twist that should be mentioned is the pending electronic linkup of futures markets. Reuters, the London-based news and information company, is preparing to launch a new service that would allow for direct trading of NYMEX contracts through an electronic trading network. Electronic trading in the wet barrel market has thus far proven unsuccessful for a variety of reasons, ranging from lack of standardization to the distrust and the unfamiliarity of market participants with the technology. But trading of established, standardized futures contracts via such an arrangement could, we believe, prove quite successful, and might be the last big innovation in futures trading. The system is at least two years away from launch, however, due to the substantial technical lead times required.

Of course, underlying fundamental problems with energy futures contracts—most notably the recent decline in WTI production that has resulted in increased opportunities to manipulate the physical WTI market—still need to be addressed. Ultimately, futures contracts are tied to the physical market, and changes in the fundamental character of the market on which futures trading is based will always affect the viability of the contract itself eventually.

Other Energy Futures: The Forward Markets

Futures markets must survive a rigorous selection process. As already mentioned, four out of every five new contracts fail. The test is severe—the successful contract requires a fine balance of homogeneity, a relatively unconcentrated market structure, uniqueness, and timing. But there are needs for hedging instruments that futures cannot provide. An alternative is to be found in the informal, unregulated market for "forward contracts."

Forward markets are simply a way for participants in a particular physical market to create a speculative forward trade in that physical commodity. Generally, one or a few of the players in the market take the lead in designing a roughly standardized contract or "terms" under which forward buying and selling is done. Examples abound. In fact, the very origins of the WTI futures market lie in the early success of the WTI spot and forward markets. A dozen or more of these informal markets have sprung up (although some have subsequently faded) over the past decade. Widespread forward trading interest is concentrated in Brent and Dubai crude oils, and in Russian gas oil, but there is specialized local trading in about a half dozen others. Following is a list of the more notable forward markets:

Crude Oil

- BRENT—The Brent crude market has become one of the most influential pricing indicators in the oil industry, clearly dominating forward spot crude trading with what experts estimate to be anywhere from 75 to 85 percent of all paper trading. Clearly the concentration of forward trading in Brent indicates the attractiveness of a high degree of standardization and liquidity in forward markets.
- WTI—West Texas Intermediate crude with delivery in Cushing, usually at the Arco pipeline; started in late 1970s and still continues to a limited extent at present.
- LLS—Louisiana Light Sweet crude with delivery in St. James, Louisiana; also started in late 1970s, but trading fell off after a lawsuit adversely affected the Capline's operator, Shell. It is one of the great ironies of oil trading that the great trading company Shell has actively discouraged trading of LLS, whereas Arco, enemy of many traders and independents, has been a reliable supplier of WTI at Cushing.
- DUBAI—The Dubai crude forward market has been in existence since about 1985 and, along with Brent, is a widely watched and quoted market. Only recently has there been much liquidity more than one month forward. Still, Dubai has evolved into what most

would call the spot marker for Gulf crude oil, which makes it important as a marker for the Far East. The Dubai market came by its position by default. Dubai was simply the largest stream of Middle Eastern crude generally available in the aftermath of the Iran-Iraq war. It has often been suggested as the basis for a Singapore-based crude futures contract, though in many ways it is unsuited for such a role.

- ANS—Alaskan North Slope crude oil, which moves into the U.S. West and Gulf coasts in sizable volumes, has evolved into a small forward market in recent years. ANS could theoretically provide an alternative crude for a domestic futures contract should WTI production continue to decline. However, the concentration of control over its production by a handful of companies is a formidable obstacle.

Products

- Russian Roulette—This Rotterdam-based forward market for Russian gas oil cargoes, in existence since about 1985, is widely traded and extremely influential.
- Littlebrooke Lottery—This UK fuel oil forward market is much smaller than the Russian gas oil trade, and is primarily an extension of UK utility feedstock trading. Nonetheless, it is being watched with increased interest on both sides of the Atlantic.
- BOSTON BINGO—A forward market for heating oil centered in Boston. The market has seen a fair amount of local trading activity since about 1986.
- Manhattan Mogas—A forward trade in motor gasoline centered in New York Harbor; it has evolved over the past year. As in the case of Boston Bingo, Chevron has been extremely influential in the development of this market—spurring trading in the contract by helping to define terms and by actively participating.
- Japan Naphtha—Periodically, trading heats up in this commodity in the Far East, driving an active forward market and spurring serious discussion of starting a formal futures contract for the commodity. However, of late, the big Japanese buyers have indicated a lack of enthusiasm for a futures contract, and the notion has been put on hold.

Forward markets are themselves in the process of evolving and are getting new attention from regulatory authorities. An interesting experiment may take place in 1988 in the Brent crude oil forward market. Several proposals have been circulated, one by the International Petroleum

Exchange, another by the First National Bank of Chicago. Each would have the effect of creating a self-regulated market with a central clearing mechanism for forward trading. If established, the market would be an experiment not previously tried in oil (although British Petroleum has for some time served as an informal watchdog over Brent trading, attempting to track the "daisy chains" to facilitate the end-of-the-month accounting process). The contract would be for 5–600,000 barrels, far larger than the 1,000-barrel contracts of a typical futures contract.

The "rumor," however, is that the proposals to establish a formal clearing mechanism will be rejected, with the current participants in the market preferring to retain the degree of control that they currently have in the less-regulated environment. Only the direct (and often threatened) intervention of the UK government is likely, we believe, to result in a change in this market to a more formal arrangement.

The key in observing all these markets, though, is to remember that they will come and go, according to circumstances and the needs of participants. Often the circumstances that give rise to these markets are serendipitous or the unexpected result of governmental action. Thus, the Brent market got its start from the concerns of UK tax authorities that North Sea producers were understating intracompany transfer prices. By looking for arm's-length prices, the authorities provided a strong incentive for the major North Sea producers to sell their crude oil to other companies and avoid the risk of government's placing unrealistic values on the crude. Absent this pressure from the UK tax man, it is highly unlikely that the major companies producing in the North Sea would have made Brent as readily available as it has been. Conversely, if the tax regulations change, the Brent market could quickly slip back into obscurity.

Conclusion

The 1980s will be remembered as the period when market risk entered the lexicon of the oil industry, alongside the geologic and technological risks that have always been present. Undoubtedly, the decades ahead will hold further surprises—we suspect that waste disposal and contamination will be the industry's next "toxic shock"—but it is unlikely that the oil world will again soon experience a period of fluctuating prices to match the past fifteen years.

The origins of the instability were years in coming, deriving from a chance mixture of corporate myopia, historical inevitability, and geologic reality. In the future, it is more likely that the amplitude of price movements will tend to shrink, but it is highly unlikely that either stability or predictability will be sufficiently restored to allow the oil industry to dismiss or ignore market risks. Reintegration will not return the stability of the 1940s or 1950s.

In spite of the hyperbole that emanates from brokers and, believe it or not, even from exchange executives, futures (and forwards) are neither inherently good or intrinsically evil. They are simply inevitable.[5] They serve useful purposes: as market barometers and financial blowout preventers for the oil industry. They will be available in a variety of flavors over the coming years, but they will never be the main course.

Notes

1. In fact, this is not the first time conditions appeared propitious for the development of oil futures trading. In the nineteenth century, a Petroleum Exchange flourished in New York. Again, in the early 1930s, when market discipline was briefly disrupted by the explosive growth of oil production in Oklahoma and Texas and oil prices fell dramatically, an oil futures market (in West Texas Intermediate) was established. And abortive attempts were made to establish oil futures markets in New York right after the Arab oil embargo.

2. For example, as raised by Ed Morse's provocative April 1986 article in *Foreign Affairs,* "After the Fall."

3. As cited by Marcello Colitti, Agip Petroleum, in his paper "The Structure of the Oil Industry in 1983 and 1990," presented Fall 1985 at the GREEN Conference, Université Laval, Quebec, Canada.

4. Price volatility or uncertainty: This provides the economic incentive for futures trading and is necessary to attract speculative interest.

Uncertain supply and demand: Volatility arises from uncertain supply and demand, making hedging in the futures market a valuable management tool.

Sufficient deliverable supplies: Supplies of a commodity must be deliverable in sufficient quantities to support delivery requirements. This requires (1) the absence of government controls over price and allocation and (2) sufficient transport and storage facilities.

Product homogeneity and perishability: Products must be capable of being standardized or graded to meet certain specifications and must be capable of being stored.

Market concentration: There must be a competitive market, broad spot market activity, a large number of buyers and sellers, with no one market participant large enough to control the flow of supply, and ample supply and demand.

Availability of price information: Price information must be readily available to all market participants.

Unique trading opportunity: A successful commodity futures contract should offer a unique trading opportunity and should not duplicate similar contracts on other exchanges.

5. Jack Evans, on the other hand, is intrinsically good.

13

Oil Companies as Multinationals: The New Environment

Louis Turner

In the 1960s, the world looked stable to all but the most perceptive oil industry executive. As an oilman (there were few women involved), he would see the dominance of the Seven Sisters, with the oil-producing governments apparently doomed to remain toothless opponents. However, he would increasingly have seen himself as a representative of a new breed of "multinational" executives—for this was the era of the "American Challenge," when people finally became aware of the tremendous surge of multinational direct investment that had taken place since 1945. To most executives, the Anglo-Saxon (predominantly U.S.) multinational phenomenon was a benign force. Certainly, it was difficult to see what could happen to challenge the U.S. domination of the international business scene.

In retrospect, those were innocent days. During the 1970s, the oil majors lost control of their upstream activities in the Third World, even in the case of Gulf Oil's coming to lose its corporate independence. New state-owned competitors have emerged from the OPEC world, such as Petromin, KPC, and Petroleos de Venezuela. The remaining oil majors survive as powerful players, but in a noticeably more complex world than that of the 1960s.

On the wider, multinational front, the era of the American Challenge now seems slightly quaint. As both Western Europe and North America strive to come to terms with the new surge in Japanese investment, those arguments about how U.S. multinational investors were poised to become the world's third great political force, behind the United States and the USSR, seem remarkably dated. In fact, what we have seen in the last two decades are two separate revolutions—one within the oil sector and one within the general business environment. The questions this chapter therefore seeks to answer are whether the oil industry has now reached a new plateau of stability, or whether the corporate environment is due for another set of revolutions so that when, in another two decades, we look back on the 1980s, we will do so with the same wry amusement that we, today, feel about the situation in the 1960s.

Oil: The Once-and-for-All Revolution

As I have argued elsewhere, the revolution of the 1970s was a once-and-for-all affair that did not just affect the oil industry but touched all resource-based industries (copper, bauxite, bananas, et cetera) that had to deal with the Third World. The "OPEC revolution" was in fact but one of a series of readjustments to a series of contractual relationships that were no longer seen as equitable and were not defensible as Third World self-confidence and capabilities grew.

In the late 1980s, the shift in power between companies and Third World governments has been made, and the only interesting question left is how the new arm's-length relationship between the two sets of players will evolve. In practice, the signs are quite promising. After all, the oil companies gave ground quite gracefully during the 1970s. Whatever might have happened earlier (such as the Mussadegh affair), there were no attempts to "do an ITT"—that is, to destabilize the OPEC regimes that were leading the campaign against the companies. That is in fact a point worth stressing, because the contrast between the oil majors—some of the world's very largest multinationals—and some of the microstates on the Gulf could not have been greater. On the surface, the circumstances for successful corporate skulduggery looked more promising that those surrounding International Telephone & Telegraph (ITT) in Chile. However, in the case of the oil companies, the multinationals decided to roll with the punches and to see what could be salvaged once the height of economic nationalism had passed.

The fact that the oil companies came out of the 1970s politically uncompromised means that they are now in much the same position as any other kind of multinational that is interested in building a lasting relationship with the Third World. They have technological, general managerial, and marketing skills, which have to be parlayed into more lasting contractual arrangements with countries that are still not easy to deal with. The key point, though, is that the oil industry faces problems that are no more serious (or light) than those faced by any other multinational. Today, then, the problems of the oil industry are really only those that face multinationals in general.

The Routinization of the Multinational Issue

If the oil companies really are but one (important) subset of the multinational community, then one can argue that they now have little to fear on the political front. As far as direct investment is concerned, there has been steady liberalization of controls on outward investment within the industrialized world, whereas even for the more sensitive issue of inward investment, controls are being dismantled—though not to an equivalent extent, for a number of smallish countries still feel sensitive about running a completely liberal regime. There are worries about national security, and there are continued concerns about the extent to which Japanese companies can be integrated into local economies. In general, though, in recent decades, there has been a steady liberalization of the environment within which multinationals do buiness, and this trend shows no sign of reversing itself.

There are probably three aspects of this trend which are worth developing. First, one can show that barriers to direct investment are steadily being reduced in country after country within the industrialized world. Second, the general process of industrial liberalization through measure such as deregulation and privatization has made important strides during the 1980s, though there are some doubts as to how far it will continue in a post-Reaganite world. Finally, U.S. determination to get investment issues treated within the General Agreement on Tariffs and Trade (GATT) framework may put a final seal on the process whereby multinational investment becomes basically a routine activity stripped of political controversy in the world's key economies.

The Attack on Restrictions on Investment

In most parts of the world, restrictions on inward and outward investment have steadily been whittled away. For instance, the steady expansion of the European Economic Community (EEC) has meant that newer members (Spain, Portugal, and Greece) have been forced to strip away their controls on multinational investment as a condition of entry into the EEC. Elsewhere in the world, Japan has increasingly been encouraging its companies to invest overseas and, more important, the authorities have been responding to foreign pressure by dismantling a large number of the controls they had against inward investment. There are still cultural reasons why this official liberalization has limited effects, but certainly at the level of green-field investments and the creation of friendly joint ventures, the formal barriers are now very limited.

At a deeper level, what seems to have been happening is that, for whatever reason, the political drive to bring multinational investments under increased scrutiny has been blunted. Within Europe, potentially radical initiatives such as the draft Vredeling Initiative and the Fifth Company Law Directive (both very much aimed at increasing the transparency of multinational decisionmaking within Europe) have been put on the back burner. In Canada, the pioneering Foreign Investment Review Agency has been turned into a very different institution. In Australia, similar developments have taken place. In each case, initiatives or institutions toward which the multinational community was deeply hostile have been watered down or shelved.

Liberalization

One further development, which can only improve the context within which multinational investment takes place, has been the very marked process of industrial liberalization that has taken place in key sectors of the OECD world since the early 1980s. In retrospect, the key event has proved to be the 1984 breakup of American Telephone & Telegraph (AT&T), though earlier developments like U.S. airline deregulation and the 1975 shake-up of Wall Street were manifestations of an underlying drive for liberalization that has now spread well outside the United States to other key countries in the industrialized world.

There are, of course, a number of ways in which such industrial liberalization has manifested itself, and anyway, it does not always guarantee that foreign multinationals are particular beneficiaries from the process. For instance, the AT&T breakup did not immediately make it significantly easier for foreign telecommunications companies to invest in the United States. What it did do, though, is increase the number of international players in this key industrial sector, for with its domestic monopoly gone, AT&T was forced to develop a global strategy for itself, forming strategic alliances in both Western Europe and Japan. The entry of such a giant player onto the world scene has then meant that other purely national giants such as British Telecom and Japan's Nippon Telephone and Telegraph (NTT) are being forced to develop global investment strategies in their turn. Such companies may not have a direct impact on the oil sector, but their arrival on the multinational scene means that the political clout of globally minded companies has been strengthened, in that the telecom newcomers are giant companies with strong political connections.

Related to the deregulation that freed AT&T from its essentially national shackles is the wave of privatizations that, until the October 1987 stock market meltdown, had steadily been picking up speed. This selling of previously nationalized companies was most marked in the UK, Japan, and France, but was having its influence elsewhere. Once again, the direct impact on the existing multinational community will not have been major, though it has generally meant that the newly privatized company is freer to make overseas investments. On the inward investment front, however, such companies are still normally treated as "national champions," sometimes protected by regulations limiting holding by foreign investors. In general, though, governments that have trodden the privatization route are firmer believers in competition and freedom for investment than not. Inevitably, the multinational business community must benefit from an increasingly liberal approach by governments to economic issues. The scale of both the deregulation and privatization campaigns during the early 1980s has undoubtedly produced a more favorable environment for the multinational investor, though we still have to see whether the aftermath of the October 1987 financial crash and the end of President Ronald Reagan's term of office may even see a partial reversal of these trends.

Investment, the OECD, and the GATT

One of the reasons why multinational investors are seemingly getting better protection than was true in the past is that key parent governments, particularly that of the United States, have learned how to use intergovernmental institutions like the OECD to develop a consensus among Western governments about the treatment that should be meted out to multinationals. For instance, one part of the (generally anodyne) OECD code on multinational investment specifies that goernments should show "national treatment" to inward investors, that is, that foreign investors should get equivalent treatment to that offered to domestic competitors. This principle was then waved at the Canadian government, whose Foreign Investment Review Agency and energy legislation of the early 1980s were clearly designed to discriminate against foreign investors. Although much of the diplomacy was a bilateral affair between the United States and Canada, the existence of generally approved principles within the OECD code clearly played its part in weakening the Canadian case.

In 1988 the U.S. drive is to get investment issues into the current round of the GATT, which, if successful, would involve a major evolution in this body's scope, pushing it beyond mere trade matters. There are two parts to this drive. The first is to get the whole service arena into the negotiating process; this could well be a major extension of the principle that all forms of corporate investment should be given relative freedom throughout the world. Although much of the initial skirmishing has been between the United States and key Third World countries like India and Brazil, this initiative has implications that go far beyond

North-South economic relations, since there is still a host of restrictions on the freedom of investment within the industrialized world's service sectors (banking, insurance, airlines, professional agencies, et cetera).

The second part of the U.S. drive—to bring TRIMs (Trade-Related Investment Measures) within the GATT framework—is aimed more narrowly at Third World practices, such as the setting of export conditions before investments will be approved. There is probably less consensus between the United States and its partners about the need for this initiative, but both the services and TRIM initiatives are a further reassurance to the multinational community that key parent governments are seeking to extend the acceptance of multinational investment by multilateral diplomatic initiatives.

The Limits to Routinization

In the core OECD world, a good part of multinational investment is now treated virtually routinely, in that it is not seen as raising significant political issues. For instance, outward investment has almost become a nonissue, with the odd exception where a country imposes some conditions regarding prior notification or sources of finance. Naturally, this does not mean that such investment is totally without critics, for at regular intervals trade unionists and others concerned about the productive base of their national economies will argue that domestic employment is being sacrificed as their companies invest abroad. However, despite these doubts, such outward investment by multinationals in the industrialized world is now about as noncontroversial as it is possible to get.

Most countries still have regulations covering inward direct investment by multinationals, even where they have (like the United States, UK, and West Germany) liberalized all other aspects of capital movements. Thus the United States retains controls against foreigners' taking stakes in nuclear energy, domestic broadcasting, domestic air transport, and coastal shipping. The UK also runs similar controls on air transport, broadcasting, and shipping.

Given that other countries are steadily moving in a similar direction, it increasingly looks as though multinational investments in low- or medium-technology manufacturing sectors, not involving the acquisition of a domestic company, have become almost as noncontroversial as outward investments. Where such inward investments involve negotiations with local or regional officials on matters such as levels of financial incentives, the discussions are increasingly kept to a technical level. What controversy remains is over massive mobile investments, which can be located in a range of neighboring countries and therefore tempt national authorities into competing on the scale of subsidies they will offer. These occasional giant green-field investments (particularly when they involve Japanese companies) raise the hackles both of local competitors with productive facilities already in place and of component suppliers concerned about the wave of secondary component investments that the initial giant investment may attract.

It is the acquisition of domestic companies that is most widely still seen to be controversial. Even where countries have been historically relaxed both on inward investment and on the principle of contested takeovers, there are still limits to what is politically acceptable. In the United States, there was the resistance when French-owned Fairchild was in danger of being sold to Japan's Fujitsu. Although the deal was not formally blocked, it was clear that a Japanese stake in the U.S. microelectronics industry raised a level of hostility completely different from that triggered by the preexisting European stake. Similarly, in the UK, there was a panicky retreat from the idea of selling the Rover Group and related companies to the U.S. competition, while the Westland Helicopter affair showed that there was a considerable body of political opinion that viewed a European solution as infinitely preferable to the U.S. one, which eventually won the day.

If there are limits to what is acceptable in countries such as the United States and UK, there are countries in which a contested acquisition by a foreign company is virtually off limits. Italy and Japan fall into this category, while France was, until recently, also extremely hostile to foreign bidders. On the other hand, one can plausibly argue that most of the movement in governmental positions has been toward greater tolerance. For instance, there has been a significant modification in the position of both Australia and Canada, two countries with particularly active screening mechanisms. In both cases, they now accept that their countries want to attract multinational investments, while the Australians also no longer insist that an incoming multinational prove that its investment is going to bring a positive economic benefit to the domestic economy. Similarly, Canada and Norway—two countries with energy programs particularly biased against foreigners—have modified their positions under heavy international pressure. Elsewhere, Japan has actually transformed an export-promoting body like JETRO (Japan External Trade Organization) into one concerned with the encouragement of inward investment into Japan. All in all, it is now possible to argue that most OECD countries now have the promotion of inward direct investment as one of their priorities, even if they have qualms about certain aspects of it.

Xenophobia and Japan

Whatever the regulations may say, xenophobia still exists. In parts of Europe, it can still be strong. Within Japan, there is little doubt that anti-foreign prejudice is still strong, but the Cable and Wireless affair, in which the British-owned company tried to take advantage of its legal rights to take a stake in a telecommunications consortium, showed that different parts of the Japanese bureaucracy had conflicting attitudes toward non-Japanese investors, however officially welcoming their formal legislation might be.

However, it is Japanese outward investment that currently attracts most debate within the rest of the OECD world—with the "Japanese challenge" having long since overtaken the "American" one as a source for political concern. Quite simply, the scale of this first wave of Japanese investment has grown so fast that it is taking time for both the Japanese investors and the host economies to decide how best to handle the phenomenon. As far as the Japanese are concerned, few of their companies had invested in the Western economies before the early 1970s, and most of them waited until the early 1980s before they really took the decision to invest in Western Europe and the United States. Inevitably, then, they are inexperienced investors, often investing to get around trade barriers, all too often putting down plants that are best described as "screwdriver" operations.

Inevitably, then, Japanese investments are coming under the kind of somewhat xenophobic scrutiny that U.S. investments in Europe were coming under at the height of General Charles de Gaulle's influence. What is less clear is whether investments from Third World countries that are emerging in Japan's slipstream (Korea, Taiwan, Brazil) will attract such detailed scrutiny and occasional emotional resistance. For the moment, investments from the newly industrializing countries do not have the visibility of Japanese ones, being very much smaller and less frequent. However, the kind of reactions seen in something like the Fujitsu-Fairchild affair could well be used in the future against high-technology acquisitions by fledgling investors from the Third World.

Conclusions for the Oil Companies?

The lessons from all this for the old oil majors is quite heartening (for them). For one thing, many of the old political bogeys having to do with multinational investment are dead. Within the industrialized world, political concerns about U.S. investment have now been overtaken by more pressing ones about Japanese investors. In Europe, for instance, established U.S. companies now join lobbies aimed at persuading governments to adopt tougher negotiating positions toward the incoming Japanese. On the other hand, xenophobia is not completely dead, which may pose some limitations to what can be achieved both in Europe and in Japan by the U.S. companies, while the European giants Shell and BP have only recently felt that U.S. public opinion has become sufficiently relaxed to allow them to take full control of their subsidiaries in the United States.

The key point, though, is that the energy sector is slowly becoming depoliticized in the industrialized world. The worst nationalistic excesses have been at least partially tackled in the cases of Canada and Norway, as a result of international pressure. The complicated privatization and partial dismemberment of Britain's electricity utility, the Central Electricity Generation Board, is an indication that that the process of depoliticization will continue, even if there will still be the occasional hiccup, when some particular investment happens to hit some xenophobic reaction. One likely source of reaction would come should one of the majors seem a likely target for investors from one of the OPEC countries—a situation that was becoming partially plausible in the UK in early 1988, when the Kuwaitis started to buy into BP.

The relationship that is more difficult to predict is the emerging one between the private oil companies and the Third World oil-producing world. Certainly, there is going to be no repetition within the OPEC world of the diplomatic pressures exerted on Canada and Norway to redress their nationalistic production policies. The right of OPEC nations to keep the multinationals out of their oil sectors is not likely to be challenged for some decades to come. On the other hand, the general relationship between the multinational business community and the leading Third World countries has been stabilized and may even be improving, as it becomes clear that Third World indebtedness means that private banking flows will remain constrained for some time to come. The age of debt renunciation may be upon us, but that of nationalizations now seems something from the past. The events of the 1970s lanced the tensions created by a set of relationships that needed restructuring. The 1980s have been a decade of minor tinkering with the arm's-length relationship that emerged. There is no reason to think that another revolution is either demanded or needed.

Therefore, looking at trends in both the industrialized and the developing world, it would appear that the oil companies have little to fear. Their future should increasingly be seen within the general context of the fate facing the multinational community in general. If that is so, then there would seem to be few worries on the horizon, for throughout the industrialized world, reactions to these companies seems to be increasingly relaxed. Certainly, the oil majors were once high up on the list of those who look for corporate skulduggery under every rock. Today, however, the successors to Anthony Sampson are writing about the banks and the Japanese. I am sure that is how the oil industry would like to keep things!

About the Contributors

Guy F. Caruso is currently the director of the Office of Energy Emergency Policy and Evaluation, USDOE, Washington, D.C. In the past, he worked for the Central Intelligence Agency in the office of Economic Research and the International Energy Agency, where he was responsible for analyzing world oil supply and demand and developments in the oil industry.

Melvin A. Conant is president of Conant and Associates, Ltd., in Washington, D.C., editor of *Geopolitics of Energy,* and chairman of the Royaumont Group on the Middle East, the World Bank Energy Policy Group (Korea), and the Advisory Committee on Energy in the School of Advanced International Studies, Johns Hopkins University. He is a member of the National Advisory Committee of the American-Arab Affairs Council, the National Advisory Committee on Energy Studies, and the Ocean Policy Committee, University of Virginia, and an adviser to the International Energy Forum of Japan. Among his many publications is *The World Gas Trade: A Resource for the Future* (Westview, 1986).

Fereidun Fesharaki is the Energy Program leader at the Resource Systems Institute, East-West Center, Honolulu, Hawaii. He is vice president for international affairs of the International Association for Energy Economics and a member of the editorial board of *Energy Policy.* As energy adviser to the prime minister of Iran (1977–1978), he attended OPEC ministerial conferences. He is the author or editor of twelve books and monographs on petroleum and related energy issues, including *China's Petroleum Industry in the International Context* and *Earth and the Human Future: Essays in Honor of Harrison Brown* (both Westview, 1986).

Paul H. Frankel is life-president of the holding company PEL, Ltd., in London. In addition to his many papers and articles, he is the author of *Mattei-Oil and Power Politics; Oil: The Facts of Life;* and *Essentials of Petroleum.* He is a Commander of the British Empire and a Chevalier de la Légion d'Honneur (France) and has been decorated by the Federal Republic of Germany and by Austria.

Herman T. Franssen is the economic adviser of the minister of petroleum and minerals of Oman. He has held senior posts in the U.S. Department of Energy and the International Energy Agency in Paris. He has published several authoritative studies on the U.S. domestic and international energy outlook as well as ocean policy.

David T. Isaak is a project fellow at the Energy Program of the East-West Center in Honolulu. He has worked for the Oregon State Legislature and the Oregon Department of Energy. He is the author or coauthor of seven books and monographs.

John H. Lichtblau is president of the Petroleum Industry Research Foundation, Inc. (PIRINC), a nonprofit research organization, and chairman of Petroleum Industry Research Associates, Inc., a consulting firm. He serves on the National Petroleum Council and is a member of the Council on Foreign Relations. He has written many articles on petroleum economics and was a contributor to the Ford Foundation's "Energy Policy Project" and project director to the Electric Power Research Institute's *Outlook for World Oil into the 21st Century.*

Amory B. Lovins is director of research of the Rocky Mountain Institute, a nonprofit foundation that fosters efficient resource use and global security. He is a Fellow of the American Association for the Advancement of Science and has published a dozen books, including *Soft Energy Paths.*

L. Hunter Lovins is executive director of the Rocky Mountain Institute and is engaged in research on resource efficiency and local economic development. She has been assistant director of the California Conservation Project and has coauthored five books on energy policy. Hunter and Amory Lovins have worked together as analysts, lecturers, and consultants on energy and resource policy in more than fifteen countries.

Alirio A. Parra is the managing director of Petroleos de Venezuela Europe S.A. in London. Besides holding many posts in Venezuela, where he played an active role in the nationalization of the oil industry, he is chairman of the Oxford Energy Policy Club, deputy chairman of the Anglo-Venezuelan Society in London, and the 1989 president of the International Association for Energy Economics.

Robert G. Reed III is president, chief executive officer, and chairman of the board of Pacific Resources, Inc. (PRI). He is a member of and former director of the National Petroleum Refiners Association and a member of the National Petroleum Council. He is also a member of and has served as a committee chairman for the American Petroleum Institute and was the chairman of the Committee for Equitable Access to Crude Oil, Washington, D.C. Before joining PRI, he was an executive of several oil companies.

M. Silvan Robinson is currently a director of Pacific Resources, Inc. He was on the editorial staff of the *Economist* before joining Shell, where he held a number of positions dealing with production, economic, and supply matters. He also served as president of Shell International Trading Company.

Ralph W. "Smoky" Snyder, Jr., is chairman and president of Ralph Snyder Associates, Inc., in Washington, D.C. He was formerly an administrator in the Office of Oil and Gas and the Oil Import Administration, U.S. Department of the Interior.

Barbara Laflin Treat is president of Royal Oak Corporation, an international oil and commodities trading firm. She also handles government relations for several international energy firms in Washington. Previously she was responsible for research on international energy markets at Harvard University's Energy and Environmental Center and a senior editor at *Petroleum Intelligence Weekly.*

John Elting Treat is president of Regent International, an international trading and marketing company, and of its subsidiary Yugo First, Ltd. He has been executive publisher of *Petroleum Intelligence Weekly,* president of the New York Mercantile Exchange (NYMEX), and an adviser on international energy policy to Presidents Carter and Reagan. He is the author or editor of several books, including *Energy Futures.*

Louis Turner is the director of the International business and Technology Programme at the Royal Institute of International Affairs (Chatham House) in London. He also serves as British convenor of the Anglo-Japanese High Technology Industry Forum and as conference coordinator for Chatham House. The nine books that he has authored or coauthored include *Industrial Collaboration with Japan, European Interests and Gulf Oil,* and *Britain and the Multinationals.*

Index

For Product Safety Concerns and Information please contact our EU
representative GPSR@taylorandfrancis.com
Taylor & Francis Verlag GmbH, Kaufingerstraße 24, 80331 München, Germany

www.ingramcontent.com/pod-product-compliance
Ingram Content Group UK Ltd.
Pitfield, Milton Keynes, MK11 3LW, UK
UKHW022000180926
475701UK00003B/112
* 9 7 8 0 3 6 7 3 0 9 9 8 5 *